EXPLORING THE ANXIETY OF BEING JAPANESE

A New Look at Nihonjinron

Exploring the Anxiety of Being Japanese

A New Look at Nihonjinron

Takeo Funabiki

Translated by Ksenia Golovina

2018

CAM RIVERS PUBLISHING LTD

First published in Great Britain
by Cam Rivers Publishing Ltd 2018

Cam Rivers Publishing Ltd
5 Canterbury Close
Cambridge CB4 3QQ

www.cambridgerivers.com
press@cambridgerivers.com

Author: Takeo Funabiki
Marketing Manager: James O'Sullivan
Typesetting and cover design: Jaimie Norman

ISBN: 9781912603169

To Coco

不安

Contents

Preface

This book is based on the revised texts of nine lectures that I presented under the title "Rethinking Nihonjinron" as part of a television series entitled *Human Lectures* which was produced and aired in Japan by the Japan Broadcasting Corporation (NHK). The texts have since doubled in volume, because I have incorporated thorough discussions on the discourse on the Japanese – or "Nihonjinron", as I will refer to it – from the Meiji period until the pre-war period in the first section of the book. In the third section I have also attempted to answer the questions and comments that I received from the audience both during and after the broadcasting of the series.

The most common questions were straightforward queries such as: "Will the Japanese continue to write on and read Nihonjinron?" and "What will become of the Japanese from now on?"

In the last text of the series, where the discussion focused on the future of the Japanese, I wrote that since many different kinds of Japanese people would be born from that time onwards there was a need for "discourse on the many types of Japanese". However, it now seems to me that this was a misleading suggestion. As American historian John Dower suggests in his book *Embracing Defeat: Japan in the Wake of World War II* – which I will refer to further in this book – there have always existed multiple "Japans" and multiple "Japanese", so it is not that it has suddenly become necessary to talk about "diverse Japanese people" with the arrival of the 21st century.

Although Nihonjinron has typically ignored the multiplicity of Japan and the Japanese, this has not been a true reflection of the Japanese themselves. It is said that the Japanese tend to "bow to authority" (*nagai mono ni wa makareyo*), as the Japanese saying goes. However, one can find defiant people everywhere, both in Japan's modern society and in the history of the past. It would be wrong to assume that the percentage of this kind of "defiant people", who one by one express their opposing opinions against the majority, is considerably lower in Japan in comparison with foreign countries. Despite the fact that societal customs and people's temperaments vary from north to south, Nihonjinron does not pay enough attention to these differences. Additionally, for instance, foreign residents (*zainichi*; a term that refers to those who are permanently resident in Japan, such as the Korean minority known as *zainichi Kankoku-jin*) make up the multiplicity of "the Japanese", but their existence is repeatedly ignored.

Why is it that, during these 150 years, discourse has presented the Japanese as a highly homogeneous people and Japan as a monolithic society, when they are in fact diverse?

There are two reasons for this. Firstly, Japan had conditions that encouraged such perceptions, such as the fact that it is an island country, that there was little human movement to and from other countries during the Edo period, and that the Japanese language was the language used across almost the entire Japanese archipelago excluding Hokkaido, which for many years was not within Japanese national borders. These conditions were taken as a given of the so-called *true Japan* even after the beginning of the modern age. Secondly, it is possible to assume that with these conditions as contributing factors, people wished to believe that Japan was a homogeneous society. Japanese people's desire to believe this can be attributed to the fact that the country's national course and its educational principles made them notice that perceiving oneself through the notion of Japan as a country was a powerful method of confirming one's existence and identity. For example, until only recently, a majority of people thought of themselves as middle class. This means that one belongs to neither the upper nor the lower, but to the middle class, in other words, to the mainstream. Put differently, it means that they wanted to think of themselves as "average Japanese". I remember how I once felt astonished when a member of a family that has a legacy of producing premiers, ministers, and other imminent political figures, was trying to talk about their family as "average" within Japanese society.

I would like to note that from an academic perspective posing the question "who are the Japanese?" leaves too much room for error and does not allow for an accurate academic response. For this reason, some scholars have dismissed Nihonjinron as "mass commodity" (Befu 1997(1987): 312-315) or emphasized that they would refrain from using such discourse as the framework for discussion.

Once we think about it in this way, it may seem that there is no sense in pursuing Nihonjinron since, on the one hand, there already exists an understanding that the Japanese are the "multiple Japanese" and, on the other, it is clear that it is impossible to produce an academically correct analysis of Japanese society through Nihonjinron. Still, as it is probably not the case that such discourse is meaningless, it cannot be dismissed so easily. We must also consider the significance of the other direct question that I introduced earlier: "What will become of the Japanese from now on?"

First of all, despite the presence of the two fateful flaws in the pursuit of Nihonjinron – the fact that the Japanese are the "multiple Japanese" and that talking about the Japanese as one group cannot produce anything of value academically – people living in the Japanese archipelago do wish to talk about themselves as "the Japanese" regardless of any such reasoning. The explanation to this lies in the fact that at a certain point in time, when the Japanese experience a strong sense of themselves as the citizens of Japan, they can guarantee unification by viewing themselves not as an entity comprised of many ("we as many") but as an entity comprised of one ("we as one"). This reasoning is not complicated. However, complexity emerges when we try to retroactively investigate what it means to be "one" in the historical foundations of homogeneity.

To summarize, "the Japanese" that are routinely made the object of Nihonjinron, even when not marked as "present-day", are still "the Japanese of today", and this means that they are believed to have a historical continuity with "the Japanese of the past". The Japanese who possess this continuity are sometimes seen as people who have the same ethical values as those once held by the villagers of the Edo period or the aesthetic sensibilities characteristic to the privileged classes of the Heian period. For this reason, in the historical span, it is as if their head is in the "present", but their body is in the past with a tail stretching far behind. Let us call these Japanese who exist as a historical continuum in the history of the Japanese archipelago the Japanese as a "cultural" being. In all likelihood, although it remains unclear to what extent these Japanese will continue to be a presence, they will not disappear overnight and will continue to exist while gradually accomplishing changes as long as the Japanese language is used, at times largely impacted by the foreign cultures (Mainland Chinese or Western culture) and at other times exerting their influence on the outside world.

Discussing these Japanese in the context of the question of "who the Japanese are", makes for intellectually engaging debates, which at the same time inspire a sense of pride. If that was it, perhaps Nihonjinron would simply become a genre that would entertain people for a long time without changing its status as an intellectual mass commodity. Nevertheless, Nihonjinron is expected to not only answer the question, "What kind of people were the Japanese?" but also provide a solution to the question "What will become of the Japanese from now on?" Talking about the examples of the various Japanese today as a cultural being as well as their inclinations should suffice as an answer to the first question. The second question, however, requires us to provide an answer on what kind of Japanese we are when we say "we as one" and what we in fact should be in regard to the present moment and near future.

"What will become of the Japanese from now on?" is naturally an urgent question that forecasts our continued existence from now into the future. Simply stated, these Japanese are a group of people who will be the citizens of Japan a few decades from now. These are "the Japanese" whose concern lies with the facts of whether and to what extent they will be able to read, write, and count, if and how many children they will bear, how diligent or idle they will be, if and what kind of leisure activities they will enjoy, and whether they will feel inclined to contribute to the Japanese society. These Japanese are the Japanese of the modern nation-state whose external boundaries are made clear by means of nationality. They are not the aforementioned Japanese as a cultural being who, like a comet, leave their palely glowing trail behind in history, but are entities who, with the exception of the deceased, can be counted up to the very last member of the population that now lives on the Japanese archipelago. In order to clarify the semantics, let us call them the Japanese as a "national" being as opposed to the "cultural" being. These Japanese – unlike the cultural beings who are anticipated to carry on as long as the Japanese language is used – are the ones who would supposedly disappear if Japan was to cease to exist. Although it does seem improbable, in modern times it is not a rare occurrence for a nation-state to cease to exist as a result of being wiped out, consolidation, or a formation of a loose alliance. For instance, this happened frequently in modern Europe.

If we work on the assumption of these two types of Japanese as a being, we could say the following. The significant majority, if not all, of the works that fall under the genre of Nihonjinron look at the Japanese as a cultural being, describing and summarizing its character-istic features, inclinations, and tendencies. However, they do not only "want to know" the nature of the Japanese from past to present, they are attempting "to find out" what kind of Japanese they will become in the future. There therefore lurks not only the desire "to find out", but also an earnest expectation and wish "to become a certain kind of people". These Japanese who wish "to become a certain kind of people" are not the Japanese as a diverse cultural being that emerge in various forms when we look back at the past, but are the Japanese as the uniform national beings implied in "we as one". It is the Japan as a homogeneous nation-state where national slogans ultimately function, even though people may speak of a "pluralist society" and "various individualities". In short, we can say that the books on Nihonjinron to date have usually started by analyzing the Japanese as a cultural being, and then proceeded to apply these theories to discuss the Japanese as a national being.

Before looking in turn at what this misalignment creates, I will first clarify the basic facts about the endeavor the Nihonjinron has been engaged in. That is, Nihonjinron has been involved in exploring what the ancient "things Japanese" as a cultural existence are and, based on them, speculating on the nature of people, the citizens of modern Japan, as well as on the way they should be in the future. If we talk about this not on the national but on the individual level, it equates to one's learning about "things Japanese" today, confirming one's presence within their continuity, and determining the kind of existence one represents as a Japanese national in its "present" shape as well as the form one should take in the future as "one of the Japanese".

Writing in this way seems likely to prompt Japanese readers to object that they do not perceive themselves as a "national" of Japan. In reply to this I will say that since the words "nation-state" and "national" were long interpreted negatively after the Second World War in Japan, they have been replaced by the words "society", "culture", and the archaic "ethnos". Even if the words are replaced and the Japanese are "objectified" as cultural beings separate from the nation state, the discourse on the Japanese remains a popular topic because what has been sensed in it is the future path of the nation-state Japan and one's place within it. When theorizing about the Japanese, one first wants to know, for instance, the differences between the European and Japanese customs or dissimilarities in the American and Japanese educational methods. However, having applied the theory about these differences, we assess ourselves – that is, the Japanese in the "present-day" Japanese state – and our own identity in comparison with "foreigners". If we delve deeper, what it really means is probing the legitimacy of the country Japan and ourselves as the Japanese in the modern world. I believe that, if the earnestness toward "the identity of Japan" had not existed, Nihonjinron would not have been necessary to the extent it is nor so widely read and enthusiastically discussed.

In the three chapters that make up the first part of the book, I will address the fact that Nihonjinron seems to be a "theory on the culture" while it is in fact a "theory on the state". In the second part, I will then examine postwar Nihonjinron in preparation for exploring the question "What will become of the Japanese from now on?" in the third part of the book.

PART 1

The Anxiety of Nihonjinron

CHAPTER 1

Why Nihonjinron was Needed

Thinking about Japan is Drawing "Comparisons"

Countless books have addressed the topic of the discourse on the Japanese – or "Nihonjinron" as I will refer to it – especially since the Second World War. In his work *Transformation of the Discourse on Japanese Culture*, published in 1990, Tamotsu Aoki suggested that "well above two thousand titles" (Aoki 1999(1990): 25) could have already been published on the subject, and it is safe to assume that yet more such volumes have been published in the last two and a half decades or so until today. On top of the fact that many of these books became bestsellers when they were published, some have become long sellers that have remained popular for several decades. There are few other topics that remain as consistently popular as this one.

Let us think about why the topic of Nihonjinron has inspired so many authors and attracted so many readers. The clue lies in considering what it means to "think about Japan (the Japanese)" and under what circumstances and with what goals people do so.

Thinking about Japan implies contemplating Japan and how it may differ from everything that is not Japan. If we would not feel these differences, in other words, if we would not notice the existence of the world outside Japan, Japan would become the entirety of our world. If this happens, there would be nothing to compare "Japan" to and it would be impossible to think anything about Japan. Thinking would become limited to what is inside. Thinking about Japan therefore first arises when one's interest turns to what is outside.

This should be similar to thinking about one's own family. If one was born and raised in a certain family and only lived within its boundaries with no other families around, one would think that one's family is "just the way it is" and would not regard it in any particular terms. Only through observing other families, how the father is gentler there, how they have more money, how the whole family goes to church every

Sunday, does one start wondering why one's household is different. Thus, thinking about oneself is comparing oneself to other people.

Put another way, while the books on Nihonjinron may be written entirely about the Japanese people, beyond the surface their texts are crafted as a comparison to countries other than Japan and people other than the Japanese. When it is written that the Japanese have a love of cleanliness, it is implied that people of other nationalities are not as passionate about it. However, this comparison is not a subtle touch within the text, but the chief purpose of the book.

The people inhabiting the Japanese archipelago started thinking about Japan when they came to the realization of what lies "outside Japan". We can even say that it was during that time that the notion of "Japan" first arose. I will refrain from speculating when exactly it was that people became aware of Japan for the first time, but if we refer to a well-known old source, it can be said that when Shōtoku Taishi, crown prince and regent of Japan between the late sixth and early seventh centuries, addressed his correspondence from "the Emperor of the land where the sun rises" to the "Emperor of the land where the sun sets…", he became conscious of his own country through comparison with China. The many stories of the *Konjaku Monogatarish*ū ("Anthology of Tales from the Past"), which was completed in around the first half of the 12th century, are arranged into three parts: Tenjiku (India), Shintan (China), and Honchō (Japan). It is very possible that those who read and heard the tales of *Konjaku Monogatarish*ū perceived Japan as one of the three countries that comprised the largest world imaginable to them. Even if the equal juxtaposition of China, India, and Japan was only within the classification of tales in the collection, it is peculiar that such a pattern of thinking existed.

Of course, people had already begun to think about "Japan", as demonstrated by the existence of the mythologies of the *Kojiki* ("Records of Ancient Matters") and *Nihonshoki* ("Chronicles of Japan") and other historical texts that had been written in the Japanese archipelago even before that. However, although this kind of perception of Japan went as far as a recognition that Japan "existed", it is unlikely that it was similar to the way in which the Nihonjinron that we will discuss in this and the following chapters eagerly examines the questions of what kind of country Japan is and what kind of people the Japanese are. This kind of interest is the awareness that is born in the process of comparing with the outside world. We can also suggest that perceiving one's own country as an object in this way often develops in times of external crisis. In these circumstances, comparing one's own nation with foreign countries is not merely an intellectual interest, but a means of handling the crisis. Thus, although *Risshō Ankoku Ron* ("On Securing the Peace of the Land") and *Jinnō Shōtōki* ("Chronicles of the Authentic Lineages of the Divine Emperors") may be the products of internal conflicts in the religious world and domestic disputes concerning the Emperor, they nevertheless display an awareness of Japan that was prompted by the social unrest of the 13th to 14th centuries and by the external crisis of the Mongolian invasions, an encounter with the might of foreign nations.

However, I believe that it was only after the 16th century that such crisis-triggered awareness of Japan developed to the stage that it constituted models for a nation. The following section sets out these state models and in turn sheds light on a certain aspect of Nihonjinron.

The Three Models of Japan

There are three main reasons why Japan came to establish itself to the outside world during the period from the Warring States period (1467-1568) until the beginning of the 17th century. Firstly, Japan became relatively more independent from the Chinese imperial system. This was prompted by the fact that East Asia was entering a state of turmoil, as subsequently expressed by the fall of the Ming dynasty in 1644. Secondly, encounters with Portuguese sailors and representatives of other European civilizations allowed Japan to come face-to-face with the world beyond China and India. During the same period, they were experiencing the influence of the nomadic people in the north who would later lay the foundations of the Qing dynasty. Thirdly, the dual political administration by the *kuge* (Imperial Court) and the *bushi* (military) was about to adopt a new state system as a result of the military assuming full authority. In the midst of these developments, Nobunaga Oda, Hideyoshi Toyotomi, and Ieyasu Tokugawa brought forth the state models of Japan that continue to function today.

Nobunaga's Japan was tolerant of Christianity, expressed interest towards Western culture, and voluntarily engaged itself in trade with Spain and Portugal. His vision for Japan and its state model allowed not only for visits from the outside but also for the Japanese to visit foreign countries, such as the delegation of four young Japanese Christians sent as ambassadors to Europe in 1582 (the Tenshō Embassy), Nagamasa Yamada's trip to Siam (present-day Thailand), and a mission to Spain and Rome (1613-1620) organized by feudal lord Masamune Date and led by his retainer Tsunenaga Hasekura. I will call this model "International Japan". Yet, it is believed that one of the flaws of this model lay in the simple fact that Europe was "too far away". The fact that the "International Japan" envisaged by Nobunaga was not established as a stable model is not only because Nobunaga died when he was still in the process of unifying the country, but also undoubtedly due to the distance between East and West. Even today, this sense of distance is one of the conditions characteristic to Japan.

In contrast, Hideyoshi's Japan can be called "Great Japan". After succeeding Nobunaga, Hideyoshi banished the missionaries from Japan in order to counteract the power wielded by Christianity as a political force from the West. At the same time, he sought to monopolize trade with Spain and Portugal, which also functioned as a channel to advocate Christianity. He also aimed at increasing his influence in Southeast Asia by dispatching ships authorized by him to trade outside Japanese waters (although there is currently a strong argument that this was started by Ieyasu, not Hideyoshi). Even so, the most famous of his East Asian political projects is the sending of troops to the Korean peninsula. Although we cannot deny the extent to which these endeavors were influenced by the megalomania that he suffered from in his later years, they were not completely invalid ideas. They were prompted by the instability of the Ming dynasty in the second half of the 16th century, when it was constantly threatened by powers such as the Mongols from the north and the so-called "Japanese pirates" (*wakou*) and Portuguese from the south. His ideas were also based on a geopolitical decision to mitigate influence on Hokkaido from the north. While Hideyoshi did not in fact succeed in overthrowing the Ming dynasty, the Qing Empire accomplished this a few decades later. The efforts of Chinese military leader Coxinga – who was born to a Chinese father and a Japanese mother – to spread his anti-Qing movement across China, Japan, and Taiwan can be seen as evidence of the geopolitical reality of Hideyoshi's pan-East Asian vision.

The model that was created and established by Hideyoshi's successor Ieyasu and that has since then penetrated each level of Japanese society, can be named "Little Japan". It is said that in establishing the *bakuhan* system of government Ieyasu was extending the system by which he had governed the small area of his home region to the whole country, and that it was an extremely "internally-oriented" and elaborate system that spread the net of its control down to the tiniest components. However, it was not Ieyasu's initial intention to adopt the "Little Japan" model; he was setting the stage for the "Great Japan" model, establishing Japanese towns throughout South East Asia, by way of encouraging the activities of ships with shogunal charters for foreign trade and other initiatives. In spite of his intolerance of Christianity, Ieyasu was deploying policies in line with an outward-oriented, "Great Japan" model through trade and other such means. He nonetheless later switched course and adopted the approach of prohibiting Japanese from travelling overseas and foreigners from entering Japan – a policy that came to be known as "national isolation" (*sakoku*) – because he concluded that, if open, his country would be unable to compete with the power of Christianity both inside and outside Japan and the Western authority that supported Christianity. The national isolation that was fully enacted after Ieyasu's death was an external foreign policy, but it in turn brought about a society that is a small wonder when considered from the point of view of population theory – a society that was capable of circulating its resources and sustaining its existence, with no plagues infiltrating from outside, only small-scale famines, and absolutely no traces of war.

These three models – Nobunaga's "International Japan", Hideyoshi's "Great Japan", and Ieyasu's "Little Japan" – emerged as a result of two factors: the necessity to adopt a certain external course as an independent country and Japan's readiness to do so in terms of its competence as a nation-state. Until that time, as an island country in the eastern frontier of the continent, it had experienced relatively little force from the outside, but with the advent of the 16th century, the wave of "globalization" that had commenced with the Age of Discovery finally arrived. This, in turn, concurred with the period of increasing instability in East Asia caused by the decline of the Ming Dynasty. The aforementioned three models, which were quickly established one after the other across a short period in response to the situations the country faced, can be viewed as an attempt to test the possibilities of "Japan" as a state system that were conceivable from the conditions of those days. All three of the models overlap with each other and yet also have clearly different focal points.

In fact, these three models continue to be seen as the three currents of Japan after the Meiji period. Japan, which was taking measures to expand its terrain in order to not be prayed on as a colony by other imperialistic countries, aimed to become "Great Japan". However, during the 80 years in which this "Great Japan" functioned as a national policy from the Meiji Restoration (1868) onward, there was a short period after Japan joined the League of Nations in the Taishō era (1912-1926) in which "International Japan" was chosen as a focus area. The discourse of "Little Japan" was also present at all times, as famously reflected by the fact that even before the Second World War journalist (and later politician) Tanzan Ishibashi argued that Japan should give up its colonies. Then, the postwar Japan clearly adopted the model of "International Japan". But this, in its turn, would gradually change into "Japan as the Big Economic Power".

It is interesting that Yukichi Fukuzawa, Inazō Nitobe, and Sōseki Natsume – the exponents of "Great Japan", "International Japan", and "Little Japan" respectively – whom I will also touch upon later in this book, were featured as national icons on the Japanese banknotes that were in circulation until 2004. This demonstrates that the three currents of "Great Japan", "International Japan", and "Little Japan" are always present without converging, and that each of their values are recognized even today. Looking ahead to modern times, with these three models always in place, when Japan goes to employ a model for its nation state, it is driven in the medium term to focus on the one of these paradigms that best fits the conditions of the times. Yet, since each of the models has its flaws, until today none has remained in use in the long term. Nihonjinron is written when one of these models replaces another, when one feels that a model has been achieved, and when that system has deteriorated.

"The Foreign" of the Edo Period

Let us return to the original topic of discussion – namely, the fact that thinking about Japan is drawing comparison with what is beyond Japan – keeping in mind that although the "International Japan" and "Great Japan" models were attempted from the 16th to the 17th centuries, the conditions were not yet ripe for them to take force, and only the model of "Little Japan", which was achieved through the *bakuhan* system's preservation of domestic order, could withstand outside forces.

In the "Little Japan" of the Edo period, which was marked by extremely limited contact with foreign countries, there was little scope for people to engage in Nihonjinron. It would be fair to say that in general it was prohibited to contemplate who the Japanese people were and what Japan was by means of comparison with foreign countries.

Once, however, when I was watching a Bunraku performance, I remember seeing one scene that to me seemed to evoke a feeling that resembled the Nihonjinron that has been present from the Edo period onwards. This was in a 1715 play entitled *The Battles of Coxinga* by Monzaemon Chikamatsu, in the scene where the old mother of the hero Watonai (whose character is based on the military leader Coxinga, who was mentioned above) is taken captive by the Chinese. Despite being a captive, this old lady is cared for well, and her merciful captors offer her luxurious foods such as fresh local fruits, deep fried duck, pork, lamb, and beef. However, she responds by saying that she would "rather have a rice ball". This scene not only aims to elicit laughter by playing on the clash between the Chinese captors' attempts at hospitality and what the old Japanese lady really wishes to eat, but also at creating a contrast between the "stodgy" China and the "light" Japan. Although it is highly likely that few of the audience members in the Edo-period had had the chance to try Chinese cuisine, one can see that Chikamatsu was working on the knowledge that they would have gained from hearsay and imagination to sharply depict Japan's characteristic features by comparing it to things non-Japanese. As opposed to adopting some form of complicated logic, he uses such a simple format to provide an image of Japan that is immediately understandable and convincing for the audience. Such a simplistic means of explanation, which could easily be criticized as stereotyping, is a common feature of the later Nihonjinron.

This therefore suggests that while Japan had its back turned to the outside world, even the ordinary folk of the mid-Edo period had some thoughts on what kind of country Japan is and what kind of people the Japanese are. Set not only in Japan but also Ming and Qing China, *The Battles of Coxinga* has an international element that is rare for an Edo period play. This, in turn, connects to Hideyoshi's "Great Japan" and its position in East Asia, as discussed above. For the audience this presented a rare occasion to compare Japan to countries other than their own. For Chikamatsu, perhaps thinking in that direction was a means of spreading the wings of his imagination.

Besides, for all it being a closed country during the Edo period, Japan continued to import Western goods through Dejima in Nagasaki (if only for a limited number of people). Only those who were able to offer enough money could get their hands on the expensive foreign books. Moreover, until a certain time a number of large-scale missions from the Joseon dynasty visited Japan, exhibiting "the foreign" to the contemporary people on their long journey from Kyushu to Edo. Later on, after the 18th century, knowledge about Ezo (present-day Hokkaido) and Karafuto (Sakhalin) to the north as well as the Maritime Province (Primorsky Kray) in the Russian Far East was brought to Edo and other cities. This was generated by the expedition that the *bakufu* (Tokugawa administration) undertook in response to the Russian threat approaching from the northern extremities.

The historical sources recorded by Edo period explorers (such as Tokunai Mogami, Rinzō Mamiya, and Jūzō Kondō) on the peoples of the north and the tribes in those areas demonstrate a curiosity toward things that differ and a presumption that the other side is inferior – perspectives that are similar to those of the classical empires of China or Rome, albeit on a lesser scale. In addition, this attitude comes so naturally to the explorers that they are not particularly aware of it.

My intention in noting this here is not to criticize the Japanese in that period by suggesting that they had a colonialist disposition. As the facts have it, while they were trying to determine policies about the settlement and development of Ezo, Japan was opened by the Western powers, so the expression "colonialist" does not fit. However, these Japanese, whose attitude toward the foreign did not even evolve into something malicious so to say, must have experienced a particular shock when they themselves became the object of curiosity and contempt – an attitude that they had never expected – when their country was later opened. Incidentally, the contemporary Russia was keen to pursue diplomatic negotiations with Japan and had begun to prepare for such negotiations by founding a Japanese language school in Saint Petersburg in 1736 and mobilizing the help that could be provided by castaways from Japan and their native language skills. At the end of the 16th century Hideyoshi had sensed the movements from the north toward Japan, recognizing that while Japan had begun to dig a tunnel from its side, the digging had already begun from the other. Then, in 1792, half a century before Perry's "black ships" were to appear, Russians dropped anchor in Nemuro, bringing with them Kodayū Daikokuya, a Japanese castaway who had spent eleven years in Russia. At that time the Russians already looked at Japan through the eyes of imperialism. However, while Edo Japan also launched expeditions to the north, imperialistic notions such as Hideyoshi's "Great Japan" model were not clearly established in the views held by the Japanese, and therefore the way they looked at Russia differed from Russia's perspective.

The Japan that was Seemingly Opened from the Outside

This external stimulus from the North gave the late-Edo scholars of Western studies and the wealthy urban merchants a sense of the outside world. In the mid-Edo period, the great intellectual Hakuseki Arai, who held notable positions and had access to information about the foreign countries' conditions, was already making comparisons with other countries (in works such as *Seiyō Kibun* ["Tidings of the West"] and *Ezoshi* ["Records about Ezo"]). Still, it was not until 1853, when the doors of the country were knocked at by the West due to Perry's arrival on the shores of Uraga – considerably closer to Edo than the distant region of Nemuro – that it developed into a subject of strong interest for ordinary Japanese.

Until then, when Japan thought of the obscure Asian world of Joseon, China, and India or as it engaged only in foreign relations with Holland, there did not emerge a strong "necessity" to consider what Japan was. There, at every level of society people subconsciously restricted the world they were living in to Japan, and some were content with being able to peek outside from there with mere curiosity in line with interests such as having a "taste for Ezo" – with exceptions such as Shihei Hayashi, the author of *Kaikoku Heidan* ("A Discussion of the Military Problems of a Maritime Country", 1791), who possessed a profound sense of the existence of the world around Japan. This was suddenly reversed when Perry's black ships flung the country open to international society in which various nations negotiated with each other.

US Commodore Matthew C. Perry's approach to opening Japan is referred to as "gunboat diplomacy", the use of force and demonstrations of superiority to sway the course of negotiations. Japan had not sensed such a stance in its non-committal encounters with Russia in the north since the end of the 18th century. As the Japanese had erroneously believed Japan to be Russia's equal, the unique sense of humiliation and threat that they felt in the face of America's "Black Ships" diplomacy was completely new to them.

Following the opening of the country, the Japanese therefore saw "Japan" as inferior to any other country – with the exception of course of other countries that were already in a subordinate position at that time, such as other Asian countries, Africa and South America. Even now, the modern-day equivalent of this feeling of inferiority can commonly be seen in so-called Third World countries. I had the chance to spend significant periods of time in such areas during my anthropological fieldwork and could always feel how deep-rooted this kind of feeling and hurt was. Such hurt and sense of humiliation and threat are all the result of the divide between superior and inferior nations that is generated by modernization. This is the overwhelming disparity in society, cultural systems, and technology by the "modern" historical stage driven by the industrial revolution in the smaller western parts of the Eurasian continent and the North America, a development which took place while Japan was refusing to negotiate with foreign countries in its long period of national isolation.

In other words, while Japan was still "asleep", the Western countries took the lead in developing industrial civilization and competing for modern progress in all fields within the political and economic framework of imperialism. After it was opened, Japan must have felt like a runner made to run in a marathon that had already started – the very last in the race. Japan had a frantic urge to catch up with the West and avoid suffering the same fate as China in the First Opium War – an urge that encouraged a vivid fear among those statesmen who could understand the international situation, and a vague anxiety among the onlookers who had witnessed the arrival of Perry's "Black Ships" and the *bakufu*'s reaction towards them, and both this fear and anxiety continued to spread without any sign of retreating.

It would be necessary to pursue this topic in more detail in order to understand the actual political conditions of the mid-19th century and the extent to which normal citizens were able to reflect upon this national anxiety. We can say that a few decades later, at the end of the 19th century, the national policy had ensured that the people of the Japanese archipelago had already adopted a certain way of describing Japan. In turn, such describing of Japan prompted a need for Nihonjinron.

The Story of "Japan" needs Nihonjinron

Here I will propose a hypothesis on the overall concept of Nihonjinron. In the following chapters I will investigate this hypothesis as I look at some actual examples of Nihonjinron and highlight and explore the specific problems that can be seen in such works.

The hypothesis is as follows:

The nature of Nihonjinron lies in its attempt to explain who the Japanese are and thereby remove the anxiety associated with the identity of the modern Japanese. The existence of this anxiety stems from the fact that in modern times Japan occupied a peculiar historical position, namely, it was not a society that belonged to the Western history that produced the "modern age". Since Japan being an outsider in the so-called "Western" modern era is a historical given that cannot be changed retroactively, the anxiety arises again and again. When the anxiety rises, Nihinjinron is written, making interpretations in line with the features of that anxiety. However, as this anxiety over identity is ingrained and unsurpassable, a new form of "anxiety" always emerges, and every time this happens a new work of Nihonjinron becomes a bestseller. Yet, by no means does this "anxiety" only increase in the event of crises involving "Japan"; it arises equally when the future of the country looks favorable, as its people do not feel certain about its success. Thus, the anxiety and the Nihonjinron as a response to it appear both when the country's power strengthens and when it fades.

Behind this hypothesis there is the story of "Japan". This is a story of the last 150 years or so. Although it started being told over 150 years ago, its existence is only possible when one looks back from the present to interpret the history of the past, so the present form of this story is about the recent 150 years, or the "modern times".

Although its subjects are the Japanese society as a system and the tens of millions Japanese people, this story talks about a single character. This singularity is not only a matter of numbers; it means that the subject's nature is uniform and not pluralistic. It is a convention connected to the structure of the story itself. The "storyline" becomes apparent when the character's nature is simplified and the society and other such abstract phenomena are personified. Through such methods, the "story" functions as a mechanism in people's thought. "People" think and make projections about themselves, having presented themselves in a way that makes it easier for them to look outside of themselves. The story "Japan" is being told as the basic material and evidence of all Japanese thinking about what Japan is and what will happen to Japan.

In this story, "one" "Japanese person" starts his journey as someone upon whom modernization has been forced and who has no choice but to compete within modernization. This seems to correspond to the events that have happened in Japan from the country's opening in the Meiji period until now. From this perspective, it becomes tempting for the Japanese to say that this story is almost true. Still, it is not true to say that Japan was "forced to", although it is thought of this way as a result of the interpretation. Was Japan opened forcefully or had it in fact sensed the necessity to open the country and took the chance that presented itself? The truth lies somewhere in between, but the idea that it happened "by force" still lingers. For instance, when a nation must accept an international treaty (such as a convention on the status of refugees) or an international system (such as a financial system), it is unthinkable that such a development has happened intrinsically. It seems that such treaties and systems are developed as a result of a process of something essentially different being forced upon a nation, similar to the way in which Japan was thrown into the competition of modernization.

While an initially reluctant competitor, Japan did fight well and achieve success in that competition. Yet, it also had its failures. If we apply a Western literary genre to this drama-filled story, it would probably be Bildungsroman, a genre that focusses on the protagonist's self-formation. An example of a Japanese work that resembles a Bildungsroman would be *Taikōki*, a classic success story dealing with the life of Hideyoshi Toyotomi. Although the story initially seems headed for a happy ending, halfway through the main character becomes constantly compelled to climb higher and higher and lives in anxiety about whether he can ascend further or whether he will fail. In fact, the main feature of the story is the idea of overcoming such anxiety.

However, the theme of the story of Japan does not stop at merely overcoming anxiety – anxiety born as a result of strongly desiring to succeed – by achieving success. If this was the subject matter, it could have been possible to write it in the form of a success story split into several parts, as the overall situation has been improving, despite a few failures in the course of these 150 years. Yet as I have already mentioned in my hypothesis, this anxiety, responsible for the creation of Nihonjinron, presents itself not only in crises, when the country is perceived to be under threat, but also when the conditions are favorable and the country is on a high. Nihonjinron was also written during the highs that Japan experienced before and after the Russo-Japanese War, and when the Japanese economy was at the height of its prosperity in the final stages of rapid economic growth in the late 20th century. On all of these occasions, one of the three models for Japan became the focus for remodeling.

That is, what I earlier described as the "unique" sense of humiliation and threat does not come from losing in the competition for "progress" under the pursuit of imperialism and modernization. It comes from the doubts concerning whether or not Japan has any right to participate in that competition at all, the doubting whether or not Japan is a legitimate runner in the race of the "modern". During the past 150 years, Japan has been preoccupied by the questions of whether it is possible to incorporate the "modern", a Western external element, and, if it is, whether it is legitimate and "right" to do so. If the country had not succeeded in that modernization, the anxiety of identity might have been less significant. It is precisely because it has actually been progressing rather well that anxiety has arisen, as in the moments of success one doubts whether things are done right, and, in the moments of failure one is gnawed by anxiety, as if acknowledging that it was not meant to be all along.

Speaking metaphorically, it is like the anxiety of identity that happens to a highly-talented child from a vassal state who receives an education through support from the government of the suzerain state and then achieves a certain success in the society of the suzerain state, as was a common occurrence in societies with "colonial conditions". For example, from what I know, it is the anxiety experienced by the children of the Pacific Melanesian society who received support from the white people, learned about their lifestyle, received an education, and then, having been accepted as pseudo-whites, obtained jobs and maintained a lifestyle of a level higher than that of the people of their native society. People like this feel alienated from both the society they were born in and the society where they were brought up and work. That anxiety can act like a spring and become the source of one's energy, but it will always hurt like a chronic illness that burdens an individual. This, for example, brings to mind the so-called "stolen generations", the children of the Australian Aborigines who were brought up in white society. The Japanese people similarly escaped from the "backward Asia" and alone succeeded in modernization from the Meiji period onward, making Japan since the late 20th century the only country that has been enjoying the position of a "pseudo-white" as a member of the financial and political summits of the major powers, such as the G7. However, the loneliness that Japan experienced after becoming an orphan of the world upon its withdrawal from the League of Nations in 1933 will never be forgotten.

This kind of metaphor may sound somewhat cruel, but the Japanese society is, to an extent, a big society. It is such that an individual can live only inside its big "well"; and, as a society, it can go on without viewing this as a big problem. It can therefore avoid perceiving itself in such a cruel manner. This is because it has more than succeeded in cultural enlightenment. However, this success is constantly threatened by anxiety.

Crisis and the Foreign: The Two Factors that Create "Anxiety"

There are always two triggers that generate anxiety: "crisis" and "the foreign". As I mentioned before, crisis comes from both failure and success. Let us start by considering failure. Anxiety about Japan's state of being emerges whenever there is a political isolation, military defeat, or economic collapse. While this anxiety also leads to discussion at a realistic level, such as if the country's approach or fighting power are inadequate, at the same time it brings about doubts about self-identity. Is not Japan's negotiation with other countries and competing with them in the international society essentially like a "handicap race" in horseracing? Is it even really accepted by the Western-dominated world and given the status to negotiate and compete there? When the country is successful, it means that the strategy has worked in practice, thus the Japanese should cease having doubts about Japan. Despite this, Nihonjinron is still written. This Nihonjinron develops a certain "theory on uniqueness", similar in a strange way to the Nihonjinron created in the case of failure. In the same way that it says that the failure happened because of this "uniqueness", it insists that the success is also due to this "uniqueness". The more this notion is elaborated, the more it leads to both oneself and others making an assessment that this success is unique and is therefore not a successor of the western "modernity", but represents, to say it cleverly, "yet another" kind of modernity. The identity therefore remains unstable. If this success is then followed by decline, the "I-knew-it" anxiety of that moment makes one experience increasingly aimlessness and crisis of identity.

In summary, crisis does not only mean "failure," but also "success", which functions similarly. "Anxiety" that comes from that "crisis" is not only discussed in the realistic dimension of overcoming failures, but also makes one think about "legitimacy" in the deeper historical conditions of the modern Japanese people.

This is namely when one becomes conscious of "the foreign" as foreign countries that form an object for comparison. The crisis in the movement of modern times is connected to the relative ups and downs of the economy and military affairs and is measured in the competition with other countries, thus bringing about awareness of the foreign. Nihonjinron, especially its most powerful examples, are written whenever such consciousness about the foreign is particularly strong.

In fact, this element of "the foreign" also functions actively on another different level. It works on the individual level when a Japanese person who is writing Nihonjinron strongly acknowledges "the foreign". Numerous people who write on the topic of Nihonjinron are driven to start writing by sensing "the foreign" and, in a lot of cases, by experiences of "studying abroad". There are too many examples of this to enumerate here. We can even roughly say that when the Japanese intellectuals go abroad and come across a certain wall or obstacle there, they write Nihonjinron in order to stabilize their identity. With this in mind, in this book I intend to look at what kind of "walls" each of them have faced, and in which direction the Nihonjinron led the authors.

Lastly, I will discuss the meaning of the hypothesis I introduced here in relation to Nihonjinron written by foreigners. In fact, from the end of the 16th to 17th century, when Japan was experimenting with its three models externally, information about Japan was presented in the form of a certain Nihonjinron. An example of this is the attempts to "understand Japan" as part of activities by missionaries in works such as *Historia de Japan*, written by Luis Frois. These books are similar to the ethnographic records of the 19th to 20th centuries, the forerunners of anthropology, which is my area of specialization. They have two dimensions: its nature as the groundwork data for missionary or colonialist activities, and the desire to "genuinely" learn about something different in detail like a natural historian. Both of them do not strictly fit into the hypothesis that "the writing of Nihonjinron is driven by anxiety". However, I would like to indicate that in their attempt to question how they should understand the "different" Japanese people within the Western framework, these works have something in common with Nihonjinron that tries to explain what place one holds within the Western modernity.

Many works of this kind of Nihonjinron written by foreigners were also produced by the foreigners who visited Japan from the end of the Tokugawa shogunate to the Meiji period. Each of the books is an "ethnographic record", or a "travel account", comprised of the afore-mentioned two dimensions. The later works such as Ruth Benedict's *The Chrysanthemum and the Sword* and Ezra Vogel's *Japan as Number One*, which I will discuss in more detail later in this book, are written as a result of anxiety towards "Japan in the modernity" in the opposite sense and are thus different from the records about Japan in the Warring States period or the late days of the Tokugawa shogunate. This is the anxiety that stems from trying to find out whether or not Japan is a changeling in the western modernity that is native to the authors. In this book I will study a few outstanding examples of this. I trust that they will serve as important sources for the examination of my hypothesis on Nihonjinron.

Note 1
In this text, in all cases in which the terms such as *nihonbunkaron* ("discourse on the Japanese culture"), *nihonshakairon* (discourse on the Japanese society) or *nihonron* ("discourse on Japan") may be more ap-plicable, I will still use the term "Nihonjinron" ("the discourse on the Japanese") for the purpose of convenience, as all of these terms address the same topics.

CHAPTER 2

"Rich Country; Strong Army": The Period of Elation between the First Sino-Japanese War and the Russo-Japanese War

Four Books on Nihonjinron

When one discusses Nihonjinron, it usually equates to looking at the written content of a particular book. However, in this book, I will attempt not only to discuss individual works on Nihonjinron but also to think about Nihonjinron as a whole and address questions such as why it is written and read. I will therefore examine not only the content of the works but also the process by which the discourse was formed as well as when, by whom, and for whom it was created, as these questions are equally important.

The nearly a decade between the First Sino-Japanese war (1894-95) and the Russo-Japanese war (1904-05) can be considered the first period in which Nihonjinron flourished. Many writers addressed the subject of Japan and the Japanese after facing national endeavors that took the form of the two wars against the outside powers. The fact that a journal under the self-evident title *Nihonjin* ("The Japanese"), first published in 1888 by a group of editors including Shigetaka Shiga, whom I will come back to later in this chapter, merged with *Nihon* ("Japan"), a newspaper in press from 1889, to become *Nihon oyobi Nihonjin* ("Japan and the Japanese") serves as a symbolic example of the period. As a response to Japan's national "crisis", the writings about Japan at that time looked at Japan by drawing comparisons between it and "foreign countries" and appealed to the growing national awareness of the Japanese. Even poet Takuboku Ishikawa, who was 18 years old at the time and yet to turn to writing skeptical works on the state and the times, started a nationalistic serial titled *Senun Yoroku* ("A Personal Memorandum of the Wartime") in the *Iwate Nippō* newspaper upon the onset of the Russo-Japanese war in 1904.

Among the many volumes produced at the time, each of the four books that will be discussed in this chapter had their first edition and English originals published during this period, became bestsellers or longsellers, and are still highly valued as the classics of Nihonjonrin and readily available in paperback in Japan. The following list shows the publication dates of these books in chronological order, along with the dates of the First Sino-Japanese War and the Russo-Japanese War:

August 1, 1894: The declaration of the First Sino-Japanese War (ended April 17, 1895)
October 24, 1894: Shigetaka Shiga, *Nihon Fūkeiron* ("The Landscape of Japan")
November 24, 1894: Kanzō Uchimura, *Representative Men of Japan* (Written in English; originally known as *Japan and the Japanese*)
December 1899: Inazō Nitobe, *Bushido: The Soul of Japan* (Written in English)
February 10, 1904: The declaration of the Russo-Japanese war (ended September 5, 1905)
May 1906: Tenshin Okakura, *The Book of Tea* (Written in English)

These four books on Nihonjinron have a few particularly characteristic features in common. One of the points highlighted in this chapter is that these common features do clearly reveal an aspect of the times in which they were written. Nevertheless, despite the presence of these commonalities, these works of Nihonjinron also clearly pursued different goals, and were influenced by the individual style of each author. These differences can also be found in later works on Nihonjinron. In order to discuss these similarities and differences, let us look at the content of each of the books.

All of the four books appear to be widely known. At least, this can be said of their titles. However, in all of the four books, the impression given by the title differs somewhat from the actual contents. I shall address these differences as I briefly summarize the content of these books.

A summary of the contents of *Nihon Fūkeiron* (hereafter, "The Landscape of Japan") by Shigetaka Shiga would probably amount to saying that it is a literary work in which a geographer explains the Japanese archipelago's natural geographic characteristics mainly in terms of its climate, marine currents, water vapor, and volcanoes, stating that Japan's scenery does not only rank as equal but as superior to that of the West and China. This description makes it seem like an academic monograph, but its actual contents range widely – one might even say excessively – from its theory on culture to its accounts on mountaineering techniques, with its general message being Nihonjinron for the masses. This has something to do with the fact that in the 19th century, geography belonged to the general humanities, which were inclined to making speculations on the characteristics of the society and people of a country – in contrast with fields such as geology, which as a natural science involved providing empirical explanations.

Kanzō Uchimura's *Representative Men of Japan* is a biography style account of the lives and vestiges left by Takamori Saigō, Yōzan Uesugi, Sontoku Ninomiya, Tōju Nakae and Nichiren Shōnin. Each of the narrations is short and written plainly and clearly. If one quickly flips through its pages, the book gives the impression of a collection of biographies of "great men" that was written by a person recognized as an intellectual responding to a request to produce a book for youngsters of about high or middle school age. However, if one starts pondering the reason why these five men were selected and grouped together in one book, and why the chosen men are described not just as "great" men but as five men who "represent" the Japanese, it gives a different flavor from that of any juvenile volume on five "great men of Japan".

Among the four books I shall introduce here, *Bushido: The Soul of Japan* is perhaps the most well-known. Inazō Nitobe perceives *bushidō* as a "system of ethics" of the Japanese and interprets the virtue and value of integrity, courage, benevolence, and politeness as well as the life and code of the *samurai*, making it a book on understanding Japan. Judging from the title alone, this book appears as if it was written by a restorationist. Yet, from the viewpoint of its composition and the way the arguments are built, its contents are different from first impressions; while mainly making comparisons with chivalry, this work discusses *bushidō* in contrast with the West and readily refers to Veblen's *The Theory of the Leisure Class* that had just been published in 1899, the same year.

The last work, Tenshin Okakura's *The Book of Tea*, along with two more of his works – *The Ideals of the East* and *The Awakening of Japan* – are often seen as the author's trilogy on the theory on civilization. While

The Ideals of the East and *The Awakening of Japan* address "the theory on art" and "the theory on culture" respectively, and their titles suggest a cultural flavor, they incorporate messages akin to political manifestos containing vehement words. As a result, upon merely seeing the title of *The Book of Tea* readers may assume that it deals with the unique traditions of the Japanese tea ceremony. However, just a quick glance at the table of contents reveals that two of the seven chapters that make up the book – "Taoism and Zennism" and "Art Appreciation" – bear no direct relation to "tea". Furthermore, as is suggested by Okakura's choice to title the book *The Book of Tea* as opposed to "The Book of the Tea Ceremony", the second chapter, entitled "The Schools of Tea", for instance, addresses not the major schools of the tea ceremony, such as Omotesenke and Urasenke, but the process of the tea plant becoming the source of a popular beverage, and most of the chapter is focused on developments in China. As briefly demonstrated in the summaries of the four books above, while the titles address *bushidō*, tea, and other such aspects of Japanese culture, the contents of the works do not necessarily fit with the respective titles. With the exception of Shiga, none of the authors is even an expert on the topics of their respective works. In other words, all these authors intended something more than providing an explanation of their subjects. Their agendas were brought forth in the context of the ongoing contemporary pursuit of "Nihonjinron". It is this discourse that made these authors write their books. This is the reason why, despite their individual contents, I group these four books together as the Nihonjinron of the time.

The Four Authors

The four authors belong to the same generation. Their birthdates are so close to each other that one could even describe them as "the same age".

They were all born during the three years between 1861 and 1863: Kanzō Uchimura in 1861, Inazō Nitobe in 1862, Tenshin Okakura in 1862, and Shigetaka Shiga in 1863. It is interesting to note that Japan was experiencing drastic changes while they were in their formative years. In 1867, at around the age of six, they all witnessed the downfall of the Tokugawa regime and the disturbances that surrounded it. Apart from Okakura, who was the son of a Yokohama merchant, they were born to families of feudal retainers, whose lives underwent radical transformations brought about by the collapse of the *bakuhan* system implemented by the Tokugawa shogunate.

It is likely that experiencing this major shift in the world at an early age influenced them in a number of ways. They must have been deeply affected by the way in which the Meiji Restoration became a complete overhaul that served as a historic manifestation of the irrevocable nature of modern "progress". Even if such a transition did not affect them deep in their hearts, the changes of that period, in terms of the actual circumstances they found themselves in, presented them with opportunities for great advancement in life, for though they had been born to military families, they had not been members of the upper class under the old regime. All four of them studied English and pursued higher education in order to make the most of these opportunities. English took the place of the conventional "Chinese books" and the Chinese language as the language of the new generation. Among them, Okakura went to the present University of Tokyo, while Uchimura, Nitobe, and Shiga attended Sapporo Agricultural College in Hokkaido. Uchimura and Nitobe enrolled in 1877 at the ages of fifteen and sixteen respectively as part of the second intake, and Shiga in 1880 at the age of sixteen as part of the fourth intake.

When we hear the name "Sapporo Agricultural College" now, it may sound like a low-level educational institution dealing with the not-so-glamorous occupation of agriculture, in a remote location with no railway access. The reality was quite different.

At that time, this college was, alongside the University of Tokyo, one of the two national institutions of higher education in the country where one could obtain a bachelor degree. With its first intake comprising of sixteen students and second intake of seventeen students – including Uchimura and Nitobe – it was literally a training institution for the elite (although the numbers of students are disputed). Sapporo was chosen as the location (its predecessor was first opened in Tokyo in 1872 but moved in 1875) as it was felt that Hokkaido, Japan's "colony" of the times, was the best location in which to educate the elite to become the future leaders of imperialism, and because the area was rich in agriculture, Japan's key industry at the time – the majority of Japan's population was still in farming even after the industrial revolution in Europe. Agriculture was also seen as essential should another colony be acquired. Besides agriculture, the curriculum covered other subjects deemed necessary for colonization and cultivation, such as geology, land surveying, and civil engineering. Moreover, the teaching was conducted in English by foreign lecturers such as the famous Dr. William S. Clark, an American missionary, who became the founding president of the college. The teaching methods included debates, which were held in English. In other words, Sapporo Agricultural College was "foreign" in terms of both its geographical environment and the language used there.

As the offspring of the warrior class entered the college, both they and the people around them believed it was the beginning of an age of "educational elites". Maybe it is even more accurate to say that they decided to study in a "foreign country" without actually going abroad. Their English skills were therefore the result of training in such an environment during their early years. These English skills would support their future work, turning them into "internationally-minded" people. At the same time, they were also greatly influenced by another factor: Christianity. Dr. Clark and many of the other tutors at the college were devoted Christians. Some of the young students, who were influenced by their tutors in all aspects of themselves as people, were baptized and became Christians. Uchimura and Nitobe, who were the best of the best among the college's second intake, became Christians along with a few students from the first intake, later forming a group known as the "Sapporo Band", and were practicing Christians throughout their lives. Uchimura in particular exerted significant influence on the academic world as a religious leader. Nitobe's affiliation with Christianity, in terms of the protestant ideal of searching for a new world, could be directly linked to his subsequent position as one of the first professors of colonization policy at Tokyo Imperial University and his work as deputy secretary-general at the League of Nations after the First World War.

Another graduate of Sapporo Agricultural College, Shigetaka Shiga, is said to have been antipathetic towards Christianity. The reason was perhaps that he studied English at Kōgyokusha, an institution closely related to the navy, where besides Western learning, great value was placed on "Japan and Han studies, i.e. Japanese history and Chinese studies" (Ōmuro 2003: 228). It is also related to the fact that he entered the Agricultural College during the fourth intake when the predominant influence that Dr. Clark had held around the times of its founding had dwindled, and backlash had emerged against the secretive Christian groups among the students of the "Sapporo Band" in the first and second intakes.

Here, I will refrain from delving any deeper into the depiction of these four men, all of whom engaged in diverse and extensive activities, but will instead touch on "colonialism", a topic to which they are all connected. At present it is common to discuss "colonialism" in terms of the "evil doings" of the major nations of the 19th to 20th centuries. However, at least in those times, it was considered something of positive "value". In other words, colonization and civilization were positioned as appropriate endeavors for a young person to devote one's whole life to. It can perhaps be compared to the fields of "development" and "international aid" that attract young people today. No doubt in the core of the "colonization and civilization" of the West lies the Christian spirit of sharing beliefs with all mankind. Therefore, the fact that Uchimura and Nitobe became Christians at Sapporo Agriculture College goes beyond the mere coincidence that the faculty members themselves were Christians, but, most importantly, it is related to Christianity as the backbone of the education provided by the Agricultural College, which foresaw the future, from the cultivation of Hokkaido to the colonization of Taiwan and Manchuria under Japan's imperialist initiatives. Tadao Yanaihara, who was responsible for colonization policy at Tokyo Imperial University after Nitobe, was also Christian, thus continuing this lineage.

The last of the four authors I have introduced, Tenshin Okakura, did not attend Sapporo Agriculture College. He did however start to learn English in Yokohama from the age of seven and soon entered the Tokyo Foreign Language School (which later became the Tokyo English School) to study English. The Faculty of Letters of the University of Tokyo, which he entered at the remarkable age of fifteen, was an educational institution where the lectures were still held in foreign languages by the foreign advisors who assisted the Meiji government (*o-yatoi gaikokujin*, lit. "hired foreigners"). Owing to his proficiency in English, he was later able to maintain a wide range of activities in the West and in Asia as an internationally-minded cultural figure. Interestingly, Uchimura and Nitobe had also studied at the Tokyo Foreign Language School before they enrolled in Sapporo Agricultural College.

As seen above, these four elite cultural figures of the Meiji period, who were raised at similar educational institutions in the same period, personally embodied the story of contemporary Japan. The leaders of the Meiji Restoration one or two generations before them entrusted this new elite, which they had created through pure cultivation in a test environment of Western culture, with the task of rapidly bringing Japan abreast of Western modernity and allowing it to prevail in the competition of colonialism. Bestowed with this role, the four men all went abroad upon their graduation from Sapporo Agricultural School and the University of Tokyo (Nitobe also studied at the University of Tokyo after leaving the Sapporo Agricultural School). Uchimura went to Amherst College (USA), Nitobe to Johns Hopkins University (USA) and then to the Martin Luther University of Halle-Wittenberg (Germany). Okakura spent one year abroad at the age of twenty-four, during which time he traveled with and studied Western art under art historian Ernest Fenollosa. All of them ventured overseas as the vanguard forces of modernity. Their high levels of English ability, familiarity with Western culture from childhood, and the fact that they were young men in their early twenties – namely, at an age when people tend to be more adaptable – all worked as favorable conditions for their ventures overseas. During their trips to foreign countries, they were able to take on duties that made optimum use of their abilities.

It is important to assess the magnitude of impact that these kinds of experiences of the "foreign" had on the Japanese intellectuals. In particular, how they were accepted had a great influence on their views of foreign countries, or in a narrower sense, on how Japan was viewed by foreigners. The most renowned novelist in modern Japan, Sōseki Natsume's experience of studying abroad, when he rather reluctantly spent time overseas in his mid-thirties and developed neurosis, is very famous as Sōseki himself talked about it afterwards. However, the periods that these three men spent abroad were a success in many ways. These men had positive experiences in the West. The success of studying and living abroad largely depends on whether one is able to establish relationships with the locals. Relationships with others hinge upon language and body. They were accepted by the Western society largely due to their ability in foreign languages. These abilities allowed them to have friendly associations and even romances with Westerners. In their personal lives, Nitobe married an American and Okakura later took on a position at an art museum in Boston, enjoying popularity among the ladies of the Boston circle of intellectuals. Underneath these successes there were also many "unpleasant" experiences related to them being from a small country in the East; however, the fact that the peak of their activities coincided with the time when this small country was significantly rising in prominence helped them to develop a positive attitude to "the foreign" and thus a better view of the Japanese.

Shiga's case was slightly different. Later in his career he occupied a certain position in political and bureaucratic circles and seized on various chances to travel the world several times, but before that in 1886, at the age of twenty-three, he set out on a tour of the South Sea Islands on the navy training ship *Tsukuba*. It is notable that, unlike the other three men who went to the West, Shiga first visited Hawaii, New Zealand and Australia, where he witnessed the situation in the Pacific colonies. I would now like to discuss what kind of difference this creates in comparison with the three other men.

"The Landscape of Japan"

Such were the experiences that Uchimura, Nitobe, Okakura, and Shiga – four men in their thirties, the prime of their lives, at the time of the then "young Japan" – accumulated before writing their works between 1894 and 1904. Let us have a look at when, for whom, and how these works were written. Firstly, two of the books were written in 1894: Shigetaka Shiga's "The Landscape of Japan" and Kanzō Uchimura's *Representative Men of Japan*.

Shiga's "The Landscape of Japan" was written shortly before the commencement of the First Sino-Japanese War. However, rather than being inspired by the imminent outbreak of the First Sino-Japanese War, Shiga was foreseeing and describing how the social climate of the age was drawing Japan toward the conflict. The book followed the same tone adopted by the nationalistic journal *Nihonjin* (The Japanese), which he played a key role in launching, as it was targeted at Japanese citizens and emphasized the pride that should be taken in the Japanese scenery. It therefore became a big seller when it was published at the height of the war, a time when news of Japan's victories had sent spirits soaring high.

It was indeed both a bestseller and a long seller that captured the spirit of the people and the time. Although I wrote that it was a book published at the height of the First Sino-Japanese War and intended for the Japanese, it is possible to assume that they were not the only readers. Judging from the *kanbun* (Chinese prosaic style) of the book, we can imagine that it was a pleasant read for contemporary book lovers. Content-wise, sometimes Shiga seems to jump here and there as he pleases, introducing such subjects as mountain-climbing techniques, which can hardly be called useful, and in this sense it is an internally-focused work for domestic readers. However, the author's resplendent writing also hints at an awareness of "foreigners" who are beyond the drama of the writers and readers of the Japanese reading circles. In this case, "foreign countries" includes not only the West but also China, as Shiga compares Japan's scenery to that of the West and notes the way in which the value of Japanese scenery has been measured against the landscape of China, as the sceneries depicted in Chinese paintings and calligraphic works had been seen as a standard of authenticity since ancient times.

While on the one hand "The Landscape of Japan" repeatedly argues that the scenery of Japan is unparalleled in the world, on the other, it seems to rely on evaluations from Westerners as the final authority with which to emphasize Japan's uniqueness. We can see this for instance where he describes one of the Japan's typical scenic views created by "water vapor" as something that "cannot be found in a foreign country" (Shiga 1995(1894): 83-84). Furthermore – and this is something that had not been said before about the Japanese landscape – he explains how the various scenes are produced by the contraction of the ground surface due to the volcanic nature of the islands and builds a comparison by saying that this does not happen in Joseon or China. This kind of comparison was not used to note that Japanese scenery was one among the many in the world, but to claim that it was equal to the Western landscape and superior to that of its Asian neighbors. There is a reason why my understanding is that Shiga wished to emphasize that it was equal rather than superior to the West.

In *Shiga Shigetaka Nihon Fūkeiron Seidoku* ("An Intensive Reading of Shiga Shigetaka's 'The Landscape of Japan'"; 2003) Mikio Ōmuro argues that Shiga was reluctant to compare Japan's scenery to that of its Western counterparts when he wrote "The Landscape of Japan", but later developed a talent for it, coming up with descriptions such as the Kiso River as the "Japanese equivalent of the Rhine". While I agree with Ōmuro's interpretation, I believe that in "The Landscape of Japan" Shiga was creating differences between his comparisons with the scenery of Asian countries and his comparisons with that of the West. For example, after referring to the active volcanoes present in Japan but inexistent in China, Joseon or England, as nature's "ultimate creation" (Shiga

1995(1894): 175), he goes on to mention the rare sights produced by basalt rocks in England and remark that they also exist in Japan, albeit not prominently. While this may seem like yet another vague attempt to assert that Japan is "number one", Shiga is in fact seeking to imply that "Japan is the same as the West".

This is a significant difference. In short, when comparing Japan's landscape to that of other East Asian countries, Shiga emphasizes the *superiority* of Japan's "unique" features, but when making comparisons with the West, he refrains from accentuating Japan's "uniqueness", instead adding that "Japan is *the same*," as if he subconsciously sensed that doing so would separate Japan from the Western modernity. While in the proud account of Japan's volcanic islands that I touched upon above he completely ignores the fact that countries such as Italy and America also have volcanoes, later in the book Shiga makes an off-the-cuff, and somewhat deceptive reference to the fact that Roman civilization, the cradle of Western Civilization, was also founded on volcanic rocks (Shiga 1995(1894): 190).

Here, one can see that Shiga tried to depict Japan as a country that was advancing rapidly and waging wars on great powers like China and Russia by portraying it as unrivaled in Asia and toe-to-toe with modern Western civilization. He attributes Japan's success to its similarities with Europe (Roman civilization) rather than Asia (China and Joseon), and noting that Japan had not shared the history of the West, looks for explanations of Japan's success in the "geographic and geological" conditions that differ from and are in a sense more constant than historical factors. However, according to Shiga's intrinsically nationalistic assertion, Japan's uniqueness is essential for maintaining its sense of identity. When he compares Japan with Britain, a nation with which Japan was building a closer relationship at the time, he therefore attempts to preserve Japan's unique identity by touching on features of Japan that are superior to those of Britain in addition to observing the similarities.

The fact that, as mentioned above, Shiga's first ventures abroad were a visit to the South Sea Islands, Australia, and New Zealand, was surely a key factor behind this tendency to vacillate between emphasizing Japan's uniqueness and noting her similarities with the West. When writing "The Landscape of Japan" he had not yet laid his eyes on the West. That is, what he witnessed of colonialism was not the prosperity of suzerain powers but life in the vanquished colonies. The aforementioned work by Ōmuro (2003) sheds greater light on Shiga's subsequent travel to the West in 1910 – a time when Japan had already ascended to the ranks of the great powers – when Shiga freely likened the Kiso River to the Rhein and the lakes of Shinshū to those of Switzerland. Just as Japan needed Nihonjinron discourse when it was working to avoid colonization, as someone who had witnessed the colonies Shiga required Nihonjinron discourse at the time of writing "The Landscape of Japan".

Representative Men of Japan

Kanzō Uchimura's *Representative Men of Japan* is in fact a revised version of a work entitled "Japan and the Japanese" that was originally published in English in 1894. In producing *Representative Men of Japan,* which was published in 1908, Uchimura removed certain sections from and made a few modifications to the original.

Uchimura started writing the initial edition the night before the First Sino-Japanese war. As the war proceeded, he referred to it as a sacred war (in this edition, the war is called the "Corean war" and there is a chapter "Justification of the Corean War"), and expressed his support for the war by adding a section on Takamori Saigō, who had advocated the dispatch of troops to Joseon. At that time, Uchimura criticizes Shiga's "The Landscape of Japan" discussed earlier, but in this text he partly refrains from such criticism, and concentrates on observing the direction of the war as it unfolds. However, by the time the First Sino-Japanese War came to an end, Uchimura had already become skeptical towards both the war and warfare in general, and by the time of the Russo-Japanese War he stood firm as an influential pacifist.

With this in mind, it becomes important to consider for whom and how *Representative Men of Japan* was written. While its original edition was written in English, this does not necessarily mean that it was not intended for Japanese readers. It is most likely that it was aimed at Japanese who would read it in the original English and that it was presumed that the book would be immediately translated into Japanese. In 1894, however, there was no need to bother explaining about figures such as prominent military figure Takamori Saigō and agricultural reformer Sontoku Ninomiya and justifying the on-going war to the Japanese readers. The purpose was therefore to defend and applaud Japan and the target audience was "foreign countries".

This did not change with the publication of the revised edition. While it was no longer advocating Japan's war but Japan itself as a historic entity, and the level at which the discussions were set out was not international society but a humanistic, intellectual and Christian dimension, the justification and praise remained the same. Nowadays it is difficult to comprehend Uchimura's personal character as a Christian and the importance of Christianity, especially to the educated youth, in this particular stage of the Meiji period.

While the purpose of this chapter is not to investigate Uchimura, who as a Christian and as a Japanese loved "the two Js" – Jesus and Japan – or elucidate his "patriotism", it is interesting to note that Uchimura's intent did not change significantly over the years. When the first edition was revised, none of the five representative Japanese were replaced, despite the removal of the pro-war chapter. Uchimura's intention was to overcome the dilemma of being Christian and Japanese at the same time. If we consider this in connection with the discussion of this book, it means surmounting the anxiety that a Japanese person may feel toward their identity as a Christian follower. The five representative Japanese were not chosen merely as "outstanding" people but also because their lives, legacies, and thoughts would have made them great "Christians". By noting Saigō's self-denial, honorable poverty, and commitment to the motto "revere heaven, love people", Uchimura identifies Saigō as someone who, while "lacking" Christian puritanism, is somehow "puritan" like Oliver Cromwell. Similarly, he depicts the respected feudal lord Yōzan Uesugi as a "paladin" who tried to bring the "Kingdom of Heaven" to this world in an age that was not yet blessed with Christianity, and neo-Confucian scholar Tōju Nakae's life as a proof that "education" existed even before Western Christianity came to Japan's salvation. Both Buddhist monk Nichiren and Sontoku Ninomiya are also introduced in a Christian context as Japanese who can be highly commended for their Christian-like values before Christianity became known in Japan.

More than anything this serves as emphasis of the fact that the Japanese had the capacity to become Christians – even before the Meiji Restoration. From his perspective as a Christian, Uchimura therefore substantiated that even though Japan did not belong to the Western civilization historically, it was both capable and competent of acting similarly to the West in the modern age. The point of this argument is consistent with the tone of the discussion about eliminating anxiety regarding national identity in the modern age and its effect does not stop at "Christianity" but functions as a prescription for Japan and the Japanese for the entire Western modernity.

Bushido: The Soul of Japan

Inazō Nitobe's *Bushido: The Soul of Japan* (hereafter *Bushido*) resembles the features and structure of Uchimura's work in terms of for whom and how it was written. Firstly, it was written in English and published in America in 1899. Although its Japanese translation came out the following year, it was mainly read in Europe and America. The book seeks to explain *bushid*ō, a reflection of Japan's unique identity, with the aim of highlighting the Western culture, namely the Christian virtues, within *bushid*ō and encouraging readers to recognize Japan as a country that is on par with any of the countries of the West.

According to a commentary by Norihisa Suzuki (Uchimura 1997(1894): 201), the materials that Uchimura referred to when writing *Representative Men of Japan* "could be easily accessed, were popular and even included children's readings". Nitobe also simply relied on materials he had read and things that he had heard when writing *Bushido*. It is beyond doubt that Nitobe possessed a wide range of knowledge, and he did not demand any additional resources about *bushid*ō in order to write the book. Rather, it is interesting that he cites numerous references from Western texts. It is also significant that to illustrate a real-life case of seppuku, a ritualistic suicide (by the Tosa *samurai* sentenced to death in the 1868 Sakai incident), he draws the description of events from a Western source rather than using Japanese-language source materials. Nitobe attempted to persuade Western readers with little knowledge of *bushid*ō to see it as a universally-discussed topic with a "modern" perspective and, fearing to make a mistake about the Western realities and wishing to avoid becoming idiosyncratic or reactionary, he cited the aforementioned works by Veblen and Hegel.

"Universally" refers of course to universality in the context of Western civilization. In the same way that Uchimura implied that the only thing that his "representative men of Japan" lacked as Christians was prior knowledge about Christ, Nitobe argues that *bushid*ō is a moral system of a dignified civilization that stands on a no lesser pedestal than that of Western civilization, adding that if one desires a higher level, that should be "Christian love" – one area that *bushidō* "too often forgot duly to emphasize" (Nitobe 2002(1899): 150). In short, although *bushidō* is undoubtedly close to the heights of Christianity and Western civilization, it is not entirely the same. Still, Nitobe stipulates that since the Japanese have long maintained this level, they are capable of ascending to the altitude of Christianity and Western civilization.

From one point of view, it is not surprising if one gets weary of the way in which Nitobe attributes everything to Christianity as it suits him. What deserves our attention is not whether this line of thought is still valid today, but how this book – which is still well-known today – was written as Nihonjinron. In this respect, Nitobe, as a Christian and a cosmopolitan intellectual, clearly struggled to bring together into one identity the two conflicting elements of Japan's uniqueness as a non-Western society and the universality within Western civilization. Regardless of the approach, the fact that people still reread and quote *Bushido* and sometimes attempt to write their own versions modeled on it (Lee 2003), is for no reason other than that they are deeply moved by the fact that it diligently addressed a straightforward yet still unsolved matter by trying to form a bridge between these two irreconcilable elements.

The Book of Tea

The last book, *The Book of Tea* is an affirmation of the "East" to the "West". In a certain sense, it is not about bridge building. It is an antagonistic assertion of uniqueness. In the two other works in Okakura's trilogy on the theory of civilization – *The Ideals of the East* and *The Awakening of Japan* – he voices resistance against the West in a stronger tone. Yet, none of the three books present a denial of the West. Rather, they must be perceived as a reinforcement of the East and Japan in a way in which the author acknowledges and then resists Western values. He argues that it is urgently necessary to speed up the awakening of the East and Japan, reevaluating oneself and recapturing the outcome in positive terms. His target readers therefore differ from those of the three works discussed above.

If we consider it in contrast with "The Landscape of Japan" – which was also strong in its affirmation of Japan, while "The Landscape of Japan" was written in *kanbun* with the Japanese readers intended as the primary audience, *The Book of Tea* and the two other works by Okakura were written in English and meant for English-reading foreigners. But unlike *Representative Men of Japan*, the envisaged audience was not English-speaking people or Japanese who could read English. One of the differences is that while the first edition of *Representative Men of Japan* was written in English and published by Keiseisha in Tokyo, *The Book of Tea* was published in New York by Fox, Duffield and Company. The book therefore targets foreigners even more than Uchimura's work. Another telling difference is that, just as *Ideals of the East* appeals to the Indians who were fighting for their independence from colonial oppression, in Okakura's mind "the foreigners", as an intended reading group, did not only include the Europeans and Americans, but also Asians and other non-Westerners under colonial rule who were capable of reading English. I would like to mark this as a difference that distinguishes Okakura's work from those of the other three authors.

As I mentioned earlier, the second chapter, "The Schools of Tea", describes how tea originated from China and how its tradition was inherited by Japan, and the third chapter, "Taoism and Zennism", discusses Chinese Taoist thought and how Zennism emanated from India and then came to Japan through China, implying a "pan-Asian" culture sphere. By doing so, Okakura emphasizes that the Nihonjinron discourse expands to become discourse on Asia and the story of Japan's resistance against the West comes into being within the story of Asia. This is perhaps what we can see when looking back at *The Book of Tea* from the perspective of Okakura's subsequent intellectual path. It is just that despite all the similarities this book shares with the three books written by the other three authors, the direction in which it embarks is clearly different.

Finally, I would like to consider a few specific parts of *The Book of Tea*. Okakura writes of the average Westerner: "He was wont to regard Japan as barbarous while she indulged in the gentle arts of peace: he calls her civilized since she began to commit wholesale slaughter on Manchurian battlefields" (Okakura 1994(1906): 217). He goes on to say: "Much comment has been given lately to the Code of the Samurai – the Art of Death which makes our soldiers exult in self-sacrifice; but scarcely any attention has been drawn to Teaism, which represents so much of our Art of Life" (Okakura 1994(1906): 217-218). The first quote is not irony but a lamentation. The underlying attitude is not that of satisfaction with Japan being recognized, regardless of the means by which this was achieved. If Japan's war is regarded as the birth of a new imperialistic state and reinforcement of this system, it means that the liberation of Asia envisaged by Okakura has become even more remote. Okakura displays full criticism towards such a situation. The second quotation seems not only to refer to the letters of praise written to the Japanese military men by Western war correspondents and military attachés, but also to Nitobe's *Bushido*. I interpret it as a criticism towards the publication of the latter.

Similarities, Differences and Testing the Hypothesis

If we summarize the earlier arguments, we will see that there are many similarities between these books in terms of their authors and when, for whom, and how they were written. The authors all share an elite upbringing and education, and were writing in a period of glory marked by Japan's victories against China and Russia. All of the books were aimed either directly or indirectly at readers from "foreign countries." All four books built their discussions on the basis of comparisons with foreign countries, and three of them were written in English. While the books cover different topics – landscape, living style, moral systems, or culture – they all pit Japan against the leading countries of the West by recognizing the uniqueness of these elements of Japanese culture and tradition while also stating that these matters are universal to the age of modernity and its world and stressing that they are thus sometimes superior or equal to that of the West not because they are unique, but because they can be compared universally.

However, when we also consider the personalities of the four authors, the differences are noticeable. As I noted above, what sharply distinguishes the three books written in English from Shiga's "The Landscape of Japan" written in *kanbun*, Chinese prosaic style, is the way in which the former works seek to position Japan within Western civilization, in contrast with the forcefulness of the latter, which emphasizes the uniqueness of Japan as an absolute value – in fact, it contains many laughable arguments. Yet, if we take a closer look, we can see that as the first books praise Japan too much, their arguments that everything already existed there before Meiji Restoration are somewhat labored. As noted earlier, in Shiga's work, amidst what seems to be him boasting Japan's superiority, we can see that he is overly concerned with the perspectives of "foreign countries". One can understand that as far as the similarities and differences go, whether to look at Japan's "uniqueness" inside universality or whether to address it as an independent subject is a matter of mere emphasis. As for "uniqueness", the four authors are not very eager to examine its true nature. They simply perceive differences as unique when applying narrow comparison with the "West" of their knowledge. What my argument brings into question is how they interpreted the identity of Japan and the Japanese in their own experiences of encounters with the foreign countries given that they could not help but see Japan's features as unique.

If we look at this in the context of Christianity, Uchimura and Nitobe's suggestions that Japan's past civilization is something that can be evaluated from a Christian perspective are a direct expression of viewpoints of the Christian members of the Sapporo Band; in contrast, Okakura and Shiga have approached the culture and landscape of Japan from the non-Western vantage point. Yet, it is a challenge to determine what the "non-Western" perspective here really constitutes. It is fair to say that Okakura, rather than taking the "non-Western" position, wrote about the "one Asia" that he wished for. Shiga cloaks his geological description of the landscape of Japan as something objective and scientific, but is on the other hand attempting to create a core of independent Japanese values by bringing out "aesthetic judgments", and the focus is mostly on rhetoric rather than logic. Thus, none of the works produce a stable notion of Japanese identity.

The question of the kinds of readers these books are aimed at reveals a number of differences, which start from whether the adopted language is English or Japanese. In terms of differences, among the three works originally written in English *Bushido* and *The Book of Tea* were expected to resonate in the Western publishing circles while it was assumed that *Representative Men of Japan* would also be studied by Japanese who can read in English. Moreover, all the authors must have anticipated that each of the three works issued in English would one day be published in Japanese, sooner or later, and the works therefore cannot be simply referred to as "English publications". Only Shiga wrote his book in *kanbun* hoping for it to become a piece that would be rewarding for many Japanese to read. I would like to take note of the fact that while Shiga created the work that required its readers to understand *kanbun*, he was a "cosmopolitan" who was to later journey around the world several times. In short, while he cites Japanese and Chinese literature, the foundations of his learning are largely Western. Therefore, despite all the differences and varieties these books show in terms of literary methods, all four authors share a common background as new Meiji elite and the capability to verse in Japanese, Chinese, and English.

If we refer back to the hypothesis on Nihonjinron set out in the first chapter, these four books were created during a transition between two identity crises. More specifically, they were written as an attempt to cast away the anxiety regarding identity that was invoked by the West's low assessment of Japan and at the same time to justify Japan's greatness with the aim of overcoming the identity crisis resulting from its improved reputation due to the victories in the ongoing war. Time-wise, "The Landscape of Japan" and *Representative Men of Japan* were written as a response to anxiety due to low self-esteem and *Bushido* and *The Book of Tea* as a response to anxiety brought on by inflated pride. However, over the course of their repeated republishings, the first two books take a stance of explaining "greatness". Of the latter two, *The Book of Tea* turns into a discussion not of greatness but of the controversy that only Japan was enjoying a high-ranking status in Asia – which comes across more like a warning than justification. This is not only due to the shift in the author's intent, but also owing to the change in the historical context of Japanese society.

If we put the characteristics of the four books simply, they are distinguished by a positive evaluation of Japan and the resounding nature of the writing style. These characteristics stem largely from the fact that the authors belonged to the elite who embodied that era. While this is something that I will discuss later, many figures, such as author Ryōtarō Shiba (an influential novelist and critic in the 1960s-90s), have described the Meiji period as "bright", yet this is primarily due to the fact that they were fortunate times when the main characters of Japan's story achieved their first success. This fortune includes the fact that people neither fully noticed the incoherence of their identities nor possessed the energy or time to suffer over it. The exception is Okakura, who was aware of and somewhat disconsolate due to the gravity and measure of this problem, and allowed *The Book of Tea* to reflect this. This "gloominess" became a characteristic of the Nihonjinron that followed, which will be discussed in the following chapter.

CHAPTER 3

"Orphans of Modernity": Shōwa's Gentle but Fatal Slope

What Followed for the Four Authors

It was not the case that the four books discussed in the previous chapter were followed by a succession of similar works of the kind that are widely read even now. The four authors each walked their own path and as they did so they each began to develop new images of Japan.

Tenshin Okakura was from the outset a thinker who developed his discourse not within the frameworks of Japan, but as part of a larger construct of Asia, "the East". It is easy to question now the extent to which he was able to visualize the actual conditions of Asia and whether it was right of him to depict "Asia" as a unified region, yet he was breaking new ground in his attempt to address Asia not as a residual category of one out of many, as it was seen by the Westerners, but as an "independent" moving body. The concept of "Asia as one" connects to the Nihonjinron that I will discuss in this chapter.

Uchimura was sharply critical of his own work on *Japan and the Japanese*, the original version of *Representative Men of Japan*, and revised and republished it under its current name, minus the chapter that justified the First Sino-Japanese war. However, as I mentioned earlier, one can see that Uchimura's attitude did not change. For instance, in the chapter on Takamori Saigo, the section on the subjugation of East Asia by Japan still described it as an inevitable result of the contemporary "state of the world" and suggested that the two grounds for invasion of Joseon were territorial expansion in order "to be a compeer with the Great Powers of Europe" and "an idea of the great mission of […] [Japan] as the leader of Eastern Asia" (Uchimura 1908(1894): 23). This relates to the stance Japan takes against "foreign countries", a topic that I will refer to in this chapter. Later, Kanzō Uchimura either lost interest in, became indifferent about, or transcended this statement of his, as he advanced from a religious and theological way of thinking to a "citizen of the world" approach. As this approach breaks away from the level of society too much, I will not discuss it further. Here I will only take note of this "breaking away" in order to briefly return to it later.

From 1920 Inazō Nitobe served as deputy secretary-general at the League of Nations. In addition to being engaged in such international work, he formed a research group, known as the "Kyōdokai", to reconsider the real Japanese society through its regional communities and folk traditions. "Kyōdo" (one's native province) in the name of the group refers to the "rural districts" in contrast to the center, and can be interpreted as Japan's "place of origin". Young Kunio Yanagita (usually referred to as a founder of Japanese folklore studies) was an organizer of this group. He went on to create works that can all be treated as Nihonjinron, but through this circle his relationship with Nitobe deepened and, partially owing to this connection, he came to serve as Japan's delegate of the League of Nations in Geneva. While a line of connection can be drawn from Nitobe to Tadao Yanaihara, mentioned in the previous chapter, with Yanagita, such a line ceases to exist. Rather than being dissociated, the connection just disappeared. I will explain why shortly.

While, as described in detail by Ōmuro (2003), Shiga shifted away from Nihonjinron from that time onwards, I will not discuss his later work. His "geographical Nihonjinron" did however bear a few descendants, including Nihonjiron works such as Tetsurō Watsuji's *Fūdo* ("Climate"), that will appear in this chapter, and Tadao Umesao's *Bunmei no Seitai Shikan* ("Civilization from the Perspective of Ecological History"; 1957).

Here, I would like to mention an episode involving Shiga that hints at Japan's attitude to the outside world after the Russo-Japanese War. In the latter half of his life he travelled around the world and visited Europe in 1910, a time when Japan was establishing itself as one of the great powers following its victory in the Russo-Japanese war and the establishment of the Anglo-Japanese Alliance. During his travels in Europe, he felt that he was treated with respect as a Japanese, or rather, owing to him being Japanese. He makes an observation that this is due to Japan's victory, "namely, to physical force, brute strength", saying that it allows him to "swagger about the European continent" (Ōmuro 2003: 312-313). Here, Shiga seems to consciously switch to a choice of words that is somewhat out of tone with the style of the rest of the work.

This "feeling of elation" experienced by Japanese travelers abroad, is determined by the expectation they had of themselves (the Japanese).

The more one fears that he will be made to feel inferior, the more thrilled he becomes when welcomed cordially. These emotions while travelling may vary widely, from feelings of elation to a sense of failure. What comes to mind is a resentful text written by the Chinese literature expert Kōjirō Yoshikawa describing the cold-hearted welcome he received when visiting post-war Italy (Yoshikawa 1976: 176-178). It is surprising to read how an accomplished scholar such as Yoshikawa, who had travelled extensively to China, falls into an emotional complex of some sort on his first trip in Europe. These sentiments can also be seen as a metaphor for Japan's lonely journey through modernity during the Meiji period. In this chapter I will also look at Riichi Yokomitsu's *Ryoshū* ("Melancholy on a Journey"), another work that was written with such a sensation at core. While we cannot say whether or not he was merely concealing his weaknesses, as people tend to do, Shiga seemed not to experience any such feelings of inferiority, living out his days as a "joyful celebrity" until the late 1920s (Ōmuro 2003: 271).

As I have noted above, with the exception of Shiga, the young men who wrote Nihonjinron during the period of national elation surrounding Japan's victories against China and Russia no longer felt the necessity to be tied to it ideologically. Uchimura, Nitobe, and Okakura extended the framework of Japan to "the world", "the international" and "the locality", and then to "Asia", thus seeking a path along which to transform the problem of "Japan's" identity. At the same time, although Uchimura's and Nitobe's writings were a reaction to and attempt to rectify foreigners' "misconceptions" of Japan, after they had achieved a certain result in this direction, the three men must have determined that by continuing the discussion at the same level they would be adopting the position of "Japanism" (*Nihon shugi*) in its nationalistic sense. One can imagine that Uchimura and Nitobe were both particularly anxious to ensure that the impact of their works did not go beyond their original intentions in this way, given that there were no new books on topics similar to theirs that were written for foreigners in a foreign language. Nitobe's later work *The Japanese Nation* (1911) is in this sense more of a general "introduction to Japan" and not Nihonjinron. Similarly, it is possible to say that Shiga, who stubbornly insisted that the landscape of Japan was unique but then relaxed his attitude by saying that it could be compared to the picturesque sceneries of the West, became driven by the mentality that Nihonjinron was not his task anymore.

The Period When Nihonjinron was **Not** Needed

As a result, no notable works of Nihonjinron were written until those of the mid-1930s to mid-1940s, which I will discuss in this chapter. Before I do so, I would like to touch on some points regarding this period from around 1905 to the mid-1930s.

First of all, the period of some twenty years between the victory in the Russo-Japanese war and the beginning of the Shōwa period in the late 1920s – during which the Taishō period came and went – was marked by comparatively little anxiety regarding identity. It was a period when Japan started being recognized internationally. For this reason, Nihonjinron did not increase in a way that would allow it to remain for the future generations. It would be absurd to hypothesize that the so-called "ordinary people" living in Japan, who did not have the opportunity to go abroad, were habitually troubled with their identity as "citizens of Japan" when there were no impending problems at the national level, such as military enlistment. Such troubles were generally only faced by the elite and "exchange students" who cannot help but come into close contact with "the foreign". However, both the assumption that the so-called "common people" were simply living quietly with no interest in the state and the world, and the belief that they interpreted the problems of identity as Japanese in a similar way to that of the elites and intellectuals are precarious suggestions. In fact, the drastic changes of the post-Meiji modernity ensured that no one was able to stay completely indifferent and uncaring towards the world they lived in and that of the foreign, regardless of their way of living. The national elites, who managed the development and the diplomatic relations of the modern state, would not have been able to do their work without guiding and educating the ordinary people on how to perceive the world beyond Japan. With this premise in mind, I agree with the general assumption that the Taishō period was a time when it was believed that modernization was progressing favorably, and Nihonjinron was not deemed necessary.

Here I would like to introduce two literary works from that period that have a strong Nihonjinron subtext, although they do not belong to this genre in a strict sense. One of them is *Tōno Monogatari* ("The Legends of Tono"), written by the aforementioned Kunio Yanagita in 1910, and the other is a pair of works, *Seihō no hito* and *Zoku Seihō no Hito* ("The Man of the West" and

"Sequel to the Man of the West"), authored by novelist Ryūnosuke Akutagawa, in 1927.

In "The Legends of Tono" one can clearly see that Yanagita, as one of the first and second generation representatives that followed the intellectuals active in the post-Meiji Restoration period, already displayed a different stance towards the Western modernity. For him, the West is neither an object of fascination to look at from afar, nor a force driving modernity with the energy generated by both affection and hatred towards it, but is a barrier, an obstacle of insurmountable strength and differences. For instance, the stronger Japan becomes, the more it seems to achieve equality with the West, but Yanagita suspects that in reality it is not being given an equal position. It is a kind of feeling that might be experienced by an uninvited guest, or an orphan adopted by "modernity". Only someone as lighthearted as Shiga was able to remain convinced that Japan had secured a nearly equal standing with the West. Yanagita, as an activist of the aforementioned Kyōdokai and as someone who was trying to uncover the unwritten folk wisdom, tried to avoid colliding with the barrier of the West head on, seeking ways to take a long detour around it by submerging himself in the inner side of Japan. "The Legends of Tono" is positioned as a work that illustrates this determination.

In the dedication at the beginning of the book, Yanagita dedicates the work "to people who are abroad". I have commented in an earlier work of mine that while this must have "several meanings," in its common meaning it is likely to render a tone that is not short of a challenge, where Yanagita offers something Japan-specific to the foreigners and the Japanese living abroad. I suggested that this dedication has "several meanings" to imply that on the surface the work was intended for people who forgot about the Japan of that kind, but on a deeper level, it was dedicated to those who may reside in the middle of Tokyo or elsewhere but perceive stories about such deep mountains as those of "foreign lands". In this sense, Yanagita may also have wanted to imply that those who were under the influence of modernization in the form of westernization were in fact "abroad" when looked at from the viewpoint of such a Japan. The perceptional change here lies with the attempt to not look at Japan in relation to the "foreign countries" of the West but to reveal "Tōno" as the internal "foreign land" and to emphasize that it is this very Japan, the Japan that possesses the people's history, that has to be explored. This and other works by Kunio Yanagita therefore do not fit into the Nihonjinron that I have in mind. Although they may be discussions about Japan that talk about Japan or discussions about the Japanese people that describe Japanese people, they are not Nihonjinron, which is "directly" aimed at stabilizing the identity anxiety of the Japanese inside the "Western modernity" by means of comparison with "foreign countries". However, it is also true that while it was not the case in Yanagita's individual works, his activities as a whole and his strategy of taking a "big detour" in approaching Japan were carried out within the construct of "identity anxiety", which generated a need for Nihonjinron.

"The Man of the West" – a biographical story of Christ – is hardly a masterpiece among the works of Ryūnosuke Akutagawa. Yet I bring it up here to make a few observations based on the crucial difference between his and Uchimura or Nitobe's stance on Christianity and their sense of distance with the West. First of all, it shows that for Akutagawa's generation "the West" ceased being something constraining that could not be reached unless one changed the language of use to English and one's manners to Western ones. Following its victory in the Russo-Japanese War, Japan had become a country that seemed to be highly respected as one of the first-rate countries of the world and a national power in terms of military affairs, as reflected in its position in the League of Nations. "The Man of the West" is an inquiry into the thought and religion of the Western modernity. The fact that Christianity is dealt with as "one of" the Western philosophies and Christ as one of the "men of the West" reveals that it was the task of the writer of those times to demonstrate that the West could be relativized. Akutagawa himself was acknowledged as a Japanese who was able to consume and relativize such "intellect of the West". Yet, I do not judge this essay in regard to whether the author in fact relativized Christianity as an ideology in his own way. What I view as important is the fact that its mode of writing and rhetoric convince the readers of this kind of possibility by means of narrating "the West" as a local part of the world and not the world itself. This relates to our later discussion about one of his successors, Riichi Yokomitsu.

The twenty years between 1910 and 1930 can therefore be described as a period when Nihonjinron was not perceived necessary. As already noted above, "discussions about Japan" did take place in the field of the human sciences, led by the ethnologist Kunio Yanagita, historian Sōkichi Tsuda, and others, as well as by the so-called nationalistic ideologues of the thought on Japan: Sohō Tokutomi, Kōzaburō Tachibana, Shūmei Ōkawa, and Ikki Kita. They, however, differ from the approach that is normally adopted in Nihonjinron, which explains the anxieties of the author and the reader in the realm of comparisons with "foreign countries". In other words, the writings of these adherents to Japanese ideology, who turned their backs, be it consciously or not, on the circumstances that made Nihonjinron necessary, either drew on the premise that, or attempted to justify the fact that, "Japan" could exist independently from Western modernity, and are thus different from Nihonjinron. Among the works we have examined in this book, they can perhaps be likened in some way to Shigetaka Shiga's stance.

There is one more reason why notable Nihonjinron was not written during that time. It is because in order to discuss the Japanese in this era one has to come close to discussing the Emperor and the underlying system. In other words, under the fairly liberal social conditions of the Taishō period, when one discusses the Japanese by comparing with the foreign countries, it turns into the "relativization" of Japan with the Emperor at its center. However, this undertaking is close to a sacrilegious crime on the one hand, and leaves one vulnerable to an attack from the right wing on the other. Since such discussions seem easy to pursue, they may also conceal the risk of the discussion going too far in that direction. While Akutagawa did carry out a kind of social critique in his novel *Kappa* and the members of the Shirakaba-ha (White Birch Society) literature society did intend to make some remarks calling for a new form of society, they were surely a little fearful as they did so.

Still, the risk of coming close to discussing the Emperor system is ever-present in our society. It is difficult to assess whether this risk subsided or mounted during the some twenty years between 1905 and the late 1920s in comparison with the times of the four men discussed in the previous chapter. Yet, we may say that in Nihonjinron, which has no meaning unless written for the "ordinary readers", this risk was potentially great, unlike the utterances made inside the academic disciplines such as the "Emperor organ theory" by a constitutional scholar Tatsukichi Minobe. Possibly, Nihonjinron, which was inspired by the comparison with foreign countries and in demand of relativization of Japan at some level of discussion, could not emerge during that very period despite the liberal nature of the times, or perhaps precisely due to it.

Four Books on Nihonjinron – Shōwa's Gentle but Fatal Slope

Once Japan caught up with the Western countries following its elation after the First Sino-Japanese and the Russo-Japanese wars, the country entered an age in which it lost a visible goal. We should even say that subsequently during the period from 1930 until its defeat in the war, it lacked a sense of direction and was straying off course. Ryōtarō Shiba gave his novel about Meiji-era Japan up until the Russo-Japanese war the title *Saka no Ue no Kumo* ("Clouds above the Hill") and if we follow this image, Shōwa period Japan could be said to have been aimlessly walking a gentle slope which is neither ascending nor descending. Many turbulent incidents happen one after another, and the country vacillates unable to calm down, with a sense of futility hanging in the air.

The four books that will be discussed in this chapter are similar to the four works reviewed in the previous chapter in that they are still widely read and even considered "classics". While they do not focus entirely on Japan, each of them is a discussion with Japan as its central subject and retains the features of Nihonjinron. They are listed below with their years of publication and relevant historical events.

1929 The Great Depression
1930 *'Iki' no Kōzō* ("The Structure of Iki") by Shūzō Kuki
1933 Japan's withdrawal from the League of Nations
1935 *Fūdo* ("Climate") by Tetsurō Watsuji
1936 The February 26 Rebellion
1937 *Ryoshū* ("Melancholy on a Journey") by Riichi Yokomitsu
1941 Commencement of the Pacific War
1943 *Kindai no Chōkoku* ("Overcoming Modernity"), the record of a symposium preceded by Tetsutarō Kawakami (published in a journal the previous year)

These four works represent a variety of genres including philosophy, the novel, and roundtable discussion. However, they have a rich commonality that transcends their differences. They are not just similar because on the surface they are works that talk about Japan, but also in their attempts to establish how "the Japanese" are positioned within "the Western modernity". Let us have a look at their content and their characteristics as Nihonjinron.

'Iki' no Kōzō ("The Structure of Iki")

Shūzō Kuki's *'Iki' no Kōzō* (hereafter "The Structure of Iki") is an unusual book. There is no other known book that has similar content or writing style. It is rather "boundary-pushing". However, it is known to the world as a classic even though these remarkable features are not recognized. In other words, this work also satisfies the requirements characteristic of classic books in that it was able to become popular without being read as on the basis of its title people assumed it must have some kind of special content.

It is most likely that people think that the book is an analysis of the concept of *iki*, a typically Japanese sensibility or value, using methods from Western philosophy. This is not entirely untrue. A very brief summary of the main points of the work would be that *iki* is comprised of three components – "coquetry" (*bitai*), "pride and honor" (*ikiji*), and "resignation" (akirame) (Kuki 1930, translated by Nara, Hiroshi 2008: 48-49) and the opposing meanings of "elegant/crude", "flashy/quiet", "prideful/boorish", "astringent/sweet" (68-101) that represent it make up a cuboid structure. Yet, even in the opening pages of the book, we come up against an unexpected narration.

> In the intensional analysis of *iki*, we notice that the first distinguishing feature of *iki* is *bitai* 'coquetry' towards the opposite sex. From the fact that *ikigoto* (lit. '*iki* affairs') means *irogoto* (lit. 'romantic affairs'), we know that this relationship with a person of the opposite sex constitutes the fundamental being of *iki*. If we speak of *iki na hanashi* (lit. 'stories that represent *iki*'), the phrase invariably refers to stories about relationships between men and women […]. What then is coquetry? Let us say that coquetry is a dualistic attitude; that it puts a person of the opposite sex in opposition to the monistic self; and that it posits a possible relationship between that person and the self (Kuki 1930, translated by Nara, Hiroshi 2008: 40).

What does the "dualistic attitude" that "posits a possible relationship between that person and the self" really mean? If this book was a new publication, it would probably be placed in a corner of books on "love and romance" theory. It is difficult to read as it explores the aesthetics of love, rather than providing tips on romance, yet when one reads it further there are more details on what flirtation really refers to and, depending on the way it is read, it could be seen as a "how-to" of flirting.

For instance, it contains what could be described as instructions on romantic gestures, from simple comments like, "An expression embodying *iki* that involves the entire body is the *wearing of very thin fabric*" (Kuki 1930, translated by Nara, Hiroshi 2008: 104-106) to detailed instructions such as, "*Ryūben* refers to sideways glance, a motion involving the eyes alone, a coquettish signal sent to the opposite sex. It is modalized as *yokome* 'sideways glance', *uwame* 'upward glance', and *fushime* 'downward glance". Looking askance at him alongside is flirtatious, as is giving an upward glance to him in front. *Fushime*, too, is used as a means of flirtation, to suggest "coquettish shyness" (108) or, "The mouth, with its realistic function as a path between the sexes and its great possibility of movement, can express the tension and relaxation required of *iki* in a notably clear way" (110); as such, it is a popular Japanese version of Kamashastra. It is indeed a philosophical analysis of *iki*, but the *iki* here is a particular cultural value that is revealed in the "world of amore", a highly specific and individual Japanese system of prostitution. It can be perceived as the sexuality of the Japanese culture found in the traditional arts. It should by now be clear to the reader why earlier I referred to the book as "unusual" among modern Japanese classics.

The reason I bring it up here is not because of this work's ability to vividly cut out a single segment of the Japanese culture, but because we can explain how it serves as a peculiar example of Nihonjinron when we look at why the author created it.

Kuki crossed to Europe in 1921 to study philosophy in Germany and France, returning to Japan in 1929. During that time he studied under Rickert, Heidegger, Husserl, and Bergson's mentorship, meaning that he entered the circles that were on close terms with such philosophers. As a baron's son, he had the financial means to do so, and he also made use of his intellect and attractive personality. Between the "language and body" that form the hinge of relationships with others in the West as I mentioned in the previous chapter, his experience of studying abroad, to the extent we know, could be deemed successful in terms of "language." It seems, however, slightly strange that "The Structure of Iki" is what he published after returning to Japan in 1930, namely, that it was the first book that he made public after having studied German and French philosophies. What is more, he did not write it after returning but completed the manuscript in 1926 while still in Europe (according to the commentary to Kuki's book edition by Michitarō Tada – Kuki

1979(1930): 201). It is clear, that he knowingly allowed his thoughts to float in the world of "eros" of the Japanese *geishas*, something that was so detached from the surrounding environment of Europe.

It is not that he was unable to accept "the West" and wrote an unusual text while secluded and fantasizing about an imaginary homeland. What is present here is a perception of "the Japanese" different from that of Uchimura and Nitobe or Yanagita. In the cases of Uchimura and Nitobe, we see the Japanese who can be on par with the Westerners, with whom the comparison is made. Yanagita, in his turn, both subjectively and methodically focuses his efforts on "the Japanese ethnos", expressed by the words "ethnology of one country", implying that it is inappropriate to make comparisons with other ethnic groups when one does not understand one's own. What Kuki had in mind – or better say what he did not have in mind – was to define the object within such frameworks as nation or ethnos; instead, he looked for meanings inside his own experience and history. Thus, even when living in Europe he concentrated his thinking on the topic that truly fascinated him. There is no doubt that he was also heavily influenced by his own mother's experience as a former *geisha* and by the fact that she was involved in a mad love affair with Tenshin Okakura. Even if we do not delve into such circumstances, we should be able to see that he himself directed his mind to the isolated world of beauty and that this conception holds the ultimate meaning for this book. More specifically, when thinking about the anxiety of identity that overpoweringly sweeps over a Japanese living in a "foreign country" through the discussion of a certain subject, he does not make comparisons with such country's phenomena and brings up something completely disparate, while at the same time employing a philosophical method of analysis that was forged within the Western civilization.

Kuki could have compared *iki* to the French courtesans or love matters of European literature. He, however, chose not to. His aim was not to show through comparison that Japan and the West were equal, or that Japan was more astounding than the West, but to demonstrate that since Japan's "world of eros" could be analyzed using Western philosophical methods, the Japanese were not some isolated existence, but people who could be handled with universal, albeit distinctive, tools – namely, that they were people who could be comprehended.

Now comes the question whether or not "The Structure of Iki" has been read widely. It is not written in simple language like *Representative*

Men of Japan or "The Landscape of Japan". It therefore cannot become a bestseller. Yet, if Nihonjinron is not delivered to many Japanese, it cannot fulfill its functions. If a work of Nihonjinron does not become a "national" piece of literature, surely it has failed to touch on the subject of the national identity? "The Structure of Iki" has perhaps the least readers among the Nihonjinron works dealt with in this book. However, the influence a book holds is not only measured in terms of how much it is read. Knowing that such a book exists, wanting to read it someday in the future, in other words, just the fact that the title "The Structure of Iki" is lined up together with its author's unusual name ("Kuki", a rare name, literally means "nine demons"), be it in the chronological tables on literature at the end of the textbooks of Japanese schoolchildren or in tables of Japanese history, conveys that *iki* too has its structure as unique Japanese aesthetics.

"The Structure of Iki" has not been read widely, but it has established itself as a classic work, thus making its remarkable title recognized, and has continued to deliver a message that things Japanese may possess a "structure" that is possible to analyze. Kuki inherited such a method from the West that he consciously turned his back on.

Created like a twin to "The Structure of Iki" is *In'ei Raisan* (hereafter "In Praise of Shadows") published by Jun'ichirō Tanizaki in 1933. I am not saying that it is similar in topic. The way Tanizaki creates his work, having concentrated his mind on a single aspect of Japanese aesthetics, is similar to that of Kuki. Yet "In Praise of Shadows" is not Nihonjinron. It is a discussion on Japan, a theory on Japan in an ordinary meaning. This is because the work was created by the irreverent Tanizaki after he had moved to Kansai, experiencing no uncertainty regarding identity in terms of his ego or the historical and cultural continuity of the Japan that he saw himself living in.

Fūdo ("Climate")

"Fūdo" (hereafter "Climate") is widely known as a work by Tetsurō Watsuji along with his *Koji Junrei* ("Pilgrimages to the Ancient Temples"). While the latter was written by a 30 year-old Watsuji (1919), created by the energy of a young man dearly attached to Japan when foreign countries were still an object of far-away fascination for him, "Climate" was published in 1935 after he spent one year studying in Germany (1927-1928) and with these experiences at the core of the vision. Aside from the attempt to transcend the bounds of Heidegger's "Being and Time", from which he drew his inspiration, and the philosophical lineage that could be traced from Herder's and Hegel's climatology, the substance of the discussion is extremely straightforward. More specifically, it divides the world into three categories – a monsoon, a desert, and a pasture – and explains at great length how the cultures and societies born under such conditions were connected to these geographical types.

It seems as if Watsuji takes discoveries from his experiences during study abroad and travels as the seed for discussion, spreads the subject to the religion and culture of each geographical category, and adopts a format of an argument analyzed under a certain hypothesis. However, to me it seems to be Nihonjinron written for the purpose of exploring the "wounds" of studying abroad.

This is not to suggest that Watsuji had a particularly negative experience abroad. It points to the problems that can be experienced even if one has been received warmly by a foreign society, stemming from a feeling similar to that of discomfort toward a given society that develops into a complex when entwined with other issues. Most of the "other issues" may be of contrasting levels of complexity for the Japanese who went abroad, but they emerge from the fact of "being Japanese". When the ball can be targeted directly at the counterpart – "the West" – the writing style becomes positive. *Bushido* and *Representative Men of Japan* fall into this category. Although Okakura's writing assumes a voice that sounds somewhat tragic, it also rings loud and clear. As I mentioned before, "The Landscape of Japan", which similarly describes the geographical environment of Japan, is on a high pitch, both from the viewpoint of the epoch and the author's personal history. Compared to this, the pitch of "Climate" is low. This is reflected in Watsuji's comment that "Japan has to get by with such a climate" – a somewhat sorrowful resignation.

This is probably a reflection of the historical environment faced by Japan and Watsuji himself at the time. In 1933, Japan withdrew from the League of Nations – following the League's approval – by forty two votes for, one against (Japan) and one abstained (Thailand) – of a resolution recommending that Japan withdraw from Manchuria, an event that can be seen as both a direct and a symbolic indicator of Japan's position at the time. We have just seen in the examples of "The Structure of Iki" and "In Praise of Shadows" that historical conditions were not uniformly reflected in the works that dealt with Japan. In contrast, Watsuji writes "Climate" as an intentional, rather than a subconscious response to such historical circumstances.

Watsuji argues that Japan is more unique because it belongs to the "monsoon" environment that is neither "a pasture" nor "a desert", and due to its twofold nature as both tropical and boreal. This geographic uniqueness corresponds to the historical conditions that one is compelled to perceive as contemporary Japan's difference from the West as "a pasture" as well as the desert societies and China in Asia (monsoon) on the international arena. This correspondence makes Watsuji think that his discussion is solid, and at least one cannot see him doubting – something that must naturally occur – that he is creating the theory himself exactly because he is trying to accommodate the historical conditions.

It is clear that in this work by Watsuji, there is an overt lack of practical knowledge about "deserts", "monsoons" and "pastures" and a lack of awareness of the differences within Western Europe. When Watsuji writes, "As the above demonstrates, we have made the structure of the human beings of the desert obvious. That is 'drought'. Drought is an antagonistic, combative relationship between a human being and the world, hence, a relationship of absolute subjugation of an individual towards the totality of humanity" (Watsuji 1979(1935): 71), it feels like a classic example of armchair theory bereft of realism. Furthermore, when he suggests that "the Chinese" are impassive, and highlights and criticizes their lagging behind, he displays a typical case of the psychological defense combining personal overconfidence and hatred towards close relatives, which stems from losing respect towards the backward China, a defense mechanism that was so prevalent among the intellectuals of the Meiji period and after.

For this reason, this book should be read entirely as an unpleasant example in which the discussion about Japan and the Japanese does not reach the level of analysis, but gives way to individual agendas and political manifestation, in which the identity issues of oneself and the country overlap inside the process of Japan's modernization. At first glance, it seems to discuss "human" civilization from a broad geographical perspective and attempts to use an equal amount of pages for each of the three classification types, but in the end, it only serves as a prolusion, a warm-up for Watsuji to bring up the subjects of "Japan" and "Japan's peculiarity" that he wanted to deliberate. The full title is "Climate – A Humanistic Study", but in fact it is "a study in Nihonjinron". We can find this schema – where an author who understands the protective methods of textual rhetoric and discussion acquires readers who are not used to examination and critique of the arguments – in numerous subsequent works on Nihonjinron.

Ryoshū ("Melancholy on a Journey")

In Riichi Yokomitsu's (this author was then considered to be "god-like" in the Japanese literary world) *Ryoshū* (hereafter "Melancholy on a Journey"), two young people (Yashirō and Chizuko) fall for each other when they meet while traveling in Europe, and eventually get married, at which point they have to face other people's love and life circumstances (that of Yashirō's opponent Kuji, and of Tōno who is one generation older than Yashirō and Kuji, closer to the author's age). A distinctive feature of the plot is that the characters inexhaustibly exchange opinions, each from their respective social standing and philosophical perspective and in conjunction with the personal conflicts of their hearts in response to the hardships of Japan of the late 1920s and early 1930s. I first read this book in around 1971, when I was still in my early twenties, upon return from studying in Paris, which was my first experience of living abroad. The novel's endless debate about how "Japan" should be assessed by the Japanese abroad and sense of mental unrest, as if one is competing with the other Japanese to "assimilate" to the local environment and cease being "a Japanese", – were familiar to me. However, when I read this novel again more than thirty years later, it did not feel the same anymore, making me think that when I had traveled abroad over thirty years after Yokomitsu had embarked on his trip to Paris, it had already become less intense, even though I was unable to realize it at the time.

When I say that "*it* did not feel the same" or "*it* was already less intense", what is implied by this "it"? "It" is the main concern of Nihonjinron, something that is referred to by Yokomitsu as "the agony of the Japanese", meaning the instability of identity of the Japanese inside the modernity – namely, the anxiety of being Japanese. The title, "Melancholy on a Journey", is also chosen to create an illusion that this "melancholy" – uncertainty in oneself that the Japanese have when looking at what is left behind and what awaits ahead in the development and changes of the "modernization" – is a feeling of "sorrow" experienced by the traveler. When this anxiety cannot be grasped, the metaphor of "Melancholy on a Journey" is applied. But nowadays it seems that "it" is not exactly the same anymore.

The characters express "it" – the "Melancholy on a Journey", the anxiety regarding identity – in many parts of the novel. These sentiments in their original form directly convey the underlying argument that flows throughout this book. Below I will recite the relevant parts in the order they appear in the novel. The novel is set between 1936 and the following year.

Yet, those who had been in Paris for two to three years treated the newly-arrived Japanese the most coldly, acting annoyed, and they were also the most fervent advocates of Europe. However, the reason why these people despised Japan was all due to the fact that all the Japanese were unable to fully imitate Europe (Yokomitsu 1998(1937), Upper Volume: 135).

When looking from here, Japan is really at the ends of the earth! (Upper Volume: 166).
(Uttered in despair by Yashirō when the couple, Yashirō and Chizuko, travel to Switzerland and lie among the saffron flowers gazing the lake.)

If we do not make an effort to participate in the world's humanism, can we advance our learning? Do you think that ethics can come to life? (Kuji)
But we also recognize humanism in the East. Of course it is there! It is slightly different from the humanism of the West. But I do not want to discuss which is better. (Yashirō)

Is there a distinction between the Eastern and Western humanism? Isn't it because there is no difference that we have faith in its ideals? (Kuji)
Are you going to eternally repeat the exercise of denying any difference between the East and the West because of your self-absorption as a member of the educated class? You have acquired this through practice!" (Yashiro) (Upper Volume: 193).
(An exchange that takes place in one of the repeated debates

between Yashirō, "the advocate of Japan" and Kuji, "the advocate of Europe".)

You do not know the anguish of human beings that is history. Can the Japanese escape from the torments of being Japanese? If you can, go ahead and try! (Yashiro) (Upper Volume: 214).
(During the last exchange of opinions in Yashirō and Kuji's many heated debates.)

What do you think, Mr. Oki, was there ever such a time before when young people had to think this much? (Kuji)
No, this is the first time such a thing has happened since the Meiji period. Although there have been a few big incidents until now […] nowadays it is difficult to understand what means what. No idea what is the better thing to do. We have run too fast since the Meiji period and our hearts have jumped out of our chests. (Oki)
Oki's words first sounded amusing, but then the members suddenly stopped talking and silently cut the lamb [on their plates], as if they had been caught by the collar (Upper Volume: 245).

Many people make a sorry scene of themselves on their return from the West, involuntarily bursting into tears of sorrow upon seeing Kobe from the ship (Lower Volume: 44).
(Kuji says to an elderly man, Mr. Oki, upon news from Japan of the February 26 Rebellion, an attempted coup d'état by radical officers of the Imperial Japanese Army. Note that the "sorrow" here is not that of nostalgia but of sadness from seeing the poverty of the Japanese port towns.)

I'll tell you why people who come back from foreign countries just stay at home? They have a high fever for which the cause is unknown and are trying to avoid the danger of hospitalization (Lower Volume: 46).

The second of the two volumes of the book, includes "discoveries", such as when Yashirō, having returned to Japan, finds Cantor's set theory in the form of the paper strips offered to the gods at Shinto shrines (*heihaku*). It also incorporates "sadness" surrounding the murder of Yashirō's ancestor by Chizuko's ancestor Sōrin Ōtomo, a Christian feudal lord, with a gun – namely, Western technology. Thus, the couple's love proceeds to marriage literally through these twists and turns.

It is no doubt unclear for those who have not read "Melancholy on a Journey" where the "discovery" and where the "suffering" are. It could be suggested that Yokomitsu was unknowingly creating an intellectual game that is in a sense nationalistic, and in another sense the complacency of an intellectual isolated from the reality of the times. However, if one understands that this is an "intellectual game" that inevitably drew in the people who tried the most to confront reality, a sympathy of another kind should arise. It is doubtful whether the characters, who were to turn thirty or so at the time the war ended, lived until the end of the war. Since the author continued to write the book intermittently until the beginning of 1945, the progression of time casted a darker retrospective shadow on the settings of the mid-1930s, the fictional reality of the book. As the generation who was compelled "to think this much" since the Meiji period and as the young elites of a military superpower, which had already turned into the world's orphan after its withdrawal from the League of Nations, they felt the necessity to remake "Japan", starting from the early days of Meiji, but were unable to figure out how to do it; hence, one of them was trying to respond to a voice seemingly coming from the depths of "Japan", another was placing his expectations on the West and universal values, and yet another was looking for a path in "the East", a painful process for them. The words "Can the Japanese escape from the torments of being Japanese? If you can, go ahead and try!" may also resonate with modern readers, even if in a categorical, overbearing, threatening, and slightly narcissistic manner.

Now, how did "Japan" look to me when I was in Paris in the early 1970s? It evoked both the feelings of "Melancholy on a Journey" and led me to consider how Japan could be remade in order to secure the "modernity" as seen in Paris and Europe. Unless we were to do so, it seemed that there would be no way for post-war Japan to become a "returnee newcomer" to the Western modernity. Of course, these sentiments overlapped with my personal history, reflection on the student protests in my university that had continued in Tokyo until the preceding year, and skepticism towards the post-war society that I grew up in.

Still, the most suitable "form" for this kind of "Melancholy on a Journey" was certainly the problem of the identity of Japan as it stood isolated in the modernity. From the scatterings of knowledge that I had in anthropology at that time, I was already familiar with a pattern of thinking that looks for multiplicity in modernity such as "another modernity". Yet the overwhelming gravity of the Europe in front of me made the expression "another modernity" sound utterly hollow. I saw this gravity in the Notre Dame de Paris Cathedral – which features repeatedly in "Melancholy on a Journey" and to which poet and sculptor Kōtarō Takamura proclaims his love in tears of ecstasy – on the first day I visited Paris. A Frenchman, having caught a glimpse of the cathedral through a gap between buildings, called it "massive", and these words became clearly imprinted in my mind.

Perhaps, none of this is strange as a manifestation of reality. It is true that seen from the West, Japan is "at the ends of the earth". The fact that humanism is both inexistent and present is generally a realistic representation and not something that one should lament. What one should do is solve this, as it is true that poverty is due to poverty, and the fact that one may not feel one's self as a result of an intercultural experience – be it a homesickness or culture shock – is also reality and nothing more or less than that.

In other words, if these experiences are supposed to be less, but exceed the expectation, they take place not at the level of reality but in the ideological dimension of values and principles, such as "anxiety". At this level, there are questions, desires, and notions such as how one wants to change Japan and how Japan should be, and the decisions and interpretations in response to these questions bring forth a "Melancholy on a Journey" and anxiety. For instance, if one asks whether Japan is the West, the honest answer would be "no". If one wants Japan to be the West, one's heart would be inevitably filled with negative emotions as a reaction to the outcome of this unrequited effort. In 1971 to 1972, I became conscious of this and stopped by Nepal and Korea on the way back from Europe, and one month there turned into an experience comparable to the eleven months I spent in Paris. In a sense, this led to a simple discovery that the "another" is in fact not the East but rather humanity.

Yokomitsu's answer to the questions present since the Meiji period – "What origin of country should and can Japan act as?" – is that it must continue its journey without a set direction, overwhelmed by "Melancholy on a Journey". Although it contains disbelief about the direction of wartime Japan and reflection on the war in hindsight, since the nature of identity anxiety and problems characteristic to Nihonjinron do not change throughout the war, both the questions and answers are still alive there.

I would like to touch on one final point regarding "Melancholy on a Journey". In this novel's illustration of Paris, there are almost no French characters, and, if they do appear, most of them are like part of a backdrop. One night, however, while in Pyongyang in Korea on his return journey to Japan, Yashirō calls for a Korean female artist-entertainer (*kisaeng*). She tells Yashirō that on seeing Kobe – a city that the Japanese bemoaned for its poverty – "she became mesmerized when she realized there is a place on earth that is so beautiful" (Yokomitsu 1998(1937), Lower Volume: 61). Here it is implied that the adoration that Japan holds for the West goes hand in hand with the disdain it holds for the backward Korea and that such adoration and disdain are nothing else but a "relative" phenomenon; yet, the novel is not written as if Yashirō or even the author took notice of the *kisaeng*'s light-hearted comment. It is we who are nevertheless able to read it this way. Here we can find both the weakness and yet the strength of this novel as something that continues to be read until now.

Kindai no Chōkoku ("Overcoming Modernity)

Let us start by looking at the content of the roundtable discussion *Kindai no Chōkoku* ("Overcoming Modernity") frequently referred to as "infamous", and of the book containing the short papers by its members (published in a journal in 1942 and as a book in July 1943).

According to its roundtable's editor and chairman, Tetsutarō Kawakami, its ideas and progress were as follows.

First of all, this roundtable – proposed by Katsuichirō Kamei, a member of the journal *Bungakukai* ("The World of Literature") and developed in collaboration with Kawakami and Hideo Kobayashi – was brought to fruition on July 23 and 24, 1942, when an eight-hour discussion was held between participants from "The World of Literature" and other members. The participants from "The World of Literature" were Hideo Kobayashi, Katsuichirō Kamei, Fusao Hayashi, Tatsuji Miyoshi, Mitsuo Nakamura, and Tetsutarō Kawakami. Among those invited were Keiji Nishitani (Kyoto University Professor of philosophy), Shigetaka Suzuki (Kyoto University Professor of history), Saburō Moroi (composer), Seishi Kikuchi (scientist), Toratarō Shimomura (philosopher), Yoshihiko Yoshimitsu (theologian), and Hideo Tsumura (film critic). A literary critic, Yojūrō Yasuda became unable to attend at the last minute. The roundtable participants submitted their papers in advance, and read each other's submissions before the event. Some of these papers did not make it into the journal but were included in the book, or appeared in the journal only. There is no need to go into the details here. Yasuda's last-minute cancellation is also interesting but I will skip the details. In his interpretation of the book, Yoshimi Takeuchi argues that such a structure of members "combines three elements, or genealogies of thought" belonging to the members of "The World of Literature", "Japanese Romantic School", and the Kyoto School, and I tend to agree with him. However, this fact is not directly connected with the discussion I am leading here.

Rather, what fascinates me is how they managed to overcome the difficulties of bringing together such prominent figures at the time. Although to explain this I will further borrow Kawakami's words, it is possible to say that feeling such as the restfulness and urge to hold endless debates experienced by Yashirō, Kuji, and Tōno in "Melancholy on a Journey" finally changed into a sense of urgency with the advent of the Pacific War, in particular, the victory in the first battle, Pearl Harbor.

Kawakami writes in the opening passage of the discussion: "If I may be allowed to say so, all of us here haven't lived through this current era – which stretches from, say, the Meiji period onward – in entirely the same way [...]. Nevertheless, our emotions have assumed something like a single pattern to them, particularly since December 8. This emotional pattern can in no way be expressed in words, that is to say, it is what I am here calling "overcoming modernity" (Kawakami 1942, translated by Calichman, F. Richard 2008: 151). Yet, as a reflection on the topic of the discussion, Kawakami states that this "modernity" does not necessarily hold the same meaning for each of the participants of the roundtable. He then proposes that the discussion should proceed with defining the meaning of the Western modernity and establishing the merits and demerits resulting from the arrival of Western modernity in Japan after the Meiji restoration. And so commenced the discussion, similar to a political talk show in the current terms but far more solemn, one that Kawakami would have compared to the League of Nations' International Committee on Intellectual Cooperation presided over by Paul Valery.

To summarize the content of the roundtable, discussions were going on at different levels of abstraction and logic, from conference presentations to giving one's own opinions, and was thus not moving forward. When the attitudes collided, it brought forth an exchange similar to the following dialogue formulated by Yokomitsu in his "Melancholy on a Journey", which could be called the basis of such discussions.

Is there a distinction between the Eastern and Western humanism? Isn't it because there is no difference that we have faith in its ideals? (Kuji)
Are you going to eternally repeat the exercise of denying any difference between the East and the West because of your self-absorption from belonging to the educated class? You have acquired this through practice! (Yashirō)

In this roundtable, Hideo Kobayashi acts as Yashirō but also assumes the hidden characteristics of Tōno. In contrast, Kuji's part is carried out by a few invited prominent scholars, especially the philosopher Shimomura and the gentle-natured scientist Kikuchi. The fact that it sounds like a parody of the discussion that took place in "Melancholy on a Journey" has much to do with Fusao Hayashi and Katsuichirō Kamei taking on the roles of the so-called "ideologists of Japan". Still, it is not of much use to take this roundtable as a comedy in my book or to treat it as gossip. Even if we point to their overt enthusiasm, try to suggest that it was the idle talk of literary men with little knowledge of science, or assess them as the intellectuals of an island country who were essentially unaware of the world's events, this would not hold a particular meaning for my book. Rather, despite the fact that it looks like so to us nowadays, what interests me is that at that point the Nihonjinron since the Meiji period was "coming to a standstill" rather than on the rise. What this symposium conceals is an excitement, a feeling of urgency, and somehow a sense of bewilderment.

This is vividly expressed in the following statements by Kawakami, Shigetaka Suzuki and Kobayashi respectively:

I'm sure that this understanding of contemporary Japanese history as world history is of concern for all of us (Kawakami 1942, translated by Calichman, F. Richard 2008: 153).

[…] this is the largely correct idea that modernity is something that is essentially European […]. Such equivalence thus refers to Europe's world domination, whose overcoming is the reason the Greater East Asia War is currently being fought. This, too, can be understood as one way to overcome modernity (Kawakami 1942, translated by Calichman, F. Richard 2008: 154).

[…] the history of Japanese literature since the Meiji period has been – to put it in the extreme – the history of misunderstanding modern Western literature […]. Now, when we have finally begun to see some sound and proper instances of reflection and research on modern Western literature, political crisis has broken out. We must somehow discover Japanese principles, and yet it is quite difficult to achieve this (Kawakami 1942, translated by Calichman, F. Richard 2008: 179).

These quotations reveal the shock brought by the events of December 8, 1941 and both the elation and bewilderment stemming from the fact that due to these developments the Japanese themselves became the central players of the unfolding events.

Until then, when Japan had reached out to the West, which it undeniably thought of as the center of modernity, in some cases it had been accepted and in others rejected, at times it had acknowledged its limitations and at others it had acquired a feeling that it had reached equality with the West, yet it had always returned to the state of "being at the ends of the earth", as described in "Melancholy on a Journey", but then excitement was generated as this very Japan found itself standing at the center of the world history. However, these were not the circumstances created by the men who assembled for this roundtable discussion, but the bewilderment arising from the developments pushed forward by the military, the rawest of all the powers of the Japanese state, towards which the roundtable members themselves felt repellence, disgust, and doubt. Yet, the ultimate reason that these men gathered was the fact that they wished to confirm through the debate an unexpected idea (or a fantasy) they had that the Western modernity – which they had been confronted with without knowing whether its gate had been open or if they had been allowed inside – suddenly turned into something that possibly could be overcome at once. With the exception of Fusao Hayashi and others, it is not that the members did not feel skeptical about this fantasy of "overcoming", albeit each to their different degree. However, what the Japanese military did on December 8 and afterwards emerged as a thunderbolt that made this skepticism itself seem doubtful. The terrorist attacks on America on September 11, 2001 had a similar impact. Given that in the case of Pearl Harbour, Japan was the side that launched the attack, its state of mind was surely completely opposite.

Was the complex question of Nihonjinron – namely, "In what meaning can the Japanese be members of the Western modernity?" – solved when Japan's modern history became the world's history? Or did this question disappear altogether by "overcoming the West"?

In the course of the discussion, the participants confirmed many times that modernity is after all "the Western modernity". In this regard, there are many statements that one might expect at an ordinary research presentation. When the members who are likely to disagree, for instance, Suzuki, say "[...] while it is perfectly fine to construct Japanese things, it seems to me that we must also gain a more thorough understanding of Europe so as to surmount civilization and enlightenment", it does not help that the response from Hayashi Fusao is a mere, "that sounds excellent" (Kawakami 1942, translated by Calichman, F. Richard 2008: 192-193).

Then, Hayashi's subsequent statement – "In addition to Europe, there is also the need for a greater understanding of China and India" (Kawakami 1942, translated by Calichman, F. Richard 2008: 193) – lacks the substantiality of, for example, Tenshin Okakura who, even if fanatically, screamed that Asia was one. When the intellectuals of the Shōwa period, who, in comparison with those of the Meiji period, have a lower ability to approach the West and who cannot look at Asia evenly, say this, we should view such expressions not as armchair theory but rather as quoting from a textbook.

These tendencies became stronger after December 8. Once the war started, they had no more "actual field" as writers. Writing became about expressing one's impression about the information provided in regard to the new state of things, and this impression was insufficient even as a decorative praise at times when the state's gigantic apparatus was in motion. Even though they did gather, with no ability to be "in the actual field", their conversation was not even consolation for the unrest they experienced as a result of the events.

When told by Kikuchi, "This might sound like flattery [...] the students all know you. Simply your research of the classics alone would be of pedagogic value", Kobayashi, who only spoke during the roundtable to comment or fill in the gaps in the discussion, answers, with embarrassment, "well, it's a bit difficult for me since my desire to finally explore the classics has coincided with my sense of the futility and deceit inherent in all explanation and persuasion" (Kawakami 1942, translated by Calichman, F. Richard 2008: 208), and the fact that after the roundtable and as long as the war lasted he remained silent showed that his judgment was right in terms of shrewd management of life. However, in relation to the "in what meaning can the Japanese..." part of the vexing question of Nihonjinron, it did not go further than him saying that at least then he was not able to solve it. Since everybody confessed almost in unison at the beginning of the roundtable discussion that up until then they had accepted the Western modernity, it only leads to the conclusion that this problem would not disappear. In some way, apart from Hayashi and Kamei, for people strong in rationalizing, the events of December 8 came as a shock that left them unprepared to develop new thinking.

Then, if they were to overcome this complex problem, namely, to overcome the "Western modernity" that forms the basis of this question, what would happen? Unfortunately, the problem of the identity anxiety in this regard inside the discussion framework they possessed only bizarrely changed its form further due to the military victory and was neither overcome nor made to disappear. December 8 simply defeated the counterpart by means of military technique, and there was no act for the intellectuals to play in. Even if – and there must have been people who thought that way – "the Western modernity" and states were completely beaten down by the war, what the record of this roundtable makes clear is that the participants of this "overcoming" of modernity did not have a faintest idea about what to do in regard to the forthcoming historical and social conditions.

The following quotes illustrate this in every respect.

(When Saburō Moroi is being asked about the future of the music.)
Nakamura: Mr. Moroi, is Western music really suitable for the Japanese people?
Moroi: I would reply by saying that Western music in its current form is not suitable. But if one could create a completely new style of this music, then I think it would be suitable (Kawakami 1942, translated by Calichman, F. Richard 2008: 175).

Hayashi: As can be seen in both Japan and China, Oriental music involves a kind of straining of the voice through overtraining or overuse. Does this same thing happen in the West?
Moroi: No, it doesn't.
Hayashi: Won't this be important in the future? (Kawakami 1942, translated by Calichman, F. Richard 2008: 176).

Kobayashi: Do you dislike Japanese music?
Moroi: No, I don't.
Kobayashi: Do you find it quite poor?
Moroi: I would say rather that it lacks a sense of development (Kawakami 1942, translated by Calichman, F. Richard 2008: 173).

This neither answers the question, nor surmounts Western music. If the only purpose of the roundtable was propaganda, it would not have led to such an outcome. However, as each of the members was a sensible person, they gathered with the intention of drawing a line of defense on their own expressions in the form of considerable doubt, expecting others to say something instead, but this lead to a situation where everybody assumed a defensive position, experiencing bitterness at heart with the sound of each overly enthusiastic statement; thus, ultimately, it was only light-hearted Fusao Hayashi who continued talking. In the end, Hayashi asked if the education of "the young airmen" was a "happy and pure" matter or "extraordinary spiritual beauty" and, with Keiji Nishitani answering that it was "healthy spiritual beauty" (Kawakami 1942, translated by Calichman, F. Richard 2008: 209), alas, the "discussion" ended.

Brief Summary

As a result of the Russo-Japanese War, Japan could not help but experience doubt about its own identity as it took a certain position among the Western countries. The four books on Nihonjinron that I have introduced here have to do with even deeper anxiety that arises from the Japanese assuming that their victory against Russia placed them among the ranks of the great powers of the West. This anxiety is akin to the dull pain one might feel when walking a gentle slope. The question whether they could live as Westerners was partially surmounted by living as such. However, their intention to compete in the same game was overshadowed by the growing anxiety of whether they were legitimate players in this game at all. I have already used metaphors such as "orphan" or "adopted child" to describe this second anxiety, Japan's concern that although it was allowed to participate in the game until the victory, it would be instantly dismissed when it won. To employ yet another metaphor, it is very much as if Japan was a "transfer student" joining the class of the modern nations.

In this chapter, I explained about "The Structure of Iki", "Climate", "Melancholy on a Journey" and "Overcoming Modernity" and the responses each of them had towards the complex problems they dealt with. As shown in the timeline earlier in this chapter, the tone of Nihonjinron in these four books gradually becomes darker inside the post early-Shōwa history, marked by drastic changes, and with the turning events placed in between the dates of their publication. If we compare them with the four books of the Meiji period, the contrast in their tone is striking. Of course, forcibly setting the problem in a way in which it states that the Japanese are trying to become Westerners would lead to no solution. It seems that the darkness of the tone lies not only with the inability to solve the problem but also with the way the problem is set. This "complex question" was carried over to after the end of the Second World War, with many works on Nihonjinron attempting to solve it upfront or in a roundabout way during the course of half a century. I will discuss this in the second part of this book. However, these four books of the Shōwa period also give us a few hints on how to break through this complex question.

To illustrate this by drawing on a single example, we can refer to the way in which the *kisaeng* in "Melancholy on a Journey" describes Kobe as "beautiful". The essence of this is that to a Japanese who returned from the West, Kobe looks shabby and desperately disappointing, while for a Korean who came back to the Korean peninsula from Kobe, it is an object of admiration. It also becomes illuminated from beneath when one says that modern Japanese history is the world's history, where "the world" means "the West" excluding all what is outside the West. There exists a misperception by which they did not see the Japanese history as "the world's history" when fighting with the Chinese, but did so when fighting with the Americans. When this misperception is detected in Nihonjinron, inside there is a way of breaking free from the complex problem of Nihonjinron.

PART 2

The Japanese People within "Nihonjinron"

CHAPTER 4

An Imperial Subject: Democratic Subjects of the Shōwa Constitution

Brief Foreword

In the first part of the book I examined the state of Nihonjinron from the Meiji period up until the Second World War largely on the basis of eight representative books of the times. By discussing each individual work, I distinguished the commonalities among them and looked at the circumstances that made the Nihonjinron essential to the Japanese after the opening of Japan by the "Black Ships" and at how these circumstances changed during the course of the first eighty years of the modern history of Japan. Its reexamination also served as a general theory of Nihonjinron.

However, even if the pre-war Nihonjinron does not differ much from the current discourse in terms of the way it is written, the Japan and the Japanese depicted there are, unsurprisingly, outdated. What it meant to be a *bushi*, or Japan's aesthetics of beauty as seen in "The Structure of 'Iki'" stray far from where we stand now. On the other hand, the postwar Nihonjinron may be interpreted as dealing with the Japanese similar in nature to the Japanese of the present day. It is not only because the postwar period is the recent past for our society, but also due to the historical factor that around the time of the Second World War Japan's self-imposed model changed from "Great Japan" to "International Japan" and has stayed this way ever since. During the seventy years since the start of "International Japan" in 1945, many works of Nihonjinron, driven by reflection on the Japanese society, Japanese culture, and Japanese people, that seemed to have fallen into ruin as a result of the "Greater East Asia War" (Pacific War), were written in order to validate the new identity of the Japanese. This, however, was not an attempt within postwar Nihonjinron to replace the previous assertions of how the Japanese were with a succession of new statements. In some cases, the same type was recreated as a result of changing the object – while it is not clear if the authors themselves were conscious of it – while in other cases, a guiding line was redrawn, thus reviving the previous discourse. In this manner, numerous books on Nihonjinron have been produced in response to Japan's postwar international status and social changes. Japan's rapid economic growth in particular has led to the appearance not only of "International Japan" but also the "Economic Giant" – a subspecies of "Great Japan" – thus prompting further transformation of Nihonjinron.

In this part I will talk about this kind of Nihonjinron. My intention is to cover approximately two works in a chapter. The reason for this is that from the standpoint of Nihonjinron, the sixty years after the war were a time when the discussion was carried out with the same "Japanese" as a target. Although their publications are a few years apart, they can be reviewed in the same way. For instance, *The Chrysanthemum and the Sword*, discussed in Chapter 4, can still be read as a book theorizing on the present-day Japanese and can also be considered fresh discourse, due to the way in which it links to the recently-written *Embracing Defeat: Japan in the Wake of World War II*. When we are no longer able to discuss the newly written Nihonjinron together with the works on the subject created since the war, this will signal that Nihonjinron has begun to change intrinsically. This is something that I shall address in Part 3.

The First Postwar Nihonjinron

We will begin our discussion of the postwar Nihonjinron precisely from the moment that postwar Japan began: midday, August 15, 1945. The Japanese before and after that point can be thought of as two separate groups: the Japanese who called out for the full-scale continuation of war, and the Japanese who accepted the change as if they had always wanted peace and democracy. However, is it really possible for a single group of people to undergo such a metamorphosis all at once? I will contemplate this question using the model of the Japanese imperial "subjects" (*shinmin*).

The examples of Nihonjinron that I will put forward in this chapter are two books written by Americans: *The Chrysanthemum and the Sword* by Ruth Benedict (1946; Japanese translation in 1948) and *Embracing Defeat: Japan in the Wake of World War II* by John W. Dower (1999; Japanese translation in 2001). The former is a research monograph by Ruth Benedict, an American anthropologist who, together with fellow anthropologist Margaret Mead, belonged to the school that viewed cultural patterns as capable of forming the personality of an individual. After war broke out between Japan and America, she was commissioned by the American government to research Japan and to learn about the enemy's land, and therefore she wrote *The Chrysanthemum and the Sword* without having had the opportunity to visit Japan. Instead of conducting a field study, she carried out research by interviewing people of Japanese upbringing residing in America and Japanese captives, and analyzed various papers on Japan, Japanese publications, Japanese movies and other materials, using an anthropological comparative method that looks at the intercultural distinctions and a functionalist standpoint that sees the actions inside a certain culture and society as connected within an overall system. Although it contains a few errors resulting from the way the materials were handled and from the intensity of interpretation, the book is filled with sharp-witted observations that more than make up for its flaws.

Embracing Defeat: Japan in the Wake of World War II was written by American historian John W. Dower. He carefully uncovered and investigated a range of materials from postwar Japan, including newspapers, magazines, and song lyrics as well as personal memoirs and oral narratives, documents from the occupation forces and other sources, and constructed a deep and far-reaching portrayal of postwar Japan. During the so-called bubble economy, interest towards Japan increased not only in the business world but also among Western scholars, but the boom has faded since. As in business, anti-Japanese sentiment revealed itself as "Japan-bashing". Yet fundamental research on Japan in America continued, unaffected by Japan's superficial ups and downs in international society, and led to admirable results such as Dower's *Embracing Defeat*. In 2000, it received the Pulitzer Prize. It is worth mentioning that the following year, the same prize was awarded to another book on Japan, American historian Herbert P. Bix's *Hirohito and the Making of Modern Japan*.

"But Then Again" and "One's Proper Station"

The Japanese people depicted by Benedict in *The Chrysanthemum and the Sword* are the Japanese of the prewar and wartime periods. I already mentioned that this book makes some outstanding observations; I would like to introduce a particularly noteworthy observation and extract from it two central ideas that are related to the discourse we are discussing.

Benedict's discovery that the Japanese people avoid competition and that they are afraid of the shame brought by losing in a competition is particularly noteworthy. This leads to a "standard generalization", made frequently in *The Chrysanthemum and the Sword*, that Japanese culture is the culture of "shame" while Western culture is the culture of "guilt", however she does not provide any details on the kind of discerning observations this discovery leads to.

For instance, there are people who regard the educational philosophy adopted in current Japanese elementary schools that all the students have the potential to earn full marks or that everyone who ran in a race should be given an award certificate as trends stemming from the postwar notion of "democratic equality". But in *The Chrysanthemum and the Sword* the description of competition in Japan says the following:

> The Japanese have always been inventive in devising ways of avoiding direct competition. Their elementary schools minimize it beyond what Americans would think possible. Their teachers are instructed that each child must be taught to better his own record and that he should not be given opportunities to compare himself with others […]. Their report cards grade children in elementary schools on marks for conduct but not on their school work […] (Benedict 2006(1946): 154-155).

If we rephrase the outdated expression "conduct" as "the presence or absence of effort", it sounds as if taken from the contemporary Japan's educational standards, but we are dealing with a description of prewar Japan. According to Benedict, the emergence of such a direction in education is due to the fact that "the Japanese avoid occasions in which failure might be shameful" (2005(1946): 157), and that "The loser 'wears a shame' for such failures, and, though this shame is in some cases a strong incentive to greater efforts, in many others it is a dangerous depressant. He loses confidence and becomes melancholy or angry or both" (2005(1946): 153). Whichever response failure provokes, the suggestion is that the Japanese are weak in the face of the shame of failure. I am sure I am not the only one who when reading this recalls the weakness of Japanese sportsmen in a crucial game or the Japanese soccer players sitting on the ground in a stunned daze following the "Agony of Doha", Japan's narrow failure to qualify for the 1994 FIFA World Cup. (Nonetheless, very recently many significantly different cases have been observed. This is a subject of discussion in Part 3).

If this passage only evokes interested acknowledgement, then there exist many Nihonjinron works that make one feel "reminiscent" when reflecting upon oneself in the described situations. The "convincing" episode with a rice ball in "The Battles of Coxinga" by Chikamatsu is precisely this. Benedict's observation stands out because it has a "but then again" element to it where she recognizes an opposite possibility, stating that after the discouragement of such a defeat Japan's real strength "lies in her ability to say of a course of action, 'That failed,' and then to throw her energies into other channels" (2005(1946): 304), thus producing a hypothesis of a higher level. It is also suggested that in addition to becoming dispirited when ashamed, the Japanese have the ability to quickly assume a different direction and different attitude, and this should be taken into account by postwar Americans, as those of the enemy country and as those exercising occupational policy when thinking about the Japanese. This is the first point that is related to the "metamorphosis" with August 15, the borderline noted in the beginning of this chapter, and that becomes important when examining the "subjects".

"But then again" is also connected to the title, *The Chrysanthemum and the Sword*. It seems that people who know the book but have not read it tend to think that the chrysanthemum refers to the flower in the imperial seal of Japan, however, the chrysanthemum brought up in the book is of another kind. It appears in the expression that a Japanese person both "lavishes art upon the cultivation of chrysanthemums", "but then again", is "devoted to the cult of the sword and the top prestige of the warrior" (Benedict 2006(1946): 2).

There is yet another passage where the chrysanthemum and the sword emerge, but they are used as a slightly different metaphor. The way in which chrysanthemums that have previously been pruned and fixed with wire racks to emphasize their artificial beauty, experience "pure joy" when allowed to grow naturally is likened to the state of the Japanese people liberated from war. Yet, Benedict stresses that the Japanese "will have to learn new sanctions" (Benedict 2006(1946): 295). The sword as shown in the expression "the rust of one's body" is a symbol of taking responsibility for one's own actions. Although it is an archaic virtue, it has the capacity to become an ethical symbol of the new free world. In both cases, the chrysanthemum and the sword function as important elements in the symbolism of the Japanese and are used to express the response by the Japanese to the kind of changes emphasized in the phrase "but then again".

The title *The Chrysanthemum and the Sword* is used to express the state of coexistence of seemingly conflicting principles, as seen in the "but then again" nature of the Japanese.

Benedict explains in a great variety of ways that this kind of "but then again" attitude is possible because the Japanese system of values is sometimes based in the Confucian feeling of indebtedness and at other times in the worldview distinctive of the Japanese Shinto, which differ from Christian morals. These explanations include excessive points where the interpretation relies on the meanings of the words slightly too much. However, if we take these away, we come down to Benedict's highlighting of the sense of order provided by fulfilling "one's proper station" (Benedict 2006(1946): 43).

Benedict argues that for the Japanese people the duty of living is to work in accordance with one's station or position. The norms of behavior are not principles; the norm is sustaining and not changing the order of the world one lives in – which may perhaps be referred to as *seken* (one's social milieu), discussed later on in Chapter 6. Failing at this means throwing one's own world, namely one's *seken*, into disorder and creating an unfortunate situation in which the entire world is "being troubled" and for which one has to take responsibility. This responsibility is not something based on the principles of behavior, but is a result of having taken action towards *seken*. An apology may take the form of a suicide. "But then again", if one is able to admit the failure, this responsibility may lead to taking a different route, where the course of action once ruled to be absolute is very quickly discerned to have been "a mistake". Dying or not dying, two completely different ways of responding to failure, are both acceptable. In a way, this connects to discussion of the level of "humans" and "the reason outside of reason" that will be taken up in Chapter 11 of this book.

August 15, 1945, marked the beginning of such a major change. This was particularly noticeable among the leadership group who had expressed their positions clearly during the war. There were those who took responsibility by committing *seppuku*, and people who suddenly showed repentance and became democrats. This leadership group spanned from army generals down to schoolteachers. These two types of people standing at mutually incompatible ends of the spectrum are completely different in terms of the expression of their acts, yet, according to Benedict's argument, they may be thought of as possessing the same "cultural pattern" within the same group. At present it is common for the theory of "cultural patterns" to face stern criticism. Still, I believe that Benedict's discovery of the "but then again" and "one's proper station" concepts function as effective viewpoints for understanding the Japanese.

August 15 as a Margin

Here I will shift from discussing the Japanese people of pre-August 15, 1945 – namely, the Japanese addressed by Benedict in *The Chrysanthemum and the Sword* – to the Japanese from that time onwards.

There are deeper reasons for me bringing up *The Chrysanthemum and the Sword* and *Embracing Defeat* alongside each other in this chapter as examples of Nihonjinron, reasons that go beyond the shared fact that they are both authored by Americans. Firstly, it concerns the times they cover. The two works focus on different periods: the former describes the Japanese before the defeat in the war, while the latter describes the postwar Japanese. When reading these two books, however, one can see that they are remarkably connected with August 15, 1945 as a margin. Besides, each depicts the Japanese from the point of view of the "subjects" (*shinmin*) to the emperor that I will refer to here. What is more, *The Chrysanthemum and the Sword* was read in the times of "anxiety", when the Japanese had lost their confidence in the wake of defeat and overreacted to MacArthur's suggestion that they had the mentality of "a twelve year old". I believe that the reason why *Embracing Defeat* was widely read in Japan as a bestseller – which is unusual for an academic work – following the release of the Japanese edition in 2001, lies with the fact that, following the collapse of the bubble economy and "monetary defeat" it was all in all a period of strong "anxiety" characterized by long-lasting stagnation of Japan. In such terms, these two works, although positioned at the beginning and end of a cycle of over fifty years since the defeat in the war, share many aspects in common and correspond with each other.

To me, for some reason it is as if August 15 fell in the middle of a year. At noon on a day at the height of summer, a time when a year's energy is at its peak, Hirohito, the Shōwa Emperor, announced by radio that the war has finished. This prompted the start of a completely different "postwar" time.

In the days before this radio announcement many believed that the war would last indefinitely. For those who had prepared to die in the war, the emperor's announcement therefore meant that they were granted their lives. The women who had faced the deaths of their fathers, husbands, sons, their whole family, or of an acquaintance or lover, also found that death was changed to life. I have been told that upon hearing the imperial rescript, many wives – my mother included – embraced the hope that their husbands would perhaps come back. While those who knew of the extreme ferocity of the war through their firsthand experiences or through hearsay, be it on the battlefield or the homefront, had believed that the only possible outcome of the war was defeat, nobody could imagine how that would actually come about. The way it happened must have felt almost like a bolt from the blue even to those people who had been able to keep themselves informed and had vaguely sensed the forthcoming surrender.

The emperor's radio broadcast on that midsummer noon truly came as a "live blessing". Thanks to this announcement in the emperor's own voice, in a strange way, "the emperor who started the war" turned into "the emperor who ended the war". The emperor who was to take lives suddenly bestowed existence. The emperor's "responsibility" for having started the war was replaced by the "achievement" of having ended it. At the same time, it was also as if the "responsibility" towards the war of each individual person listening to the radio evaporated in the midsummer heat, disappearing together with the misery that had happened to the non-Japanese Asians. With the events surrounding August 15 as a boundary, there emerge two Japans and two types of the Japanese people. What is the trick that lies behind such a great shift?

The fact that in the announcement the emperor did not specifically say that Japan had "lost" the war has often been highlighted as the use of rhetoric to cover up Japan's defeat. It is undoubtedly so. However, imperial rescripts following Japan's victories in the First Sino-Japanese War and the Russo-Japanese War both contained the word "victory" only once each, and then once in the text admonishing Japanese citizens to respond to the victory modestly. Japan has displayed surprising humility in case of winning too. Although it might have had significance for Japan's international stance, obscuring what can be obscured while using exaggerated expressions was not a trick but the basic rhetoric of imperial edicts.

Having said that, the trick seen in this very edict announcing the end of the war, the shift in the logic in its text, require special attention. The edict states that the tide of the war had turned against Japan and that the enemy had begun to adopt cruel methods. It suggested that if allowed to continue, the war would lead to the destruction of the Japanese nation and the human civilization as a whole, hence, for the sake of humanity, it was necessary "to affect a conclusion to the present situation" and for Japan to walk the difficult road to the "construction of the future", without which Japan would fail to keep pace with "the progress of the world". "Japan's defeat" is replaced by a higher issue to be addressed, namely the risk of "the destruction of the world". Regardless of how ingenious the shift in this statement is, the question is why people who were exhausted, who killed the enemy, and lost relatives and people close to them, were able to listen to such manipulation. It is precisely because of such a mechanism – which one might call a "trick" – that the Japan before and the Japan after August 15, two worlds which are 180 degrees apart in every respect, are connected by a narrow margin of merely one day.

The New "Imperial Subjects" Generated by the Emperor's Announcement

There are two important points as to why this broadcast wielded an outstanding effect: the fact that it was read by the emperor himself, even if through the radio, and the fact that it was addressed to his subjects in the second person.

Before August 15, 1945, only very few people, such as politicians, military personnel, and civil officials, had had an opportunity to hear the voice of the emperor. In other words, only imperial appointees, and even among them only those who were officially appointed by the emperor – Cabinet ministers, generals, privy councilors – the figures surrounding the emperor and central to the state system, had heard the emperor's voice. However, in the radio broadcast, which had albeit been recorded in advance, the emperor addressed at once tens of millions of ordinary citizens. Regardless of how strange the emperor's voice sounded to the listeners, or rather the fact that it was not a well-modulated voice but rather an oddly frayed voice like a Shinto prayer, it became something "to hold on to" with augmented strength to cut deep into people's hearts. In fact, after the emperor's speech, an announcer offered a summary and interpretation of the imperial rescript; personally, I have never read or heard about this in people's "memories" of the radio broadcast of the imperial rescript. They became agitated from listening to the emperor's voice, so the subsequent announcer's voice carried no meaning for them. Although it came much later than similar initiatives by Roosevelt and Hitler, this radio broadcast by Hirohito can be said to have been the first propaganda in Japan to make highly effective use of the media.

Another important point is that the live voice addressed "the subjects" in the second person (*nanji shinmin*). From the Meiji period onward, there were cases in which the recipients of the imperial rescripts and edicts were defined as "the loyal subjects" (*chūryo no shin*), but when a rescript or edict is addressed to ordinary Japanese, either the second-person "people" (*nanji yūshū*) or the second-person "subjects" (*nanji shinmin*) is commonly adopted. *Yūshū* has a similar connotation to that of *shinmin* and means "the people of state". However, these two words are different in terms of how they are used. For example, in an imperial edict aimed at encouraging the citizens after the 1923 Great Kanto Earthquake and in the rescript celebrating the 2600-year anniversary of the imperial era, "ye, the subjects" (*nanji shinmin*) is used. "Ye, the subjects" also appears in the Imperial Rescript on Education in the Meiji period and other sources. In contrast, the declarations of war and peace treaties of the First Sino-Japanese War and the Russo-Japanese War, employ "ye, the people" (*nanji yūshū*). "Ye, the people" is also used in the declaration of war on the United States and the British Empire on December 8, 1941. Yet, when that war ended in Japan's defeat, the rescript was addressed to "ye, the subjects".

Namely, "ye, the subjects" is used when an imperial edict addresses ordinary Japanese in a closer and a little more "familiar" tone, for instance when it is consoling the people after a difficult experience such as an earthquake or encouraging them to make an effort in regards to something. On the other hand, following the start of the war, "ye, the people" was used in order to encourage the people to hold strong. With such examples of its usage, "ye, the subjects" was adopted as the form of address in the imperial rescript of the end of the war. The imperial rescript could not merely say that the war was lost. It had to make the defeat sound convincing and prompt people to lay down their weapons. It was, however, also necessary not to cause too much disappointment about the "failure" in the war. It was essential to invoke a sense of motivation toward nation-building. Thus, I think that it was imperative to use "ye, the subjects", the same form of address that had been used to console the people following the Great Kanto Earthquake or adopted in the Imperial Rescript on Education during the nation-building of the Meiji period.

In addition, one of the striking parts of this rescript is the line in which the emperor asks how he would atone to the spirits of imperial ancestors if the Japanese nation were to be destroyed and human civilization made extinct. This remorse towards the ancestors is understandable when it concerns the destruction of one's home, but it is strange that the same repentance to the ancestors is expected toward demolishing human civilization. Or, rather than being strange, placing "human civilization" before the mention of the ancestors (as is the order in the Japanese text) may be interpreted as rhetoric that positions the subsequent apology to the ancestors as a public, rather than a private matter. This expresses the strong extent to which Hirohito, as the contemporary successor of the imperial family, was highly conscious that he should not destroy that family with his reign. It is also for this reason that I consider it skillful propaganda that pursued the dual goal of preventing revolution against the "national polity" (*kokutai*) centered on the emperor, and bringing citizens together under his leadership to commit their efforts to nation-building.

Finally, it was epoch-making that the emperor's call to the people was transmitted over the radio. In English, the word that corresponds to *shinmin* – "a subject" – originally refers to people subordinate to an absolute royal authority. Still, even though they must be unilaterally obedient to the king, equality is guaranteed among the subjects themselves. However, among the Japanese under the Meiji Constitution there existed a "state hierarchy" clearly associated with the importance of one's existence for the state. Even when addressed as *shinmin* (the subjects), as seen in this word's nature as a Japanese compound of two words from Chinese Confucianism – "shin" and "min" –inside the concentric circle with the emperor at the center, the ordinary Japanese are positioned as the "second-class subjects" (*min*), of the outer circle, as opposed to the aforementioned "first-class subjects" (*shin*), who surround the emperor. When these second-class subjects, were suddenly called *nanji shinmin*, or "ye, the subjects", by the voice of the emperor himself, bypassing the *shin*, it implied that the emperor was consoling them for the "shed blood" and "ravage" that had befallen them as "innocent people". Here, due to the defeat, the second-class subjects became "the subjects" directly connected to the emperor for the first time and, paradoxically, it is only when the imperial system faced the threat to its existence that a structure in which all Japanese became "the subjects" was possible for the first time.

The Meaning of **Embracing Defeat**

Dower's *Embracing Defeat* depicts how the Japanese came to terms with the defeat after this radio broadcast, and how they accepted democracy. Dower states that the Japanese did not despair or slip into turmoil about the defeat and that "the ideals of peace and democracy took root in Japan". He writes that these ideals "found expression through a great and often discordant diversity of voices" (Dower 2000: 23). This is easy to comprehend when the model of treating the Japanese as "subjects" (*shinmin*) is adopted. The substance of the word "subject" lies with the passive stance, characteristic to its existence, that one's personal safety and prosperity is ensured by receiving something from the king. This passivity may have been the reason why "the ideals of peace and democracy" did take root in postwar Japan.

Nevertheless, "the subjects" refers to people under an absolute monarchy. The state as the "democratic subjects" would inevitably lead to discord. Why then, when democracy was conferred from above in the form of an ideal rather than reality, was there not a split due to the fundamental discord between being subjects and the democratic principle of independently determining the policies of one's own society? Here, Hirohito responded with an indifferent and irresistible force to "the left wing" powers that sought to use this rift as a lever for political movement to bring about social change. More specifically, the emperor responded with a series of approaches to his subjects, starting with the radio broadcast of August 15.

First, on January 1, 1946, the emperor issued a general rescript entitled "The Humanity Declaration" (*Ningen-sengen*). It immediately appeared in the newspapers, informing the people that the emperor is not a living god. To be exact, they learn that the emperor recognizes that he is not a living god. The emperor appeals to the people in a slightly one-sided way by stating that the connection between himself and his subjects is not "based merely on myths and legends" but on trust and affection. While the text of the rescript is the culmination of deliberations between various figures and political organizations around the emperor, one can see the emperor's intention to directly approach the Japanese people during the state of emergency and the sharpness of his political intuition. This rescript is concluded with the words "trusted people" (*shinrai suru kokumin*). Although it was prior to the establishment of the Democratic Constitution and the Meiji Constitution was still in place, surprisingly the rescript said "the people" (*kokumin*)!

The emperor then made a tour around Japan, with the exception of Okinawa. In fact, this was the emperor's second tour across the country. During his regency under the Taishō Emperor, he had traveled around the country's prefectures, including Okinawa as well as Taiwan and Sakhalin (Hara 2000: 252-254). There is no doubt that for the emperor himself such tours were inspired by the closeness between the British Royal Family and the British nation that he witnessed during his visit to Britain while he was a Crown Prince. In truth, after he assumed the position of emperor, it became difficult for Hirohito to do such things, possibly making him discontent about the "deified" role that had been assigned to him. The radio broadcast, "The Humanity Declaration" and the national tour were practical activities that supported Hirohito's ideas. One of the reasons why the fundamental discord between the ideas of a subject and democracy did not lead to a fissure can be attributed to the emperor's tactics. This eventuated not only in the "second-class subjects" (*min*) acquiring the possibility of becoming "subjects" (*shinmin*) but also in the fact that the new prime minister Yoshida Shigeru and foreign minister Mamoru Shigemitsu, who signed "Shin Shigeru" and "Shin Mamoru" ("Shin" [subject] indicating humility towards the emperor) respectively even after the war, were able to find roles in accepting the democracy as instructed by America while preserving their consciousness as first-class subjects as in the prewar period (about Shigemitsu, see Dower 2000: 287-289). Moreover, Dower tells us that even Sanzō Nosaka of the communist party, a leader occupying a completely different position, "made the astonishing announcement that there was no other recourse but to appeal directly to the emperor" at the May gathering of 1946 (Dower 2000: 262-263).

We need to remark on one more side of the emergence of these postwar subjects. This is the role of General MacArthur, which Dower artfully describes in *Embracing Defeat*. MacArthur's part was also crucial when the democracy by the subjects was rising. Him being like a "monarch" in terms of both his personality and actual conduct paired with the fact that the Japanese people referred to him as "our father" (Dower 2000: 233), was just right for the "subjects" model that was initiated among the defeated Japanese. We can say that it was the duo of Hirohito and MacArthur that strongly produced the "subjects".

With the Hirohito's radio broadcast the *shin* and *min* of the *Chrysanthemum and the Sword* turned into *shinmin* ("the subjects"), and, as "the paradox […] of an authoritarianism that offered the promise of democracy" (Dower 2000: 229), were granted the peace constitution through the authorities of MacArthur and Emperor Hirohito. Dower insists that the Japanese of that time did not just receive the peace constitution, but "embraced" it and then made it into the democracy of their own. However, in this new constitution the citizens were referred to as *kokumin* as a translation of "people". If we think about the construct here in terms of the words "subjects" (*shinmin*) and "people" (*kokumin*), we can say that in response to the emperor (in the text approved by MacArthur) addressing the citizens as "people" in this imperial rescript, the pacifist constitution, people acted as "subjects" by filling the roadsides of the emperor's tour in welcoming crowds and inundating MacArthur's postbox with tens of thousands of letters.

This attitude as subjects can still be seen as a narrow and yet perpetual current among the modern Japanese. Directly, it exists at present in the form of an abnormal feeling towards the emperor. I am not referring here to anything in line with the superficial acts of waving the Japanese national flag during the public audiences with the emperor at the imperial palace at New Year. There exists something that subconsciously permeates one much deeper and wider. It is vigorous affirmation towards the emperor's existence, which, without making its reason clear, assumes that in the absence of the emperor, something negative will happen to Japan as a country. Politics is an art of communal existence that transforms the values and principles present in society into reality. If one of the conditions of the politics is that "the emperor" as a given is an indisputable part of it from the very beginning, then in logical terms it is incongruous. It stops being nonsensical only when the people under this government think of themselves as "subjects" from the outset.

CHAPTER 5

The People: The Emperor's People of the Meiji Constitution

Lamenting Japan's Ruin

In 1983 Ryōtarō Shiba started a series of opening essays in the journal *Bungei Shunjū* under the title *Kono Kuni no Katachi* ("The Form of this Nation"). This was when Shiba was 62 years old, 10 years before his death. It was during the final stages of the bubble economy and various barometers were presenting Japan as "number-one", but while Shiba's writing style was lucid as ever, his depiction of Japan was rather gloomy. The third essay, which sets the tone of the series, starts as *mugen nō* (a category of Noh plays about ghosts and supernatural beings). When one meets "a giant slimy shapeless thing" at Asajigahara, that thing, that "deformed monster", announces itself as "the modern age of Japan". More specifically, the "monster" is a reference to the forty years from Japan's victory in the Russo-Japanese War in 1905 to its defeat in the Pacific War in 1945. After the period of the prosperous Japan, from the late days of the Tokugawa shogunate through much of the Meiji period until 1905, a mysterious thing akin to a devil came to life, disappearing after the defeat in 1945. Shiba sees the times that arrived after the war as defined by "crudeness" (*gara no warusa*) (Shiba 1986-1996, Essay Number 8), something that could also be observed in the late Edo period and that should be held dear. Shiba starts his observations by stating that only this period, these forty years between the late Meiji period and the end of the war, make no sense, as if it was not Japan where the events of those years took place.

It is believed that Shiba wrote this essay to his 23-year old self, a confused soldier in the days of the defeat, in an attempt to find an answer to the reason for that reckless war. In fact, all of his works are of a similar nature. The forty years after the Meiji Restoration were followed by a forty year long period of "disconcertion". Then, forty years after the war, Shiba started writing "The Form of this Nation". I do not think that Shiba wrote this essay only to solve the controversy of the past. He sensed among signs of fear that the collapse of the bubble was to happen in Japan a few years after the start of this serial publication and, while feeling annoyance towards those people who were unable to see it coming, set about writing a warning that after this forty years of discord, another great collapse may be awaiting all of Japan. This discourse on Japan by Shiba was thus also created in context of anxiety – anxiety about the future.

In 1905, the year of Japan's victory in the Russo-Japanese War – a year which Shiba refers to as a "turning point for Japan" – Sōseki Natsume started writing novels in earnest, creating many works, from *Wagahai wa neko dearu* ("I Am a cat") to *Meian* ("Light and Darkness"), within just eleven years. Among them, *Sanshirō* (1908) is a "postwar story" depicting the younger generation in the wake of the Russo-Japanese War. The protagonist Sanshirō comes to Tokyo at a time of anxiety and elation, a time when people are dissatisfied with the lack of reparations Japan has received from Russia for its victory, and apathetic following their accomplishment, but at the same time there are over one hundred million applications to buy stocks against 99,000 stocks available in the newly constructed Manchuria Railway. At the beginning of the novel, in a train bound for Tokyo, Sanshirō meets a man who later features as "Professor Hirota" and is easily defeated when Hirota responds to the suggestion that Japan will gradually progress following its victory against Russia, with the words "Japan is headed for a fall". (Natsume 2002(1908), Collected Edition 5: 292). Professor Hirota's words are incredibly famous – it is said that Sōseki had the foresight to see what was going to happen to Japan from that time onwards. That time was the beginning of Ryōtarō Shiba's "forty monstrous years". It means that there were people who were aware of the impending events. However, not only in this phrase but throughout its text *Sanshirō* serves as the most dynamic depiction of the Meiji state through its portrayal of the students of Tokyo Imperial University, the contemporary women, and the intellectuals. It then links to *Sore Kara* ("And Then"), *Mon* ("The Gate"), and *Kokoro*, continuing to illustrate a slightly divergent form of the "people" that the Meiji state was supposed to produce.

Let us examine the people from the stance of the Nihonjinron by Shiba and Sōseki.

The Late Tokugawa Rōnin as the Forerunners of the Japanese "People"

I saw Ryōtarō Shiba only once, at a lecture in the mid-1970s. Although his hair had already turned white, he seemed very youthful. With a cheerful tone, he talked about the young *samurai* of the late Edo period, recounting the tale of a *samurai* who, in the midst of a heated quarrel, angrily threatened another with the words "Are you capable of dying?", to which the other answered "Of course I am" and immediately sat down under the eaves at the side of the road and cut his stomach open. Shiba spoke of such "outlandish events" that happened during the late Edo period and reflected the young men of the time, and while he did not praise such acts, he seemed to find them endearing in a sense.

Shiba's "The Form of this Nation" is a collection of sketches. It can be interpreted as a work that was written with the intention of putting together ideas and thoughts that could not be turned into a novel or a coherent text as hints and short representations. The story jumps between various periods, but, as if each of the parts has magnetic force, they point to a certain direction. Shiba is occupied with finding a flow that leads to modernity – how Japan became a modern state in the Meiji period, which occurrences took place on the way to it, what efforts were undertaken, and what kind of people were involved in them.

Let us take, for example, the essay entitled "The Society of the Muromachi Period (1336-1573)" (Essay Number 74). Here Shiba writes that while the Muromachi period was a time when elements of Japanese culture such as the art of Noh, Japanese gardens (*nihon teien*), and Japanese etiquette (*gyōgi sahō*) originated, the political life, in its turn, was characterized by such episodes as a *samurai* named Mitsusuke Akamatsu losing his patience and secretly attacking Yoshinori Ashikaga, the sixth Ashikaga shogun, in response to the strategic attempts of the Ashikaga shoguns to reassign their vassals according to their will. At the end he concludes: "It was unusual that although Mitsusuke left the capital in a leisurely manner, not a single feudal lord tried to assassinate him. This event, which took place in 1441, helps us to understand what kind of an age the Muromachi period was". In other words, behind this political strife was a world of personal resentment, male homosexuality, and treacherous attacks. It means that while Japanese culture might have already been established, the political system, and the form of the nation were still far from being properly established. According to the author, it was only in the Edo period that this belatedly turned into a cultural system. However, he further reasons that even in the political system of the Edo period, each feudal domain was referred to as a *kuni*, the term that is currently used to mean "country", so in order for the country "Japan" to emerge, people had to become conscious of the "state", a concept transcending their domains. Everything is written in a tone that is very typical of Shiba, and yet surprisingly lacking in sarcasm.

Shiba employs his finest rhetoric in his description of the system of the Edo period: "If we highlight the voice only of the diversity of the nearly three hundred feudal domains, the Edo period could even be described as an international society inside Japan" (Essay Number 14). Based on this way of thinking, it follows that those people such as the young *ronin* in Shiba's story, who had deserted their clans – or as one might put it, had fled their *kuni* – broke down the internal borders of the feudal system. The young *ronin* of the late Edo period who are portrayed in Shiba's popular novels – Ryōma Sakamoto, Shinsaku Takasugi, and Zōroku Murata – all died in the years around the Meiji Restoration. While none of them played an active role in the Meiji state, according to Shiba, they could already be regarded as "people" (*kokumin*). Moreover, one of Shiba's favorite historical figures, shipping merchant Kahei Takadaya, who was captured and taken to Russia, albeit in the times slightly preceding the late days of the Tokugawa shogunate, could be said to have lived as a lone "Japanese national" in the Russian state.

To summarize, in Shiba's thinking the "people" of Japan emerged naturally, even if pressure from the foreign powers was the driving force. Moreover, the energy that generated this emergence had already been accumulated over the long history leading up to the late Edo period.

Dropouts from the Switchboard of Civilization

History has it that the Meiji Restoration took place in 1868, but preparations for the emergence of the "people" that are said to have been born with it had begun some time before. The removal of the *han* (feudal domain) borders due to the abolition of the *han*-system accelerated this process by which the "people" were established. However, if the "people" had existed before the Meiji Restoration, it is natural to think that the attitude of the late-Edo warriors was still present even in the Meiji period. This is how Shiba recognizes it. Shiba suggests that this attitude, which he believed continued to be present until the Russo-Japanese War, was namely the crude "realism" that the warriors hold towards such things as the military and the war. Shiba's view of the history of the Shōwa period is that this realism – which is akin to the realistic approach that was characteristic of Edo merchants or Japanese businessmen after the Second World War – was lost. Instead, the forty years following the Russo-Japanese War were marked by madness, led by the General Staff Office and the prerogative of supreme command controlled by the military elite.

This is a convincing point. When we look back now, we see how much the state ran off track following the Russo-Japanese War. However, if this is true, there is a question that we have to consider: Who were the people who lived in those "forty monstrous years", in particular, the first twenty years of the Shōwa period? They did not appear unexpectedly. They were the same Japanese, the Sanshirōs, in Shiba's words, the people who were brought forth and raised by the sound Meiji state. The question that may cause contention regarding Shiba's historical view is why the unsound system, the "monster", was born from the healthy system of the Meiji generation. A possible answer is that as the second or third generation takes place of the generation that initially made the efforts toward modernization, they are unable to comprehend the true essence and hardships of those efforts, and therefore they have pride in place of memories. Let us consider whether this was really the case, whether the explanation is really so simple, by taking a look at the "second generation" that appeared in the novels by Sōseki Natsume.

Sōseki himself was born in 1867, just when Japan was on the verge of the Meiji Restoration. He became a young adult twenty years later than the *shishi* activists of the late Edo period and twenty years earlier than the Shōwa period's generation of "madness", thus giving him a position from where he could observe both. All the protagonists of Sōseki's so-called trilogy of *Sanshirō* "And Then", and "The Gate" – namely, Sanshirō ("Sanshirō"), Daisuke ("And Then"), and Sōsuke ("The Gate") – were born around 1887, approximately 20 years after the Meiji Restoration, and belonged to a generation who were adolescents in the years following the Russo-Japanese War. Sanshirō and Daisuke were graduates of Tokyo Imperial University, while Sōsuke was a graduate of Kyoto Imperial University; if they had existed in reality, they could well have become the national leaders who acted as the accomplices of "madness" from the late 1920s to the mid-1940s, the first twenty years of the Shōwa period, at a time when they were in the prime of their lives.

In "The Form of this Nation" (Essay Number 62) and in a supplementary article to *Sanshirō* (Collected Edition 5) in the complete works of Sōseki from the publishing house Iwanami, Shiba refers to the metaphor: "switchboard of civilization". This brilliant metaphor implied that Tokyo Imperial University served as a "switchboard" that was circulating civilization from Western Europe to each part of Japan. In other words, its graduates themselves were like "electricity" that was distributed to the various regions and various fields and, becoming the "light of civilization", illuminating every corner of Japan. They were the very "people" (*kokumin*) who constituted the core of the state that was established. The way the future of the state was to unfold depended on the efforts by such elites to sustain the country.

One of these young elites, Sanshirō, notices that his world is divided into three parts after he moves to Tokyo and enrolls in Tokyo Imperial University: the old world that he left behind in the countryside that "carries an aroma of the times preceding the 15th year of Meiji"; the unchanged world that the students inhabit, which is "coated in moss" and "layered in dust"; and the colorful mundane world of "silver spoons, champagne, and beautiful women" (Natsume 2002(1908), Collected Edition 5: 363-366). That was the world that surrounded young people after the Russo-Japanese War. Faced with these three worlds, Sanshirō humorously concludes that "there is nothing better than calling over one's mother, meeting a beautiful wife, and dedicating oneself to studies" (Natsume, 2002(1908), Collected Edition 5: 365). The amusing nature and nonchalance concealed in these words are in some sense the same as those felt by the modern-day students of the University of Tokyo, my own university, one hundred years later. Sanshirō's dream, however, is crushed when the beautiful Mineko leaves him. What became of Sanshirō as a result of this failure? He may have met another slightly more "commonly" beautiful person and accomplished his initial goal. However, his future from that time onwards may not have been that uneventful, as reflected by the way in which the novel concludes with Sanshirō muttering "stray sheep" – a well-known theme within the work which may have been intended to epitomize the feeling of the adolescents of that period, who would get lost in the face of what lay ahead.

In "And Then", Sōseki depicts one of the possible ways in which Sanshirō's life could have developed, in the form of Daisuke, a Tokyo Imperial University graduate who sponges off his parents and spends his days doing nothing. His father, who was a young man in the closing years of the Edo period, is a successful national figure, somewhat of a hero who participated in the founding of the Meiji state. His older brother is a member of the second generation of national elite, who has obediently worked at his father's company since graduating. Only Daisuke is listless, and the people around him feel they have no idea what he is thinking. On top of this moratorium-like stop to his life, Daisuke ends up having a romantic relationship with his friend's wife, and denies himself a chance to be an elite citizen as a result.

"The Gate" portrays a couple that lives such a secluded life. It shows two people whose lives are only marked by one kind of change: the passing of the seasons. Sōsuke, the protagonist of "The Gate", can perhaps be linked to "Sensei" (mentor) from *Kokoro*. "Sensei" would have belonged to an earlier generation than that of Sanshirō, Daisuke, and *Kokoro*'s narrator, "I". At the same time, it is interesting to note that Sensei, who stole his friend's loved one, is affected by the death of the Meiji emperor, commenting that it was "as though the spirit of the Meiji era had begun with the Emperor and had ended with him" (Natsume 1914, translated by McClellan, Edwin 1968: 245) and is inspired to take his own life following General Nogi's ritual suicide. Thus, after the Russo-Japanese War, the people whom Sōseki depicted in his serialized novels published in the *Asahi Shimbun* newspaper were such people who had dropped out from the "switchboard" of Meiji civilization.

The People who Read about the "People" by Sōseki

I would like to approach this theme from two viewpoints. Firstly, in his novels Sōseki clearly indicates the lack of direction of the Meiji state. He weaves into his novels the various incidents that occurred in that period such as the suicides, corruption, and crimes due to the recession that followed the Russo-Japanese War, the assassination of Hirobumi Itō by a Korean, and the events (accusations of conspiring to assassinate Emperor Meiji) related to the trial and execution of socialist Shūsui Kōtoku. By introducing the issues surrounding such incidents whenever needed, Sōseki manages not to lose touch with society in these three books, all of which can be described as dealing with "love-triangles". As these works by Sōseki were initially published as serialized novels in a newspaper, they were presented amongst such social conditions and accidents, and its characters are portrayed not within the closed space of the occurrences between the love-struck men and women, but surrounded and perplexed by shifting social conditions. They are descriptions of the people who were not carried away by the subsequent forty years of madness, and – particularly in case of "And Then" and "The Gate" – they are descriptions of the elites who voluntarily chose to "drop out". Just as Sanshirō thinks to himself "stray sheep, stray sheep", Daisuke exclaims "It's moving, the world's moving…"at the end of "And Then". Both Sanshirō and Daisuke are predicting the future. When we consider these predictions alongside Professor Hirota's comment (*Sanshirō*) that Japan was "headed for a fall", we can see that when the characters of Sōseki's novels, including Sensei in *Kokoro* realize their position as elites, they emerge as an embodiment of a predicament by which they are forced to choose between throwing themselves into the falling country as elites, or dropping out and falling on their own.

The second viewpoint relates to the people who read Sōseki's novels, namely, members of the educated class. Perhaps they read his works in the newspaper before going to work at the public office or to study in the university library or, maybe on breaks in their military service. The newspaper might have included reports conveying nation's crises or glorious achievements. At that moment, in Sōseki's story published on another page ("The Gate"), a man quietly living in his humble home, lays down on veranda and tells his wife that he "does not understand" the Japanese characters for "near" and "now" (Natsume 2002 (1910), Collected Edition 6: 349). The fact that many people were reading this story solely about a man who lacks a sense of the "near future" and "now", the most important concepts for the development of the state, and who retreats from the society step by step seems to be an important fact to consider when contemplating the "forty years of madness" mentioned by Shiba.

The fact that the image that Sōseki, a so-called "national writer", portrayed of "the people" was that of "the people" dropping out of their role in the "switchboard" – in contrast with another "national writer" Eiji Yoshikawa's portrayal of prominent Japanese swordsman Musashi Miyamoto, who strived to train himself, or in contrast with Shiba's *shishi* activists who attempted to create the future – combined with the fact that Soseki's stories depicting these dropouts were widely read, demonstrates that the "forty years" cannot be completely dismissed as what Shiba calls a "different country", that cannot be thought of as Japan (Essay Number

81). During the forty years of Taishō and Shōwa following the forty years of Meiji, it was not just the country made of the General Staff Office and the automated puppets obedient to it. At the least, Sōseki's readers were aware of the doubts about the route the country was about to embark on and of the issues concerning one's position within the country. Yet, it cannot simply be said that Sōseki's readers were unable to drop out even if they wanted to and dispelled their melancholy only inside novels. While reading the clear models of the characters, Sōseki's audience was at the same time living through a different lack of direction. In other words, when realizing that they belonged to the switchboard, Sōseki's readers did not view "the anxiety of being elevated" that had followed the feeling of accomplishment after the Russo-Japanese War in terms of being compelled to choose between either dropping out or staying, regardless of whether they, each as nationals, were the backbone or the periphery of the electric current emanating from it. Each of the works of this trilogy by Sōseki end on a note of anxiety arising from the inability to find a clear solution to their troubles, as all of them end in portraying the characters unable to make any decisions, wandering like "stray sheep". I explained in the first part of the book that this inability to find a clear solution originated in "modernization" brought about by the West. Naturally, we can say that Japan's "modernization" succeeded in some sense, and that at the stage of the victory in the Russo-Japanese War it not only became a strong country internationally, but experienced a sudden rise of "Taishō democracy" and urban living in the first half of its subsequent "forty years of madness". However, inside the state restrictions of Japan it was a challenge to build the "civic society" that would have secured personal freedom and rights and was indispensable for maintaining this democracy and urban life. In the end, the modernization that was making headway in Japan did not result in an identical copy of Western modernity, but at the same time, it could not generate "another modernity" that can be described as "unique" to Japan.

In sum, the characters of the four books discussed here – from *Sanshirō* to *Kokoro* – were not the people who held the concerns of the Meiji period Nihonjinron outlined in Chapter 2, but rather were shaped by Sōseki as the ones who anticipated the "complex question" disputed in Chapter 3 as a part of the Shōwa Nihonjinron. They had already begun to experience the loss of direction that followed Japan's success – what Shiba described as "(inviting white) clouds above the hill". The goal that had been aspired to "for the time being" was lost upon achieving victory in the Russo-Japanese War. However, there was no long-term vision of the society that could replace it. The uncertainty and lack of clear solutions reflected in Sōseki's novels emanate from such circumstances of the epoch. In the world of these novels, a character, unable to overcome perplexities in the end of one story, appears in the next story as having made a certain decision, living as a dropped-out deviant.

The readers, however, did not expressly drop out, and continued to live as "ordinary individuals" between the reality of being "modernized people" and uncertainty towards this condition. This existence is also comparable to having the upper body of a citizen of Western modernity but a lower body that is constrained by the *seken* (one's social milieu) that I will discuss in the next chapter. Kenzō from Sōseki's novel *Michikusa* ("Grass on the Wayside") falls into this category. As Sōseki himself quit his job at Tokyo Imperial University and began to work for Asahi Newspaper Company instead, he may also seem like a dropped-out "deviant", yet the stable income and the reputation he earned in return evolved out of his cautious consideration for the *seken*, equaling him to "an ordinary man", like the majority of his readers. Sōseki's novels, which portrayed such dropped-out personalities, remained equally widely read as national literature after the author's death and continue to be read today, due to "the "feeling of sympathy" the readers experience towards the novels' characters, the "anti-heroes" of some sort.

Among them the elites who were born during the Meiji period and who directly bore the burden of the forty years of the "monster" managed the state without a clearly determined long-term direction. Rather than a far-reaching goal (for instance, like the "clouds above the hill"), they were considering the "present-day world affairs" as seen in the circumstances that changed before their eyes every second. The result of continuously tackling these changes in a haphazard way was the "foolish" "other country" lamented by Shiba. In Chapter 12 I will once again comment on these elites who did not "drop out", referring to them as "Shiba's dilemma".

We are presented with an uneasy problem. We cannot solve it by passing judgements from an advantageous standpoint from which we have a view of the past. As I mentioned in Part 1, the question for Japan was defining the meaning of its modernization and finding the source of its ideas and directions. To employ the vocabulary I have used to describe Nihonjinron, it was the matter of obtaining one's identity as the Japanese in the modernity. After the first generation of Meiji succeeded in the easily approachable task of modernizing Japan externally on a material level, the second generation had to look for the ideas and directions for modernizing Japanese society internally.

In Riichi Yokomitsu's *Ryoshū* ("Melancholy on a Journey") there is a passage questioning whether there had been times since the Meiji period when the youth had to think or to suffer that much. When one is urged to make the choice between dedicating oneself to the state or not, what is one supposed to do when it turns out that this state is not what one thought it was? Should one think of dedicating oneself to the state in terms of devoting oneself to the ethnos? The solution to these situations did not emerge even in the course of eighty years since the Meiji period. Yet the task received by Japan then remains unaccomplished even now.

Status as "the Subjects" and Function as "the People"

Thus, "the people" (*kokumin*) discussed above are opposite to "the subjects" (*shinmin*) from the previous chapter. Upon seeing these two chapters' titles, you may have questioned whether it is right to first discuss the postwar Japanese by means of an archaic word like "subjects" and then the Japanese of the Meiji period using the word "people". This is a viewpoint I adopted in order to set the two epochs apart with the help of these two words. In reality, both the subjects and the people have coexisted since Meiji as two models of the Japanese.

The *shishi* activists described by Shiba, who were preparing their national consciousness in the run up to the Meiji period, noticed that by promoting the emperor they could break down the barriers of the feudal system, on the surface, at least, destroy the class system, and create a "people" devoted to the state. They then achieved this through the concept of *shinmin*, or the "subjects", the term combining both *shin* and *min* ("the subjects" and "the people"). Under the emperor, as a subject, one loses the status of belonging to a class, such as that of *samurai*, farmers, artisans or tradesmen. Yet, "the subjects" is the word used in relation to the emperor, while "the people" relates to the state. If "the subjects" is a signifier that expresses status and entitlement, "the people" refers to function and actions. Dower also suggests this in his comment that "during the war years, *kokumin* had been a familiar word in propa-

---

gandistic sloganeering, essentially synonymous with "the Japanese" or even "the Yamato race" (Dower 2000: 382). In contrast to the passive and static subjects, "the people" can be used to denote the individuals devoted to the state, including its positive nature in terms of ambitious aspirations. While the term *hikokumin* (in which *hi* is a negative prefix) – "unpatriotic person" – has been used as a rebuke, a chastisement, a discrimination to express one's lack of attitude and actions towards the state, if the word *hishinmin*, a "non-subject", was to exist, it would cause difficulties in categorizing according to status. For instance, it would have meant that the people of the "colonized territory" could not be classified as the subjects. In either case, in a situation where these two words are used as suits convenience, when the citizens are called "the people" at a political level it is not being used to suggest mature people of the modern nation-state.

Now what about the present-day Japanese? I already explained that in the Shōwa constitution the word *kokumin* was employed as the translation of "the people", and it is only natural that those preparing the new constitution avoided the word "subjects", which was distinctive to the Meiji Constitution. A later theory explaining the logic behind turning "the subjects" into "the people" notes that while "the subjects" does not include the emperor, "the people" have the emperor as one of them. It became a word to represent the idea that when the country unites against a challenge, the emperor participates in this union.

However, after MacArthur left Japan and life had become stable, the actual conditions changed again. The emperor and the conservatives surrounding the emperor once again began to detach the emperor from the people and hide him behind the veil. With nowhere to direct the energy that the people had directed towards the emperor as subjects, and as it became common sense to criticize the idea of "being a subject" as anti-democratic, this sense that the Japanese were "subjects" found no opportunity to reveal itself – the prince's marriage and similar occasions did not present enough grounds for this – up until Hirohito's illness and passing, namely the end of the Shōwa period, in 1989.

I think this sense that Japanese people are "subjects" is still not completely gone, even today. This connects to the fact that the present-day Japanese are people who live with multiple models, multiple faces, and multiple phases. I do not think that the model of being a "subject" only relates to a "passive" attitude towards the imperial family. For instance, the model of being "subjects" is reflected in developments such as former prime minister Junichirō Koizumi's popularity after 2001 – similar to the people's stance towards MacArthur after the war – with its "active passivity", an entrustment to take risks at any rate, in other words, a sort of populism. Rather, isn't the model of "the people" that seeks to promote national interests more present now in the prolonged recession, when Japan constantly fails in its attempts to advance and to awaken political and economic circles? The reason why Japan – the nation that secured wealth and military power in the prewar period and economic restoration and the status of a kind of superpower in the postwar period as a result of a combination of the governability of the subjects and the commitment and effort of the people – has now come to a halt, is because the combination of these two has stopped working.

The models of "an independent individual" and of "a citizen" in-evitably appear in such times and are particularly strongly promoted now in the context of economic and cultural globalization. I will address these models the next chapter.

Note: This corresponds with Dower's statement that "In fact, there is not even such a thing as "Japan". Rather, we have to discuss 'Japanese cultures' and 'Japanese traditions'. We have to refer to it as 'Japans'" (Dower 2001: xiii-xiv, "Foreword for Japanese Readers", Japanese edition).

CHAPTER 6

"Citizens": A Vertically-Structured Society and Seken

The World the Japanese Live In

In my discussion on the concept of "the people" (*kokumin*) in the previous chapter, I noted examples of Sōseki's protrayals of Tokyo Imperial University graduates who were supposed to become leading national figures but instead voluntarily "dropped out" from their role among "the people" contributing to the country after experiencing the torments of love triangles with their friends and the women they loved. I also argued that the readers of such novels, even if they themselves were the exemplary "people" who had not dropped out, sympathized with the anxiety of Sōseki's characters and their inability to find clear solutions. Such conflict with the world is a subject matter in Sōseki's literary works from *Wagahai wa Neko Dearu* ("I Am a Cat") onward and, as seen in *Michikusa* ("Grass on the Wayside"), is something that Sōseki himself suffered from in real life.

Historian Kinya Abe attempts to determine what this "world" is about through discussion of the phenomenon of *seken* in a series of works: *Seiyō Chūsei no Ai to Jinkaku – 'Seken'-ron Josetsu* ("Love and Personality of the Western Middle Age: Introduction to the Theory of 'Seken'") (1992); *'Seken' to ha Nani ka* ("What is 'Seken'?") (1995); *Gakumon to 'Seken'* ("Learning and 'Seken'") (2001), and *Sekengaku e no Shōtai* ("Invitation into the Theory of 'Seken'") (2002). Abe notes that "the problem of one's existence inside the Japanese society" is a "key theme" running through all Sōseki's works (Abe 1995: 180). Abe asserts that apart from the framework comprising the concepts of society and individual that was imported from Western scholarship, in Japan there exists the traditionally lived *seken* and "world" (*yo no naka*), which strongly control the actions of the Japanese. He suggests that unless we realize this it is impossible to understand Japan and the Japanese.

An indication that "the society" and "an individual" in Japan are largely different from those of the West can be often observed in Nihonjinron. The discourse commonly covers the kind of chicken-or-egg arguments in which one side suggests that Japan struggles because it lacks independent individuals while the other retorts that this is exactly how things should be. However, there are in fact very few works that have thoroughly analyzed this matter from a theoretical viewpoint rather than a fruitless never-ending argument. Among these works, Chie Nakane's *Tate Shakai no Ningen Kankei* (hereafter, "Human Relations in a Vertical Society") (1967) is, together with the *The Chrysanthemum and the Sword*, both one of the most famous Nihonjinron works and at the same time the most intensely theoretical of the works that are read as Nihonjinron.

"However You Look at It, the Human World is Not an Easy Place to Live"

What is this *seken* that Kinya Abe addresses? The quickest way to explain it is to say that the world that a Japanese person lives in at the moment is their *seken*. However, it is difficult to objectively know the substance of something that penetrates a Japanese person through to the bones. I will draw upon the definition that Abe employs as a working hypothesis (1995: 16).

> *Seken* is a ring of relations connecting individuals, and though it does not have bylaws and contracts, it links individuals with a strong bond. However, an individual does not create *seken* of their own accord. A person somehow lives in it as if there exists a place for oneself there.

Abe goes on to state that "in *seken* there are things that have a form and things that do not". He demonstrates the *seken* that "has a form" with examples such as alumni reunions, companies, haiku poetry societies, literary circles, university departments, and conferences, and explains the *seken* that "does *not* have a form" as "the relationships with neighbors and with those with whom we exchange New Year greetings cards (*nengajō*) and gifts". Abe specifies that the rules of this *seken* include participating in funerals and religious ceremonies. *Seken* could also be the participants of a group tour celebrating together inside a train, and as all the other passengers are just people outside this circle, *seken* for the time being, consideration is not given to them or any inconvenience that might be caused to them. Abe also notes that strong rules regarding *seken* are not to disgrace the *seken* one is a part of and not to "cause trouble" for the *seken*. These are not the relationships akin to those present in the West, in which either tangibly or conceptually individuals as autonomous entities create laws and agreements "of their own accord". Instead, an individual person is given one's "proper station" – as it is described in Benedict's *The Chrysanthemum and the Sword* – within the *seken*, and as long as "they keep to the rules of the *seken*" is able to maintain some position there "regardless of their abilities" and without having to compete (Abe 1995: 22).

However, Abe does not only put forward this concept of *seken* because it is effective for thinking about Japan. It conceals Abe's own mission, that is, his desire to rethink the pursuit of academic scholarship (*gakumon*) in Japan. Namely, it implies that the fact that Japanese academics have translated the Western phenomena of "society" and "individual" with the terms *shakai* and *kojin* and sought to apply these to discussion of Japan was not only a mistake at the level of analysis, but negligence at the deeper level of scholarship itself, namely neglecting to recognize the notion of *seken* that the Japanese really live in. The very fact that this negligence is allowed to continue reflects the existence of *seken*. In other words, it is typical within the concept of *seken* for a journal paper to be reviewed inside the *seken* of the academic conference and to be deemed fine as long as it maintains a certain position there. Abe, who was a specialist in Western history, must have come up against *seken* when living in Japan as a scholar and realized that this *seken* itself is an important research topic for him. Sōseki's novels also repeatedly portray the suffering – as opposed to comfort – that living in their *seken* brings the characters. It could be suggested that this is directly demonstrated by the following well-known passage from Sōseki's *Kusamakura*:

> If you work by reason, you grow rough-edged; if you choose to dip your oar into sentiment's stream, it will sweep you away. Demanding your own way only serves to constrain you. However you look at it, the human world is not an easy place to live (Natsume 1906, translated by McKinney, Meredith 2008: 3).

Until arriving at this idea, Sōseki – like Abe – spent time abroad, researching English literature in England, before returning to Japan. Sōseki felt the difficulties of living in *seken* throughout his life. Looking back to the discussion raised in Chapter 1 regarding the four Meiji-period authors who spent time abroad, Sōseki's time spent studying abroad was a "failure" in many ways. He did not gain any positive experiences, neither in the literary research he conducted in Britain nor in his interactions with British society. Perhaps because his background and career differed from those of the four Meiji-period authors, Sōseki was unable to freely enjoy life in the West like they did and his experiences abroad therefore contain elements that seem more to anticipate the "Melancholy on a Journey" of the Shōwa period.

The Significance of the Theory on Seken

What is the significance of Abe's theory on *seken*? The concept itself had already been raised by Benedict in *The Chrysanthemum and the Sword* and it overlaps significantly with the comparisons of Western individualism and Japanese collectivism that are made in various Nihonjinron works. However, Abe presents a completely new viewpoint.

This point lies precisely with the fact that Abe extracted the wording *seken* from the contemporary everyday Japanese. This is not to say that he simply found a good term to express the theory. He would deserve criticism if he had pulled this word from Western philosophy or "aspects of the contemporary times". What distinguishes his theory is that the word *seken* has been commonly used by Japanese people to explain their lives – as seen in the expression "but the public (*seken*) are not so forgiving" (*sō wa itte mo seken ga yurusanai yo*) – and that there is an abundance of cases in which it was used dating back to the Asuka and Nara epochs, suggesting the possibility that this phenomenon itself can become an object of academic examination.

Abe insists that our only option is to admit that the world we live in is *seken*. This is equal to admitting that "society" and "individual" in their Western meanings are not in effect in Japan. For instance, under the premises of the *seken* theory, such ideas as the development of "civic society" or the promotion of "public awareness" are invalid, given that the concept of "civic" does not imply its Western meaning. I do indeed know from my own modest experience that civic activities prove fruitful in Japan even when they are marked by such a discrepancy. By no means can we suggest that Abe's theory indicates that such activities and their outcomes are meaningless. I believe the modern achievements of the Japanese "civic" activities are of value and that Abe's theory of *seken* is effective in relation to the various problems that emerge inside these activities, in the form of human conflicts or dissatisfaction with the way this work is pursued. Our civic activities and the movement to change "society" are in a sense difficult to resolve due to the fact that in reality we live not in the society but in the *seken*. In other words, I would like to point out that, when we subconsciously consider it on the assumption of the presence of society, the individual, and Western citizenry, it becomes impossible to provide an answer to the crucial question of Nihonjinron: "Who are we inside 'the Western modernity'?"

Before Abe's theory saw the light, Nakane had analyzed these controversial points in her "Human Relations in a Vertical Society".

The Classics Gain Fame, but Not Readers

When addressing Chie Nakane's "Human Relations in a Vertical Society", I am prompted to make the cynical comment that "the classics" are works that have reached the stage at which their titles are widely known but their contents remain unread. This is not fame but misfortune. For instance, as I mentioned in Chapter 4, many people think that the chrysanthemum in the title of Benedict's *The Chrysanthemum and the Sword* refers to the flower in the imperial seal. This is a trivial misunderstanding, but I wonder how many people know that the "vertically-structured society" discussed by Chie Nakane is a comparison with the "horizontally-structured society" and that the archetype of the latter is not in the West but in India. One might assume that this kind of thinking is characteristic only of those who have not read the book, but even many people who have read it might suggest that Nakane argues both that a "vertically-structured society" is exclusive and that a "vertically-structured society" does not provide an individual with space for free activities. (The answer is that both are wrong. This will become clear by the end of this chapter.)

In his book *Nihonbunkaron no Hen'yo* ("Transformation of the Discourse on Japanese Culture") (1990), which I referred to in Chapter 1, Tamotsu Aoki divides the postwar Nihonjinron into several stages. According to Aoki's stages, Nakane's book belongs to the first half (1964-1976) of the phase of "affirmative recognition of peculiarity". Aoki argues that along with *Nihon no Keiei* ("The Japanese Management") by Kunio Odaka (1965) and *'Amae' no Kōzō* ("The Structure of 'Amae'") by Takeo Doi (1971), which I will discuss in Chapter 8, Nakane's "Human Relations in a Vertical Society" overthrew the general notion of viewing the peculiarities of the Japanese in negative terms.

I do not disagree with this statement in particular, but if I was to adopt the terms "positive" and "negative", I would use them in a slightly different way. I believe that rather than individual authors being positive or negative, it is the state of society that can shift from positive to negative depending on the times. In positive times, positive books are often written. However, I find it interesting that books that were produced in negative times and then read as disapproving of Japan, are subsequently re-read in positive terms upon the arrival of favorable times. For example, people who saw democracy as the ray of hope in the midst of postwar anxiety must have felt negated upon reading Benedict's suggestion in *The Chrysanthemum and the Sword* that Western democracy is not suited for Japan. However, when reading the same part after gaining a certain degree of confidence, they may have thought that Japan has its own democracy, and since democracy is a system that cannot be separated from culture, it is only natural for each country to have its own democratic path. Moreover, there are cases when a book written in a negative tone stays unread during the favorable times that follow, in other words, during periods when Japan is on the rise, and comes under the spotlight anew when negative times ensue.

As I explained in the first part of this book, regardless of whether the country is on the rise or on the fall, Nihonjinron is written and read as a result of the anxiety of identity caused by these vicissitudes. Nakane wrote her book in a time when Japan was on the rise and making a clear recovery. Having said that, it was not free from anxiety. The compulsion to think that Japan was not achieving its recovery simply by following the West but was expressing something unique stems from a desire to justify that recovery and an anxiety that one will not gain clarity without this justification, even with that recovery right before one's eyes.

The Inside and Outside

Similar to Abe, Nakane opens up a discussion by referring to the issues of research method (Nakane 1967: 10-20). There are two kinds of discourse on the society and culture of Japan: discourse that attempts to explain and bring order to Japan by means of theories borrowed from the Western social sciences, and discourse that extracts the Japan's unique phenomena by making comparisons with those of the West and tries to grasp the society and culture of Japan through such discussions. The former tries to measure traditional Japanese clothing in centimeters and meters instead of Japanese inches and feet, and when it inevitably arrives at odd figures, it discards them with the suggestion that Japan and its institutions are "old-fashioned" or "backward", even if they are crucial for Japanese society. Nakane argues that although the latter discourse cherishes these odd figures because it does so excessively and because it uses ideas forged by the efforts of Western scholarship and the theoretical results "in a negative sense", "it is extremely poor theoretically and rather possesses the weakness of a 'whim'-like hypothesis (that lacks theoretical consistency) (Nakane 1967: 18).

Nakane therefore attempts to uncover the social structure in Japan from the position of a social anthropologist. In building her theory to do this she employs such notions as place and status, inside (*uchi*) and outside (*soto*), and vertical and horizontal, and adopts India as an "extreme object" of comparison. Below I will provide an overview of how this discourse is structured.

First of all, "place" does not make any distinction according to one's status. This is used in a sense where it refers to a group of people determined "by place", when a group is formed by certain "quotas". "Determined by status" expresses the opposite meaning. While any group is constructed through both place and status, in Japan the collective consciousness is rooted strongly in "place", whereas in India "status" is a strong element, as observed in the caste system.

In Japan, a typical example of a group formed through place is a household (*ie*). For a household, the authoritative structure of a master of the house (as a status) does not present a problem, and it is organized by means of such "frameworks" as communal life or farming. Since the status inside the group is irrelevant in the case of a household or a company, it may, for instance, occur that when someone says they are "from XX television", one might think he is a producer or a camera operator when in fact he is a driver" (Nakane 1967: 30). This form of "collective consciousness" connects to the fact that "the Japanese people refer to a workplace, a company or a district that they belong to as 'ours' and those of an opponent as 'yours'" (Nakane 1967: 30). One can see that of Abe's two types of *seken*, this group formed by "place" corresponds to the "*seken* that has a form". In her explanation of inside and outside, Nakane also introduces an example similar to Abe's description of a group tour on a train: "We can observe the laughable situation in which the very same person who has jumped in front of a stranger to secure a seat for himself, offers his seat to a person he knows well (especially a senior at work), regardless of how tired he himself may be" (Nakane 1967: 47). Here we can interpret "inside" as one's own *seken*, and "outside" as everything else.

Vertical and Horizontal

Nakane discovers a vertical structure inside such a group in Japan that is formed by place and that is strongly conscious of inside and outside. This is revealed through comparison with the horizontal. A common mistake that may occur here is connecting the vertical with an authority-based hierarchy and the horizontal with social equality. However, the vertical and the horizontal should be viewed as the lines of abstract structures. Nakane explains it in the following way (Nakane 1967: 26-27).

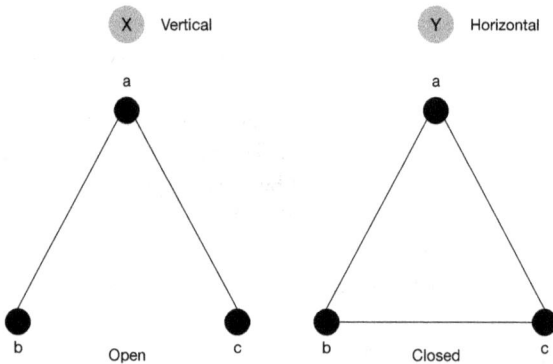

Figure 1: Figure modified from Chie Nakane's "Human Relations in a Vertical Society"

Firstly, if we employ two groups with different structures, such as X (vertical) and Y (horizontal), it will look like this. If we follow a hypothesis that each of the groups is comprised of the equal number of individuals, if they are abstractly shown by points a, b and c, we will arrive at Figure 1. The difference in these two structures is firstly that all the constituting members of X are connected only when "a" stands at the top while in Y all the members are mutually interconnected. Secondly, the X structure is always unlocked towards the outside, as seen in its open bottom, while Y is sealed-off.

From here, if someone else were to join the groups, in X one of the members would look after them, making entering easier. In Y, the approval of all members is necessary for somebody else to join. A classic example of a closed group akin to Y can be found in British "members clubs". In such clubs, "statuses" such as aristocratic lineage and position in society are crucial elements and, moreover, they have to be recognized by all members of the club. This represents that the vertical structure is open, while in contrast the horizontal structure is closed. Further, in the X structure, the newly arrived member forms a pseudo-"parent-child" relationship with the person who looks after him or her.

We can derive various points from the theoretical explanation of this structure. For instance, since in the X structure the vertical circulation of information and the chain of command have a solid foundation, the group demonstrates outstanding effectiveness even in the absence of strong leadership. However, if the system differs, sectionalism occurs due to the weakness of the horizontal relations, thus preventing the organization from functioning. This can frequently be observed in Japanese public offices. Additionally, these vertical relations are ordered by means of the external conditions that are unrelated to qualifications such as one's age, the year or term of one's enrollment, and this order – or "one's proper station", as it is referred to in *The Chrysanthemum and the Sword* – has to be followed precisely. For example, even in the academic world, at a conference research meeting, where the only condition guiding the discussion should be logic, the participants stick to an "order" determining who should deliver their remarks before whom. Interestingly, since the main requirement for becoming a leader is not necessarily one's ability, the leader at times makes up for their lack of abilities by utilizing their subordinates, while the subordinates who are most likely to feel frustrated with work due to the fact that they have potential, effectively take on the leader's work responsibilities. Moreover, by supporting the leader, it is also possible to influence the horizontal positions in which one can normally not intervene. As a result, the vertical organization "that seems to be a rigid one with an overemphasis on order and a complete lack of elasticity, at the same time provides the individuals with the scope to engage in surprisingly free activities" (Nakane 1967: 153) (Figure 2).

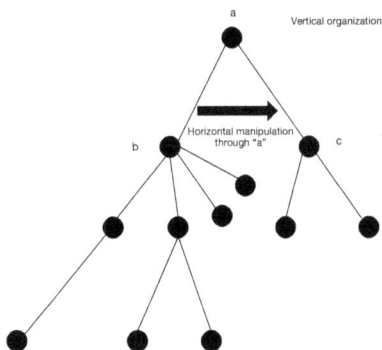

Figure 2: Figure modified from Chie Nakane's "Human Relations in a Vertical Society"

What Starts from Current Japanese Society

The model of "the people" (*kokumin*) and even more so that of the "subjects" (*shinmin*) are terms that set off warning bells in political discussion due to their connection to nationalism. In contrast, it seems that there is no such caution regarding the word "citizen" (*shimin*). For example, the phrase "creation of citizens" (*arata na shimin sōshutsu*) functions like an ever effective talisman that is unlikely to ever be denied by anyone. However, once we come to know Abe's "*seken* theory" and Nakane's concept of a "vertical structure", we should wonder whether "a citizen" exists in Japan at all. First of all, if we take an independent individual of the Western type who interacts with society based on his own initiative, we would have to admit that Japanese society is not comprised of such individuals. In some sense, the "enlightenment" of the Japanese has been pursued since the Meiji Restoration in the hope that such "individuals" would come into being, but it is true that the circumstances did not turn out this way.

Chie Nakane's "Human Relations in a Vertical Society" has the subtitle "A Theory of a Homogeneous Society". A "homogenous society" is different from a "homogeneous race". It is not connected by pseudo "blood relationships" or ideological "values"; its essence lies solely within the principle of structure. Since in a "homogeneous society" one gains belonging to a group by means of place, one loses that affiliation once one leaves the place. More specifically, if one is absent for too long, one's "seat" is taken away. In other words, the individuals are required to be fully present at all times. As a result, a single individual cannot, in principle, belong to two groups. For instance, if a relationship with a group is a qualification and if the affiliation to the group is decided through a contract based on this qualification, then belonging to two groups simultaneously is also possible. From a perspective of social security, it is risky when one dedicates both his body and soul to a certain group and is always ready to share the group's fate. Of course, if everything goes well, it can be a good choice that provides emotional stability, but it is still a gamble. Common sense would suggest that it is more advantageous when an individual has a few group affiliations. Then, there is the drawback that in a society there are multiple groups with different natures, but this also creates vitality. Both vertical and horizontal societies have their respective benefits. It is true that Japan has created a vertical society that takes advantage of increased homogeneity, having to a certain extent won in its risky gamble.

A slightly more precise description of the idea of Japan as a vertical society would be to say that in Japan the principles of a vertical society function to some extent stronger than those of a horizontal society. Any society, be it India, Europe, or Japan, is positioned between these two polar models, even if it is somewhat tilted towards one of the two. Not every "civic society" is an ideal horizontal organization. For this reason, it is feasible for Japanese society to explore its possibilities as a "civic society" between the two models at opposite ends of the spectrum while employing their two principles.

At the same time, the reason why Abe wants us to understand how strongly *seken* affects our lives is firstly because it is impossible to move forward from a wrong starting point, whether we do so theoretically or practically. It is necessary to objectify *seken* rather than being subconsciously tethered by it.

Secondly, it is because it is important to know how to live inside this *seken*. Abe says: "I do not think that *seken* will completely disappear from Japan's society. However, I do think that we should consider how an individual can exist within *seken* in a more uninhibited way" (Abe 1995: 158). The works of Abe and Nakane show us that in order to turn this individual into a "citizen", there is no other place to start than the here and now of present-day Japan.

CHAPTER 7

Craftsmen: The People Who "Make Things" Rather than "Saying Things"

The Japanese Are Craftsmen

Despite a number of hitches in the run up to its establishment, a private university known as the Institute of Technologists was established in Saitama in spring 2001 with the aim of providing students with the skills needed for professions related to production and craftsmanship in fields such as machine electronics, timber construction, and architecture. Its Japanese name, *Monotsukuri Daigaku*, literally translates as "Craftsmanship University", and the concept behind its establishment is described as follows:

> The Institute of Technologists was established with the support of the government and industrial circles as an institution to educate aspiring individuals who possess the "skill" and "soul" of craftsmanship and in turn develop the industries grounded in manufacturing and craftsmanship. The term *monotsukuri* in the institute's Japanese name is made up of *tsukuri*, meaning "creating", and *mono*, which may refer to both "things" and "humans", thereby reflecting the principle that "creating things means creating humans".

To put it in an exaggerated way, this is a "challenge" to the mainstream assumption in the West that a university is a place to pursue the wisdom of the abstract dimension of things, an assumption that has been followed since the early modern period. Are "skill" and "soul" things to be pursued at a university? However, far from coming up against resistance, it seems that this challenge has been warmly welcomed by society. As the above statement reflects, in Japan, there already existed a stronger assumption that great value should be placed on one's "skill" and "soul", which predates the idea that universities are places for the study of the "abstract dimension". This form of the aesthetics of living, which can also be found in Tenshin Okakura's *The Book of Tea* or the "secret art" of chrysanthemum growing of *The Chrysanthemum and the Sword*, has a much longer history than the university system imported from the West. Nowadays, universities are expected to produce useable knowledge and tangible profits, in the name of "cooperation between industries and academia". In short, amidst the trend by which all universities are expected to engage in "production", the Institute of Technologists is not so much a novel exception, as a form that universities should take.

Japan has a long history of craftsmanship (*monotsukuri*). In March 2000, NHK launched the documentary series *Project X: Challengers*, a series which tells the story behind the development and introduction of products and technical innovations of the past such as the VHS or the bullet train, in many cases focusing on the "unsung" technicians and project leaders who put their hearts and souls into the fruition of such projects. It has enjoyed great popularity for a number of years and is frequently rerun, no doubt in response to requests from viewers. The stories move many viewers to tears. The program invokes strong feelings of empathy toward fellow "unsung heroes" and "the real Japanese". It portrays the wisdom, values, and emotion present in daily life in Japan – a new form of "folklore" for the television generations.

The Japanese folklore expert Tsuneichi Miyamoto's work *Wasurerareta Nihonjin* (hereafter, "The Forgotten Japanese") (1960) conveys strong affection for such "unsung heroes", the people who "make things rather than saying things". Non-fiction writer and journalist Shin'ichi Sano discussed the book as part of the *NHK Human Lectures*, the series that served as the starting point for this monograph. Poet, composer, and TV personality Rokusuke Ei's bestseller *Shokunin* (hereafter, "The Craftsmen") (1996) is also a collection of memoirs about such people. It paints a portrait of the Japanese people who silently go about devising ways to improve living. Although the title of this chapter is the people who "make things *rather than saying things*", not everyone is like this in reality. Among the people introduced by Miyamoto there were many who were rather loquacious, and the characters in Rokusuke Ei's book – including Ei himself – are all very talkative. However, it is common in our world for people who only talk but do not leave written records to vanish unknown as if they never said anything. People like this tend to be called "the commoners" (*shomin*). Unlike the categories with clear connotations, such as "subjects" (*shinmin*), "people" (*kokumin*) or "citizens" (*shimin*), this is the category of "the others", which is in some way characterized by the fact that it has no characteristics. One feels comfortable in Japan when calling oneself "a commoner" because, referring back to the discussion in the previous chapter, one lives inside the vertical organization of *seken* and can always define oneself through such an ordinary thing as keeping the conventions of that *seken*, without being judged in terms of one's talents and qualifications.

However, it is wrong to assume that people with no outstanding characteristics do nothing. Rather, they are people who do something ardently, people who work hard. I argue that if we capture the most distinctive aspects of the "commoners" among "the others", we will encounter the "craftsmen". This leads to the conclusion that most of the Japanese are craftsmen and in fact it is precisely so.

Being a Craftsman is a "Way of Living"

To learn about these craftsmen, let us start with Rokusuke Ei's "The Craftsmen". Ei was prompted to associate with craftsmen following the enforcement of the metric system and the prohibition on making and selling the carpenter's square (*kanejaku*) and the kimono-maker's measuring stick (*kujira-jaku*), tools that had been used to measure in the former Japanese unit of length, the *shaku* (similar to the "foot"). He was determined to put an end to such a nonsensical rule and dared to "violate the law" by producing and selling such tools. Any line of this book by Ei allows one to picture the faces and the work of the craftsmen. Let me explain by citing a few passages. "The world of the apprenticeship system created not only things (*mono*) but humans (*hito*) too" (Ei 1994: 38). This is exactly the objective of the Institute of Technologists mentioned above. The method of passing down skills adopted in apprenticeship systems nowadays remains the topic of attention for cultural anthropology and cognitive sciences. The Institute of Technologists can be seen as an advanced system, as opposed to a return to traditional values or reactionism.

> For this reason, craftsmen do not only make things. In the case of gardeners, there are craftsmen who cultivate things and those who prefer not to do so. Farmers can be craftsmen that either grow vegetables or pick them" (Ei 1994: 27-28, Ei's own words).

This is precisely what I sought to imply when I said that "most of the Japanese are craftsmen". We tend to think of ourselves as "craftsmen": farmers see themselves as "rice makers", editors see themselves as "book makers", and those who work at automobile factories and design studios see themselves as "car makers". Rokusuke Ei also describes himself as the "radio craftsman".

Moreover, there are several features that are common to craftsmen, among which "busyness" is a key characteristic. In fact, Ei makes a number of clever remarks on what it is to be busy, at one point commenting: "If you have time to eat or go to the toilet, you're not busy at all" (Ei 1994: 4). While getting to understand craftsmen we notice that "busyness" is not just a state, but an attribute of a "craftsman". They enjoy being busy, and convey this even when saying that being busy is very, very tiring. Ei comments on this by saying:

> In this sense, being a craftsman is first of all reflected in one's physique.
> I met many craftsmen whose bodies had changed because of their work.
> Craftsmen's hands reflect this.
> Hands change to better suit the work, and when I see this, it seems to me that being a craftsman is not work, but "a way of living" (Ei 1994: 138).

In terms of their way of living, craftsmen serve as a model of the Japanese. The craftsmen's model is easy to understand. There is no need to delineate similar points such as in the case of "subjects", "people", and "citizens" or to define subtle differences. You may understand elements of this as a real feeling. This feeling is linked to the "concreteness" of things.

Both Ruth Benedict and Chie Nakane employ the word "tangible" in their books as an important term to describe Japan. Nakane writes that since the members of a Japanese group determined by place do not have something similar like their qualifications in common, it becomes necessary to be directly "in touch with (relate to)" each other on a daily basis in order to enhance the group consciousness (Nakane 1967: 54). For "humans" this translates into trusting relationships with the closest people perceptible by touch. If we think of this not in terms of humans but "things" and their "tangible" nature, it reveals that in Japanese society, things that are happening "on site" – that is, concrete things rather than abstract theories – are trusted.

The *Project X* documentary series tells the stories of a number of different projects, and each episode climaxes with an inspirational moment in which we see the awareness, ingenuity, and hands-on wisdom with which the innovators approached these concrete things. This sensation towards things is an extension of the past relations of the Japanese with things, relations that have culminated over many years – as for instance in the case of "chrysanthemum growing", a topic that I have referred to extensively. Additionally, I would like to emphasize that this does not mean simply creating something "efficiently" but also doing so "thoroughly", which is an endeavor supported by the so-called "sense of beauty" (*biishiki*). One would not have to devote all one's energy to the task if the only criteria were effectiveness and precision. What encourages such dedication is the sense of "beauty", a desire to bring harmony to one's own world, as well as the values of doing something "properly" and "thoroughly".

"Ingenuity" is Important

In Tsuneichi Miyamoto's "The Forgotten Japanese" there are many utterances and descriptions similar to those that I have cited earlier. First of all, he describes the Japanese of the old days as "busy". He quotes an elder of Nagura Village (currently part of the town of Shitara), Aichi Prefecture, who says:

> Since we have worked without a break, we cannot feel satisfied unless we work, even now that we have aged. This is already my nature, so nothing can be done about it. No matter what anyone says, we should be allowed to work (Miyamoto 1995(1960): 81).

However, Miyamoto also makes it clear that "ingenuity" is necessary, stressing that "for everyone, ingenuity is more important than work". Miyamoto goes on to quote the elder recounting how his father encouraged him to make his own tool for transporting loads:

> It's all very well to keep on saying "work, work, work", but it is not enough just to work like a bull or a horse [...]. My father once complained that we should stop borrowing the rack from others,

that we should be able to make our own, and rely on our own ingenuity rather than someone else's, which led to all the villagers making their own racks [...]. By the way, the work flowed much smoother once each household had got their own racks.

Miyamoto adds: "since then people have been using their own ingenuity and nowadays no one burdens others" (Miyamoto 1995(1960): 96-97).

This is somewhat like a compact version of an episode of *Project X*. Such lively images of farmers devising new tools and methods are often forgotten amidst the stereotypes from popular stories and movies in which all farmers do is suffer in agony. However, as I will discuss in Chapter 10, the farmers of the Edo period and modern times were in fact ultimate ecologists who devised ingenious means of living up until the finest detail, transforming their village into the ultimate recycling-based societies. Miyamoto fills the chronicles about his own birthplace and records of his travels across Japan with such stories by people who create and devise things. These were tales not of the past, but of the ordinary rural communities until around the time of the 1964 Tokyo Olympics, albeit with some regional differences.

Let us consider two more remarkable points highlighted by Miyamoto in "The Forgotten Japanese". The first of these is the great extent of people's mobility. The term *seken-shi* ("master of the world" [Miyamoto 1995(1960): 214]; see Chapter 4 on *seken*) refers to a person among the villagers who has traveled extensively since youth. Although they were certainly not great in number, each village had a "master of the world" of their own, who channeled the information from the outside. When I carried out fieldwork in Inasa District (currently Hamamatsu City), Shizuoka Prefecture, I also had the chance to hear many interesting stories from an elderly man who had visited many places as a travelling actor in his youth. Moreover, in a certain village in Shōnai Valley, Yamagata Prefecture, which I visited regularly, a man who had gone to the Tokyo division as a soldier before the war later assumed such a role as the village's supply of information. Tsuneichi Miyamoto himself was an extraordinary "master of the world" who visited every corner of Japan, listened to people's stories, and told them to the world.

We should also not overlook the stories about women in Miyamoto's book. In this book there appears a story about one man's love affairs, under the title "Tosa Genji" (the title borrowed from "The Tale of Genji") (Miyamoto 1995(1960): 131). This is an account of a man, who, akin to a "master of the world", is unable to settle down and moves from one place to another as if dependent on the gentleness of women's hearts like Prince Genji. Yet here too Miyamoto records the radiant words of the "forgotten Japanese".

> You must have also had special feelings for a woman. I feel sorry for women. Women understand men and take care of them, but men who understand what women feel and treat them kindly are rare. I think that we should take care of women. Kind-heartedness that has been shown is not something that can be forgotten (Miyamoto 1995(1960): 157).

The relationship between men and women described here relates to the Japanese model of "the commoners", which is slightly different from "the craftsmen". I will return to this point once again in the following chapter, which addresses women.

The Transformations of the 1960s

I wrote earlier that the Japan depicted in "The Forgotten Japanese" is the country of the 1960s, up until around the 1964 Tokyo Olympics. I was a child at that time and I remember how laborers who had come to Tokyo from the rural areas for work were engaged in the hurried projects to prepare facilities such as highway roads and subway lines. On the contrary, the projects introduced in *Project X* are mostly from the years that followed. The reason I called *Project X* "'folklore' for the television generations" is because it picks up from where Miyamoto's depiction of folklore ends in the early 1960s. This shift is due to the fact that those who were "farmers" up until the 1950s emerge as the "craftsmen" in the worksites that generated Japan's rapid economic growth from the late-1950s to the early 1970s.

As this chapter on "craftsmen" has looked at the documentary series *Project X* and the Institute of Technologists as examples of projects that draw on the beauty and technique of Japan's manufacturing and crafts-manship, you may think that the old "craftsmanship" of Japan is a phe-nomenon that has taken shape in the present times. However, this is not what I have in mind or, to be precise, not the only thing that I mean.

The tradition of "craftsmen" under discussion here is broader than the so-called "craftsmanship" of the works of art; it is something that was present not only in the craftsmen, but all the regular people of Japan, whether they were craftsmen, farmers, or merchants (or even academics). All Japanese, especially in the social system of the Edo period, have ensured that they are "industrious" and have the capacity to work actively, and exercise wisdom and ingenuity in their lives. This is what I wished to imply when I wrote that being a craftsman is a "way of life". While there are many craftsmen among the people who appear in *Project X*, accurately speaking these are the people whose way of life can be defined as "exercising ingenuity in life".

Through these examples, I have shown that being a "craftsman" is not just an occupation but a way of life of the Japanese in general. I would like to finish by explaining why phenomena such as *Project X* or the Institute of Technologists currently capture the hearts of such a large audience so successfully. The answer lies with the fact that we are now again at the stage at which we need Nihonjinron. As I explained earlier, Nihonjinron is created and read during times of anxiety. There have previously been two turning points at which Japan's anxiety was at a peak: the Meiji Restoration and Japan's defeat in the Pacific War. It is now at a third turning point. In the first two cases, Japan's response was led by the state under the slogans "prosperous country, strong army" and "economic revival" respectively. Moreover, while both points had their positive and negative aspects, they generated a successful outcome relatively fast. However, presently there exists recognition among people of a stage of structural transition that starts with "the collapse of the bubble economy and defeat in the money wars". Japan is exploring the new course that it will take amidst this anxiety. Yet, we have to contemplate whether Nihonjinron will have the impact that it did before on overcoming this anxiety or whether its necessity has begun to wane.

In the past ten years, I have taken part in dialogues about the course of Japan at different lecture events and workshops. On those occasions, someone would inevitably voice the idea that one has to return to craftsmanship as the starting point and rethink Japan from there. There were strong arguments that Japan, as it faces such difficulties, is essentially the country of craftsmanship, and although much is said about finance, IT, or the software industry, the real strength of the Japanese is in the making of things. On the national scale, this refers to the Japanese government's initiatives to promote a "nation based on the creativity of science and technology". It is also created with the intention of finding a means of survival in the traditions of artisanship and the model of the Japanese "craftsmen".

However, when these matters are discussed not only as technical problems, but also as a way of life, the Nihonjinron emerges. Craftsmanship appears not only in the revitalization of industry, but even in the revival of moral standards and the recreation of values. The craftsman's way of life is talked about in terms of the down-to-earth making of things in extreme contrast to a way of life where one is "floating in a bubble". It seems that there has been a tremendous increase in media coverage of devoting one's life to such "craftsmanship". "Craftsmanship" also fits with the catchphrase "harmony with the environment". There is, however, no point in judging its merits and demerits based on moral preferences.

I would like to stress a few more points to connect this subject with the discussion on the present-day necessity of Nihonjinron, a subject that I will pursue in Part 3. Japanese society has turned to "trust of tangible things" for help before on more than one occasion. Society attempts a reconstruction by going back to the strengths it previously accumulated. Going back to basics cannot be bad. There is no need to give up on the old advantages. However, what one should be conscious of is that "trust of tangible things" means "distrust of intangible, abstract things". There is vulnerability toward abstract theories and systems. It has nothing to do with the intellectual ability of the Japanese, but with their sense of values. Things are conducted with the reliance on hands-on ingenuity and empathic attitude, and not on decision-making stemming from general principles. The work is done swiftly. The fact that in the old Japan, the two turning points, the Meiji Restoration and defeat in the Second World War, were followed by rapid catching-up and recovery is down to the strength of this hands-on work. When pursuing and following the others' success, it is not efficient to consult with the fundamentals and make decisions based on them. However, when failing to perform higher-level checks in accordance with the general rules and abstractions, there is a risk of overlooking failure and thus magnifying it. This has to be taken into consideration when attempting to discover certain values in the "craftsmen" model.

To summarize this chapter, we should say that "The Craftsmen" by Rokusuke Ei, *Project X*, and the philosophy of the Institute of Technologists have all been written and read as one more Nihonjinron at a time of anxiety and lack of sense of direction. These publications and programs carry significance as Nihonjinron because the craftsmen who are featured in them are not just people who make things, but also people who represent the "way of life" in which they are unsung heroes who exercise their ingenuity. The reason why Miyamoto's "The Forgotten Japanese" – which depicts the disappearing generation of Japanese rather than the new one – still resonates now is because it is reread not as the thing of the past, but as the "way of life" of people and society, a way of life that links to the future, even if we do need to take into account the points of caution I mentioned earlier.

CHAPTER 8

Mothers and Geisha: *Women Who Care*

"The Anatomy of Dependence" in the Present Day

Nearly fifty years have passed since the publishing of Takeo Doi's *'Amae' no Kōzō* (hereafter "The Anatomy of Dependence"; 1971), which analyses the psychological structure that originates from the dependence of children on mothers (*amae*) as a feature characteristic to the Japanese. It seems that during this time the tendency for children to be spoilt by their mothers has diminished.

In 2003 I authored the book *Niseiron* ("The Theory of Second Generation") (originally published in 1998 as *Oyako no Sahō* ("The Etiquette of Parent and Child Relations"), a collection of interviews with the children of famous figures on the hardships associated with their background and the know-how learnt from their parents. As a result, I am sometimes requested to give lectures on the subject of "parent-child relationships". At one of such lectures I had the chance to address a few hundred people – mostly mothers – on the topic of methods of encouraging independence. It seemed that everyone was extremely passionate about "encouraging" such a trait. Let us imagine a stereotypical scene of two parents telling their only child – that is, as opposed to "four or five children" as it may have been in former times – to stop clinging to mother and to become a little more independent. A child given such a scolding may feel fed up even from merely being talked to this way, and may either tell his parents to "stop bugging" him or show no reaction at all. The lecture-meeting seemed to be an opportunity for parents to discuss the best way to handle such situations.

If Takeo Doi's "The Anatomy of Dependence" has had an influence on such a stance of the latest generation of parents, my impression is that its effect has been too strong. Put simply, isn't it that in the way parents raise their children there is *not enough* indulgence, and *too much* independence? However, I did not think that the parents who visited my lectures were too strict. Instead I felt that it was the very fact that the parents did the thinking for their children about how to be independent that was in fact interfering with that independence. This kind of involvement from parents – or to put it negatively, this kind of "meddling" – falls within the scope of "dependence" (*amae*), yet it does not bring out healthy dependence. My audience would surely have been surprised by my suggestion that such a thing as "healthy dependence" could exist.

The second generation I met when working on "The Theory of Second Generation" have all been facing the challenge of becoming independent from their parents since a young age. Their "already successful" parents, in their turn, have been careful to not let this success overwhelm their children. Doi suggests that in human relationships "dependence" means "behaving such that one is relying on the kindness of the counterpart" (Doi 2001b: 65), and in the relationship described above between a successful parent and his or her child, this dependence is established on a deep level. It represents mutual trust and yet an ability to maintain distance.

Doi does not discuss "dependence" exclusively in negative terms. Yet, similar to the fate of the classics I talked about earlier, there is also a misunderstanding about "The Anatomy of Dependence". Let us start by dispelling that misconception.

Is "Dependence" Good or Bad?

In the revised edition of "The Anatomy of Dependence" published in 2001, Doi writes as follows:

> Since this book was originally published, when something bad happens in our society, people say, "that is the structure of dependence" […]. Certainly, this book does describe cases in which the effects of dependence are not favorable. In particular, since the war there have been vociferous advocating of the importance of independence, and with the development of this social mindset, "the anatomy of dependence" was turned into a synonym for something negative (Doi 2001b: 3-4).

As mentioned earlier, Doi provides the following simple definition of dependence: "In human relationships it means behaving such that one is relying on the kindness of the counterpart". The "naivety" (*amasa*) of "relying on kindness" is the essence of the "dependence" (*amae*). Doi believes that this emerges within the mother-child relationship from the newborn stage onwards.

> In short, dependence is the word that indicates the child's need of the mother, a need that arises after the infant's mind has developed to a certain extent, and once they become conscious of the fact that their mother is a separate being to themselves (Doi 2001b: 105).

Since this is a process that is indispensable to character building, it may also be observed among the people of the West, but "in the West, where personal freedom is valued, people belittle the dependence-like emotion that corresponds to *amae*, so there is not even a word that could be conveniently used to express this emotion" (Doi 2001b: 122). Further, Doi takes the stance that this emotion exists in the human relationships of any society, and that the difference in it amounts to whether there is a single word like *amae* to denote it, and correspondingly whether this emotion is strong or weak and whether it is looked upon favorably or negatively. He states that when he first looked at the Japanese culture and society that he belongs to after becoming conscious of *amae*, he realized that it is present in every part of life even among adults.

Although there are some shifts in Doi's ideas about *amae* between the original and the revised edition of "The Anatomy of Dependence", let us summarize Doi's viewpoint of *amae* from the perspective of the revised version published in 2001. Doi suggests that there is no problem if the kindness relied on is returned as kindness and fed back between the order. He believes that dependence is intrinsically a good thing, even though it may have negative sides. Further, he thinks that the fact that dependence can be expressed with the word *amae* is something that the Japanese should even take pride in.

In these terms, it would be wrong to interpret "The Anatomy of Dependence" as a criticism of the dependent nature of the Japanese or as encouragement to reconsider dependence in mother-child relationships.

However, what happens if we apply the *amae* mentality of human relations to the characteristics of Japanese society, such as Benedict's "the culture of shame", Nakane's "vertically-structured society", or Abe's *seken*? It is possible to explain that dependence is a component of such theories. However, if we view the dependence present in such systems as responsible for creating these systems, the discussion will lay itself open to the error of oversimplification.

While I find it enlightening to read Doi's wide-ranging discussion of Japanese culture and society from the position of *amae* and his statements illustrating phenomena that correspond to *amae* within Western discourse, there are times when I feel that *amae* is progressing on its own beyond the control of Doi himself. It seems that Doi too was aware of this. In the 2001 edition of "The Anatomy of Dependence" – as part of an article marking the 30th anniversary of the original edition – he highlights the importance of the revised edition, admitting that in the original he had applied the concept of *amae* to various phenomena like a "magic wand" and "undeniably lacked scrutiny in exploring the concept".

Let us look at the problems present in Doi's discussion. If dependence is universal to humanity, it is necessary to explain why it is particularly strong among the Japanese. It would be difficult to try to explain this by comparing the differences between the intensity of dependence present in Japan and elsewhere, because it is incredibly difficult to measure this intensity. This is especially the case in the societies other than that of Japan, which do not have a specific word to express "dependence". For instance, among native English speakers there are no criteria determining which actions should be deemed as originating from "dependence" and which should be deemed as originating not from dependence, but, for example, from "love".

However, some certainty can be guaranteed when the "quality" of the notion is tested not as a difference in intensity, but as a problem of the value concept of the Japanese-language *amae* in Japan or as a problem of "interpretation" when the Japanese forgive or criticize a certain action with the help of the word *amae*. I believe that this is an efficient way to apply the theory of *amae*.

The Origin of the Illusion of Motherhood

Having said that, as Doi himself writes, since the title of the book "The Anatomy of Dependence" has become genericized, the situation is no longer in his hands. Doi thought that "the Japanese would not change their perception of dependence as an essentially positive thing", so he was surprised that "drastic social changes followed and the tendency to regard dependence in negative terms spread across the country" (Doi 2001b: 117-118). The mother-child relationship that *amae* originates from became the target of increasing criticism as "the anatomy of dependence".

However, alongside the criticism of dependence in mother-child relationships, there is also frequent coverage in the media of cases in which mothers abuse or struggle to show love to their children. Psychoanalyst Shū Kishida addresses this topic in his work *Hahaoya Gensō* ("Illusion of Motherhood"; 1998 revised edition), suggesting that it is absurd to assume that it is a given that a mother will love their child. He states that maternal affection is a shared social illusion that children raised this way would later take care of their parents. Therefore if value can be found in children becoming independent and leaving their homes and if mothers have an opportunity to become socially "independent", as is the case in modern Japan, the shared illusion of maternal love starts falling apart. There he explains that when a mother fails to find maternal affection in her heart for her child it is only natural that she wonders whether she is entitled to be a mother, given that the concept of maternal affection initially developed as a social tie, rather than something private.

Here we encounter a certain problem. According to Doi, for a child to become an adult – in other words, to gain independence – in Japanese society the relationship of dependence on one's mother is important. Yet, if, as Kishida suggests, it has become possible for a mother to become autonomous without being socially dependent on her children and if the illusion of motherhood has started to fade, the independence of mothers comes into contradiction with the independence of children. Namely, for a mother to become independent, it is better to not take the trouble of indulging one's child. For a child, however, "positive dependence" is necessary to gain autonomy – this is where the contradiction lies.

The current change in mother-child relationships is a rather significant – and in some ways confusing – decrease in the significance that "mothers" hold for the Japanese. Quoting Daisetsu Suzuki, Doi wrote that while in the foundation of the Western people's thinking there was a father, for the Japanese people it was a mother that unconditionally embraces anything and everything. On a similar note, in *Embracing Defeat*, Dower noted that the farewell letters of the Japanese people executed as war criminals presented their mothers as an object of affection that transcends everything, including the war and their crimes (Dower 2000). It is not that such an image of mothers does not exist in other societies. Hence, the problem here is not the comparison with other societies but the fact that mothers have been given a special position in Japanese society. Doi concludes from this that while "dependence" is not characteristic to Japan alone, the way it is expressed makes it particular to Japan. The change that is underway is the process of depriving "mother" of the "special" value it previously held.

In a way, this is happening for a reason. It can be explained from the point of view of a "mother's" status in the system of *ie* (household) in the Japanese society. The current image of a "mother" is connected to the mother's position in the system of *ie* from the Edo period onwards. According to Chie Nakane, *ie* is the smallest unit of a vertical organization, almost like a management body. Each member occupies his or her own place and works accordingly. Sōseki's "And Then", which was discussed in Chapter 5, depicts the way in which the Meiji period sons are dominated by the head of the household while younger sons are dominated by the eldest son.

Among these people, the mother is someone who came from outside as a bride. For her to gain a "proper station" in this household it was necessary to bear children. The sons she gave birth to were of great importance as they secured her existence in the *ie*, and a place for her in her old age. From the son's perspective, the mother is an object of affection and not a fellow competitor in the struggle for the patriarchal right, so there are no conflicts between the two. The daughters will leave the household eventually; therefore the *ie* for them is of secondary importance, and hence there is no rivalry between them and the mother either. On the contrary, the sons are in a competitive relationship with their father; there is also friction between brothers and sisters, stemming from the difference in their gender. Within such interwoven relations, the mother and child, or strictly speaking, the mother and son relationship are free of conflict. Reversely, their relationship gives rise to a sort of partnership. For the mother, her son, namely, the eldest son is a mainstay, a pillar who secures her ties to the household and who eventually becomes the household itself, ensuring her place in it. For the son, the mother is the only non-threatening figure.

This is how the mother image developed from the perspective of the children of the Edo-period *ie*, which was at the stage of agricultural civilization making it possible for the mother to become someone to whom they could turn to for consolation on all fronts, transcending all other ordinary occurrences. Of course there were a number of irregular situations involving stepchildren, stepmothers, parental divorce or husbands marrying into their wives' families (known as *muko-yoshi*), but there continued to be a societal structure that extended "special" status to mothers.

Changes to the Mother Image and the Situation Surrounding Dependence

Nowadays, however, there have already been significant changes to the position of the *ie* as the social unit. Since the shift from agricultural to industrial civilization, agriculture has ceased to be the main occupation and it has become rare to find households that possess farming fields that have been passed down through generations or merchant families with long-standing businesses. Yet, even if the economic foundations that used to sustain the *ie* have disappeared, the *amae*-dependence that was present in these households, the structure of affection originating in mutual interdependence, continues to exist. This is due to the fact that, aside from the changes to the economic activities and forms of the household, the custom of childrearing within the family, by which people bring up their children in the same way they were brought up, does not easily change as it is something acquired through bodily experience. The values and conceptual constructs within society are continued through "physical techniques" such as childrearing.

Moreover, the importing of the Western concept of "love" to Japan is thought to have helped such a mother image to maintain its existence. However, currently this image is in need of final change as a result of new and different ideas and values generated by industrial civilization and urban living, such as children's independence, the growing roles of women in society, and the concept of a person being an "individual" prior to being a family member. Although these changes are not all moving in the same direction, there is no doubt that the image of a mother as it was in the stage of agricultural civilization is weakening. In particular, Japan has seen the development of social phenomena such as "parasite singles" (single people living with parents into their early thirties or even longer), that may seem like a step backwards, but they represent a situation in which an underlying factor is economic dependency rather than a revival of psychological dependence functions.

The transformation of the image of mothers generated by the shift from the agricultural to the industrial civilization is a painful process for any member of the society, as it signifies the loss of previous values. For instance, since the number of women working outside the home has increased, there are naturally less mothers who are always "in the home" when one comes back from outside. Of course, it is difficult to assess how many such "privileged" women akin to "full-time housewives" existed during each of the epochs; yet, for the reasons I explained earlier, mothers unquestionably played the role of comforters, in other words, they were the figures who "took care" of the families. Such an image of mothers was firmly established among the values of our society.

This image was further expressed in the art of Japanese woodblock prints, poetry, and literature and became an object of longing. The thought that it does not exist in reality anymore invites a strong feeling of loss. Yet, for us Japanese, the real problem is not only to do with the time lag of change, when the old image lingers despite the fact that the new reality is emerging. Even if we try to accept the fact that the image of mothers created in agricultural civilization is unable to survive, we are bewildered by our inability to depict a new image of mothers that would replace the old. Having witnessed various situations involving young men and women that make us question whether the reasons for these happenings lie within their families, we have no other choice but to seriously consider *amae* and "mother's love".

I would like to stress that I do *not* think that there has been an increase in the number of mothers who do not love their children. At the same time, the number of mothers who are unsure about how to love their children has been on the rise. I think that their doubts are valid. Rather than attempting to avoid these doubts, we should recognize that they represent a path that the society has to follow. Naturally, the "father's image" and "love" itself become the object of these doubts. When we re-examine *amae* as a part of this process, we also contemplate the problem of the mother's independence and the child's independence. We must recognize that although the changes have started, the finish line is still a long way ahead.

Orientalism Under the Name of Geisha

The reason that the romanized spelling of the Japanese word *geisha* has become an established term in every language lies with its originality and uniqueness. What exactly was so original and unique about it? Edward Said's book *Orientalism* (1978) clarified this fact and is thus helpful when addressing the subject.

Said researched how the strong and dominant Western powers depicted the foreign lands, the colonies represented by the East or the Orient (with the Arab world at center in this case), and the expressions they used to do so. He reveals that the Western side, through its gaze filled with unobjective curiosity and contempt, described the East as sometimes backward, sometimes irrational, and also erotic. Said outlines the process by which this image later also establishes itself as the dominant view in the East, the object of this gaze. He calls this kind of outlook towards "the East (Orient)" orientalism.

Inside this orientalism, the ruled, the colonized, is often portrayed as a woman. The misbalance between the male and female gender roles in society is utilized as it is to express the superiority and inferiority between the West and East. For this reason, if love were to be born between the two, it would always be between the man of the ruling country and the woman of the colonized one and not the other way around (Note 1).

For instance, French writer Pierre Loti created exotic stories that took place in Turkey and Tahiti exactly from the standpoint of orientalism. He later visited Japan and portrayed a Japanese woman in the novel entitled *Madame Chrysanthème* (1887). It is thus unsurprising that this work is also written as an exotic story similar to his previous novels in which he depicted women from Tahiti. Puccini's opera *Madama Butterfly* is partially based on Loti's *Madame Chrysanthème* and can also be said to have been created as a work of orientalism. In a way both are stories about an irresponsible Western man and a Japanese woman and are – it must be admitted – rather shallow in terms of their plots.

However, these stories are not just about a sexual adventure with a woman from a foreign land under the category of orientalism. In fact, both O-Kiku-san, the protagonist of *Madame Chrysanthème*, and Cio-Cio-san, the protagonist of *Madama Butterfly*, are not constructed as "merely *geishas*". O-Kiku-san is the daughter of "a woman who used to be a *geisha* in Edo" (Loti 1937(1887): 142), while Cio-Cio-san is the daughter of a bankrupt military family. The foreign men somehow manage to "marry" these two women with "the middleman" as a matchmaker. In this sense, it is not that they were only involved with "prostitutes" as objects of sexual desire.

What does this slight difference imply? On the one hand, there is a Japanese woman as the sexual object of a foreign man, a scenario in which romanticism and eroticism collide and that seems to be easily comprehensible in the framework of orientalism. However, simultaneously, in the host country, Japan (the Orient), there are different cultural values and a system applying to women and their sexuality inside which women represent a different existence to the one that is perceived from the outside. Even inside the dramatic plays, the Westerners visiting Japan become the participants of this system.

In addition, this system of "prostitution" in Japan is only a part of the Japanese "system relating to women and sexuality". A *geisha*, who is involved in the system of "prostitution", is part of a larger system relating to "women who provide care", similar to a mother within the household system of *ie*. In every non-Western country that Loti visited there must have been a "woman" that could accept such a visitor from a foreign land as him. In Japan alike, these women emerged as fantasy creatures inside his orientalist thinking. However, the difference is that these women were part of the Japanese "system of women who provide care". While the men from the West looked at the Japanese women from the viewpoint of Western men, they themselves were at the same time integrated into the Japanese system. It is within it that they discovered *geishas*. For someone looking at Japan from the outside, this was a considerable difference and it lead to the situation in which *geisha* started to be used as a term to include all the women in Japan. This is the meaning of this difference. Japan's "system of women who provide care", in which such occurrences are possible, is thus original and unique.

The Matrix of Mother and Geisha

At the root of the system involving Japanese women and sexuality there is a matrix (Table 1) of mothers and *geishas* that sets out the traditional division of women.

Of course, mothers do have sex and *geishas* do get pregnant. However, a mother is not a proactive performer of sex acts and *geisha* cannot give birth as *geisha*.

It is known that in Japan, married couples in rural areas procreate for a short period of time and cease engaging in sexual activities relatively early in comparison with their Western counterparts. This tendency is reflected by trends such as women feeling ashamed about giving birth later in life, or the belief that sex "does not exist" for elderly individuals, a topic that has recently attracted considerable discussion. So, what happens to couples who have become sexually inactive? In addition to caring for her father-in-law and husband, the wife lavishes increasing motherly affection and energy on her children. I already mentioned that this is where the depth of *amae*-dependence, a tendency unique to Japan, is generated. Since the Edo period, men have had a large assortment of *geishas* of all kinds to enjoy extramarital sex with, from expensive to moderately priced ones. Regardless of how inexpensive an extramarital sexual affair with a *geisha* was, it could only happen if one had the money to afford it. However, the fact that the possibility was always present, and the fact that – just as "an extramarital sexual affair with a *geisha*" does not make sense as an expression since a sexual affair with a *geisha* is a socially accepted "marital deviation" – society allowed "extramarital" sexual affairs are important points determining the existence of "the system of women who provide care".

This *geisha* cannot give birth to children. To bear and raise a child she would have to renounce her position as *geisha*. However, if she does not formally marry, she will not ensure stability for herself and her child, so more often than not *geisha* in such situations would entrust the child to the father and resume their role as *geisha*. The final scene of *Madama Butterfly*, in which Cio-Cio-san hands over her child to her American husband, is precisely a projection of this Japanese system involving women and sexuality. In the fictional world, Cio-Cio-san possesses both the personality of a mother and that of a *geisha*. Otherwise, she could be viewed as someone positioned in between the two. What does this position imply? O-Kiku-san and Cio-Cio-san are called Madame Chrysanthème and Madama Butterfly rather than carrying their husbands' surnames. These names do not merely function as terms of endearment; they highlight the fact that the two women are not officially "married" and only acting as lovers. That is, between the mother and the *geisha* there is the "mistress" (*mekake*), another role that exists within the "system of women who provide care".

MOTHER		GEISHA
Gives birth	Children	Does not give birth
Passive	Sexual acts	Active
A man inside a family	The object of care	A man from outside a family

Table 1: Mother-geisha matrix

However, here it is important to take heed of the obvious fact that *geisha* occupied the lowest position in society and were devoid of freedom due to financial debt. There is no point in popular discourse stating that all *geishas* really are a type of cultural figure like an *oiran*, the glamorous courtesans of the Edo period, or a high-class "courtisane" like the character of Marguerite Gautier in Alexandre Dumas' *The Lady of the Camellias*. However, it is true that in the system of Japanese social and cultural values *geisha* was given a value different from that of a Western "prostitute" and served as an important cultural symbol and cultural factor in Japanese literature and art. As I mentioned in Part 1 when discussing Shūzō Kuki's *'Iki' no Kōzō* ("The Structure of Iki"; 1930), *geisha* represented the world of *iro*, a crucial element of the Japanese culture. In addition, as I already indicated, in Japan the existence of a "prostitute" formed a set together with a wife and mother of a family, and was accepted by society as a sexual object for men.

The Japanese *geisha* discovered by foreigners turns into a sexualized "woman of a colonized land" within the framework of orientalism, but within Japan's "system pertaining to women and sexuality" this word refers to a different female role or sexual aspect. In other words, when thinking from the perspective of the matrix of mothers and *geishas* that serves as the traditional framework, if a Japanese woman like Cio-Cio-san or O-Kiku-san was to emerge as a sexual companion for foreign men, she was not a Japanese *geisha* but a *geisha* as perceived by foreigners to be a sexual partner with whom an official marital relationship cannot be formed. Impossibility of marriage was probably due to the fact that her partner was a "foreigner".

Women who Provide Care

The charm and functions of geisha do not stop at her being a sexual object. In Japan, *geisha*, alongside mothers, assume a gender role of physical care. When a Japanese woman appears as *geisha* in front of foreign men, the heroine of their fantasies and delusions is a woman who provides "care" – be it in the stories of Loti, Hearn, or in the more recent *geisha*-novel *Memoirs of Geisha* by Arthur Golden (1997). These women who provide care remind me of the recollections by a man from the story "Tosa Genji" in Miyamoto's *Wasurerareta Nihonjin* ("The Forgotten Japanese"), in which he says "women understand men and take care of them" (Miyamoto 1995(1960): 157). There is a need to discuss how this sentiment existed as the one-sided ideology of men and what kind of a fantasy and then delusion it turned into from reality. However, here I would like to emphasize that in order to sustain these fantasies and delusions the reality has been continuously reinterpreted and the "system of women who provide care" has existed as a mechanism producing everything from maternal affection to sexuality for Japanese men.

In other words, as I mentioned in the first part of this chapter, while in Japan women took a direct part in production such as agriculture, inside the home (*uchi*) they have acted as caregivers for their fathers-in-law, their husbands, and their children. They have provided their fathers-in-law with what is currently known as elderly care (*kaigo*), their husbands with sexual care, and their children with motherly care. I already explained that the proportion of this care aimed at children grows as the mother's position inside the household becomes stronger. Thus, when the husband goes outside of the home, theoretically, it is a *geisha* who provides them with sexual care as long as the husband is a "worthy gentleman" (*kaishō no aru otoko*). In fact, it is known that during the Edo period, when the matrix of women and sexuality was established, *geishas* had as their partners a large group of consumers which included not only husbands who cut off their relationships with their wives, but also second and third sons, who could not marry as they did not have sufficient resources, warriors during the alternate-years they spent in residence in Edo, seasonal workers, and other men who were single for some reason. The customers of the modern sex industry, which is the transformation of the earlier system, are predictably just the same – husbands, single men, and employees who have relocated for work without taking their families, who go there for similar reasons. The matrix of women and sexuality functions nowadays as well.

While mothers and *geishas* clearly have a different occupation, the gender roles of a mother and *geisha* are not so clearly distinct. In other words, in Japan, a woman is "simultaneously a mother and a *geisha*" for a man. She cares for a man at times as if he were "a man" and at times as if he were "a child". This is not limited to the household, and in society and various societal settings of *seken* (one's social milieu), a woman has performed a *geisha*-gender role as the woman who "serves tea" (*chakumi onna*) in the office. This gender role of all women who provide care, similar to the tea servants of the Edo period, is permeated with a sexual tone, albeit in differing levels of intensity. In situations in which a Japanese bar proprietress is addressed as "mama" and she adds the diminutive suffix "-chan" (usually used for children) to the names of the customers, there are no clear lines distinguishing her as a mother or a *geisha*, the customers as "children" or "men", and the presence or lack of sexual nuances.

Note 1

For instance, it is not hard to imagine who will assume the male and female roles respectively in a romantic movie that is jointly produced by Japan and the US. In this sense, it is interesting to see what happens in a similar Japan-Korea joint production. When I refer to foreigners here I imply Westerners. This is because *geisha* is an image that was created inside the outlook that could be called Western orientalism. The reason why Koreans, Chinese or South-East Asians do not seem to feel the charm of *geisha* to such an extent is because no relationship of the kind exists between Japan and Asia. Rather, we can say that with the advent of modernity, Japan has started looking at the neighboring Asian countries through the prism of orientalism. This brings us back to the story of the *kisaeng* in Yokomitsu's "Melancholy on a Journey".

CHAPTER 9

The Samurai *and the Salaryman: The Men of the Pen and the Sword*

The Samurai as "Noble Savages"

In the previous chapter, I explained the reasons behind the certain charm that the *geisha* stereotype of women has continued to exert over foreigners for a long time. One was the sexual appeal of *geisha* within the framework of orientalism, while another was the positioning of not only *geisha* but of Japanese women in general as "women providing care" inside the Japanese "system pertaining to women and sexuality". The Japanese who live within this very system are not particularly conscious of the distinctive nature of women's role as caregivers.

What are the reasons that the *samurai* – another stereotypical icon from Japanese culture – still remains an image of Japanese men? Firstly, the image of the *samurai* is constructed as yet another stereotype within the framework of orientalism in which the superior West looks upon the men of the inferiorly-positioned East. Although it does not treat the West and East as equals, it represents an attitude by which traditional values such as male courage are regarded with certain respect as they mirror similar virtues possessed by Western men. It is comparable to the way that the Arabs are viewed as "noble savages" in the movie *Lawrence of Arabia*.

This perspective is characteristic of how the field of natural history, a forerunner of cultural anthropology, and other disciplines looked upon people of other races and upon other cultures. This is the view that was also influenced by the 19th-century theory of social evolution that saw other cultures as antiquated and yet "noble" but at the same time "savages" if judged on the basis of benchmarks of civilization. It seems that the warriors that Japan sent abroad as its emissaries to Europe at the end of the Edo period were all "evaluated" in this way. Because of their formal behavior and manners these outcasts of modern civilization were treated with a mix of slight ridicule and a moderate level of respect, and this is the "orientalistic" gaze that has been cast from abroad on Japanese men ever since. This image is powerful in some ways even nowadays. For instance, it can be seen in how the baseball player Ichirō Suzuki has been perceived by the American audience. Just as they began to recognize his talents, they would often describe him as a *samurai* whenever he would assume a batting position with his bat held high in the air (possibly, this analogy was at the back of Ichirō's own mind).

The notion of "noble savages" created by the West essentially reflects the way in which such cultures purposely confined themselves to the tradition of such thinking and continued to dwell on the idea despite the realization that it is perishing. It was a characteristic of Western European nations in the modern period to describe any culture other than their own as "perishing". This may be a reflection of Europe's own nostalgia towards its own path of transformation.

However, in contrast to these images established by the West, Japan went through the Meiji Restoration following the end of the Tokugawa shogunate and attempted to drape itself with "modernity", as if cladding itself in armor. This can be seen in the caricatures created by French cartoonist Georges Ferdinand Bigot and the symbol of the Rokumeikan building, complete with western-style ballroom and banquet halls for entertaining western guests in the early Meiji era. Japan made efforts to imitate the West and to consciously escape from the *samurai* image. *Chonmage* topknots were cut off, Western-style clothes worn, and attempts were made to create the "world of champagne" that fascinated Sōseki's protagonist Sanshirō. This was in accord with the West's intention, to the extent possible, to "indoctrinate the savages" by means of civilization and Christianity, and presented little wonder. The Westerners knew from their earlier experience of colonialism that such human efforts were inevitably limited, yet the rapidity with which Japan tackled modernization did seem to be of a different nature than that of East Asia and the rest of the "Orient". It came as an even bigger surprise when these endeavors resulted in Japan's victory in the Russo-Japanese War.

General Nogi and "Bushido" (The Way of the Warrior)

Let us then consider what defines the image of Japan. The years surrounding the Russo-Japanese war were not only the period when Japan was most highly regarded by the United Kingdom, United States and all its Western allies, but also when its image fluctuated between that of the *samurai* and the imitator of the West. In the accounts of the Western correspondents who followed the Japanese army in the Russo-Japanese war, there was an overlap in the two misaligned images of Japan as a land of *samurais* reborn into a new nation and as a small imperial power experiencing new and sudden prominence. When presenting its image to the outside world, Japan itself not only emphasized the features it had "in common" with the West, such as state institutions and military power, but also in contrast used its "identity" as "noble savages", as a country that has the *samurai* tradition. In other words, this differs from the Japanese reluctance to draw attention to the image of *geisha* in that the Japanese also actively emphasized the *samurai* image.

For instance, in the acts of Japanese Imperial Army General Maresuke Nogi in the Russo-Japanese war, one can see that – whether intentionally or not – he was conscious of the foreign military officers and correspondents and sought to present the image of the warrior (*bushi*) that they might depict in their newspapers. Judging from his personal history and other accounts, General Nogi himself was like a baseball player who is famous not for his scores but for the unforgettable impression he leaves.

Nogi had a few failures in his military career and during the Russo-Japanese war his strategies often turned out to in fact hinder the Japanese forces from making progress. However, his appearance, the tragedy of losing his two sons on the battlefield, his "heroic" greeting of the defeated Russian General Stessel and his later "ritual suicide" (*junshi*) following the death of the Emperor Meiji all create the impression of a dying breed of noble warriors, a variation of the image of a "noble savage". I believe that this somewhat helped to conceal Japan's clear imperial ambitions.

Inazo Nitobe's *Bushido: The Soul of Japan*, which I looked at in the first part of this book, also highlights a similar image of modernized "noble savages". However, in that monograph, the modernity and the noble savagery are described in a two-pronged manner. On the one hand, the book argues that the same concepts as Western chivalry, philosophy, and morals exist in the Japanese *bushidō* as the spirituality and ethics of the Orient, having drawn on the traditions of Buddhism, Shinto, and Confucianism. This conception also fitted with Japan's efforts to ensure the abolition of the great powers' extraterritorial rights and to secure equal diplomacy. The main purpose was to emphasize Japan's commonality with the West, arguing that it possesses a history of the same level, and that modernization was therefore more than possible. Another point stresses Japan's uniqueness and distinct identity. After all, the description and photographs of blood revenge and ritual suicide in Chapter 12 of *Bushido: The Soul of Japan*, entitled "The Institutions of Suicide and Redress", must have astonished the Western readers. In an attempt to accomplish modernization, all Japan did was to cling to the very end of the procession to modernization. However, by continuing to emphasize its distinctiveness, Japan insisted that it did not belong to the end of the line.

It is rather odd that Nitobe, a Christian, extolled suicide. There also remains the question of to what extent Nitobe was personally able to uphold *bushidō* values, which placed women as figures hidden in the background, without them conflicting with the principles he shared with his American wife. For some time, Japan continued to face a dilemma as "the Orient" that belatedly achieved modernization, as it had to emphasize both its similarity to the West and its unique identity – despite them being mutually contradictory at some level – in order to avoid being placed outside the realm of Western modernity or becoming the very last in line. However, it is rather difficult to highlight both of these characteristics in a balanced way. Even such an intellectual as Nitobe, who possessed an unbiased international perspective, seems to have either experienced a feeling of certain "elation" or a slip of the pen while praising Japanese uniqueness in *Bushido: The Soul of Japan*. This happened in spite of the fact that Nitobe had very limited experience as a warrior given that he had witnessed the Meiji Restoration at the age of six and been baptized when he turned sixteen.

The Model of Living in the Moment

At first, one emphasizes Japan's ostensible similarities with the modern nation states of "the West", but once one begins to describe the country's identity one becomes overly excited and loses precision, hyperbolizing its uniqueness as if catering to the "orientalistic" framework of the counterpart, the West. This not only appears in the Nihonjinron that took the form of written works, but can also be observed when a Japanese person engages in a discussion with a foreigner. This has inhibited outsiders in their attempts to understand Japan. For this reason, the image of *samurai* brought up here is one that the Japanese themselves find difficult to approach.

To give it another thought, both the *samurai* and *geisha* are commodities that are circulating abroad. They are not utilized in Japan but have been made for the use of foreigners. However, now, when the concept of "warrior" is in the distant past, and when there are many Japanese who have never seen a *geisha* in their lifetime, Japanese unconsciously project an orientalistic gaze on their own "past", similar to that of the foreigners.

In the past, authors such as Kafū Nagai and Seiichi Funabashi wrote novels featuring the *geisha* world, known as the *karyūkai* ("flower and willow world"), but this tradition has ceased to exist. On the contrary, although a few works about *geisha* emerged after the works of Loti, it was the aforementioned *Memoirs of a Geisha* (1997) that adopted this theme after a long period of silence. *Iki no Kōzō* ("The Structure of Iki") is not a novel, but an analysis of the aesthetics of *geisha*. The reason why it stands as a lonely monograph that has not been revisited by anyone since is not because it thoroughly covered everything on the subject, but because the very object that could lead to further reconsideration of this aesthetic vision, the "world of *iki*", seem to have disappeared altogether. Thus, although *geisha* have survived to the rest of the world, *geisha* as seen in Japan have practically vanished.

However, the so-called "water trade" (*mizu shōbai*), or night entertainment business, and "adult entertainment industry" of the present do not exist in complete separation from Japan's tradition of "women who provide care". This is where the continuity of the Japanese "tradition" lies hidden. It may also remain alive among young women, such as those who read *Puratonikku Sekkusu* ("Platonic Sex"; 2000), Ai Iijima's semi-autobiographical novel about a girl who runs away from home and becomes involved in the adult video industry.

Among the books on warriors, an equivalent of "The Structure of Iki" as it applies to *geisha* would be Yukio Mishima's *Bunka Bōei Ron* ("Discussion on the Defense of Culture") and *Hagakure Nyūmon* ("An Introduction to Hagakure"). Leaving aside the question of Mishima's true intentions, the fact that he chose to create such an "anachronistic" book in the 1960s – a time significantly distant from the era when the warriors' consciousness was alive – and his ritual suicide later in life can only be viewed as Mishima's attempt to write and act as a *samurai* as seen by foreigners, as if having "retrieved" what had once been lost, rather than as a genuine "warrior".

Then, there is Eiji Yoshikawa's *Miyamoto Musashi* that is known to have been read by the pre-war Japanese – a generation that was already separated from the era of the "warriors" by a number of generations – as an educational novel that provided its readership with a model for character building. It can be suggested that the fact that the remake of this work, Takehiko Inoue's *Bagabondo* ("Vagabond"), is widely read by youth nowadays reflects a reimporting of the concept of *samurai* to Japan. However, it seems that the third-generation "neo-*samurai*" has emerged as a new image to follow the "warrior" and *samurai*. If we call it "postmodern" we would neither hit nor miss its essence, but since the latest work is written in the form of manga, its hero Musashi Miyamoto is positioned not among subjects related to great people, life, or reasons for living, but rather as a popular "character" of such genres as sports, fantasy and games. In addition, while the book could potentially be linked to the realms of "life" and "reasons for living", we should know from the onset that it does not provide the threads to make such a linkage possible.

The present-day utilization of such a "*samurai* model" has certain limitations and it is unlikely to earn mass appeal again in the near future. In contrast, the warrior model – having gone through the Meiji period and experienced defeat in the Second World War – has turned into a certain dominant model for the postwar Japanese: that of a salaryman.

The Transformation from the Warrior to the Salaryman

It is commonplace to point out that the salaryman is a transformation from the warrior. The company is compared to a feudal estate and salarymen to the retainers.

Yet, it is "literacy" (*bun*) rather than "military" (*bu*) that the salarymen have inherited from the warriors (*bushi*). In the neighboring Korean peninsula, the positions of military officers (*bukan*) and civil officials (*bunkan*) were clearly distinguished inside the Confusion ideology, and naturally the latter had a superior standing. In the case of Japan, the warrior fulfilled the roles of both a military and a civil official. It was only natural that the role as a civil official took greater priority during the times of prolonged peace. However, with the advent of the concluding days of the Tokugawa shogunate, as the warriors unsheathed their long-dormant swords, their "military" (*bu*) side was not gone. From the Meiji period onward, the elite in Japan was split into two groups: the military and the rest. The public officials and private citizens belonged to the "literacy" (*bun*) sector.

The generalization could perhaps be made that throughout the eighty years from the Meiji Restoration until the end of the Pacific War, the "military officials" (*bukan*) were mostly in charge of both the core system and the vital parts of the country, albeit with some changes surrounding the location of power.

When Japan's military was disbanded after the end of the Second World War, the civil aspect of the two sides of the warrior came to the fore. Setting aside a number of other figures, the military and the salarymen took the central roles in the 80 years preceding and the 60 years following 1945 – the borderline year – respectively. Before I go on to explain this below, I would like to note that public officials are also included in the salarymen. While it may sound strange, in fact the public officials in Japan refer to their respective ministries as "our company" (*waga sha*).

Led by these salarymen, Japan reached the peak of its external economic power at the end of the 1980s. The way this happened in reality is still fresh in the public memory, and it is a prevailing formula to discuss this in combination with the "incident" known as the "bursting of the bubble". "Formula" means that the story of "Japan" is structured around a tragic downfall as its plot. I believe that this formulation does not accurately represent the situation. I do not believe that Japan is currently undergoing a tragedy. What is happening now is an "economic recession" and not the kind of tragedy in its pure sense, the kind that occurs once in a century. The collapse of the bubble economy is a tragi-comic skit, and if a tragedy is to happen, then it will occur at some point later in the future, when the underlying problems responsible for the current recession start surfacing in their real form. The form that they may take is either "war" or the collapse of the whole economy as a result of the fall in government bond prices, rather than a mere bubble burst.

I will return to this subject briefly in Part 3, but I will leave a thorough discussion of the topic to another occasion. Here, I will talk about the salaryman model by referring to two Nihonjinron works, one written before, and one written after the second half of the 1980s.

"Japan as Number One": The Bright Side of the Salaryman Model

Ezra Vogel's *Japan as Number One* (1979, translated into Japanese the same year) is customarily referred to as a book that describes the long-gone times when Japan was called "number one". This is a mistake. Japan is still "number one" in a significant number of the aspects described in this book. A look at the book's table of contents reveals such examples as outstanding technology in some fields, high levels of school attendance rates, a substantial education in basic sports, knowledge-sharing aimed at achieving consensus, group cohesiveness, the quantity and quality of education-targeted television broadcasting. On the whole, such themes dealt with in the book as the laborers' willingness to work, the managers' dedication to problem solving, and the public officials' loyalty towards the state – while recently in question – remain the characteristic features of the Japanese people. These are precisely the features of the Japanese that are largely described with the word "salaryman".

These traits are currently being disputed because they do not translate into economic results, but although these features of willingness, dedication, and loyalty are undergoing changes, they have not disappeared. Hence, *Japan as Number One* is still readable nowadays. In particular, the fourth part of the concluding chapter "Can the Japanese Model Survive Success?" predicts the problems of the severe economic downturn that followed the end of the bubble economy (*Heisei fukyō*) and is thus astonishingly accurate.

Why is this book misunderstood, as if its subject is some kind of joke (number one)? In order to address this problem, let us look at how this book was written. It was created not in the late 1980s when the mirage that Japan was perhaps "number one" surfaced, but ten years before that (1979), when Japan was not yet in fact "number one" at all. Furthermore, in the context of the book the phrase "number one" should not be thought of as meaning "the best in the world". Instead, "number one" naturally refers to the comparison of America and Japan, and it should be perceived as follows: "Which country is ahead? Surprisingly, it seems that Japan is actually ahead in many areas". In other words this book is both Nihonjinron that served as an early warning to American readers that America may lose its status as "number one" if nothing changes and, as if mirroring this state, simultaneously "the discourse on America" that is engaged in rethinking America.

I read this book while in England, immediately after it was published, and felt the discomfort one experiences when being praised too much. Exactly at that time a series of over ten special programs on Japan, entitled *Inside Japan* was aired on British television, and I remember realizing upon watching a scene where a policeman drops by a farmer's house to have a cup of tea that such relationships between policemen and citizens would have been impossible in England and even more so in America. However, when considering this book dispassionately, one realizes that it is a work targeting the general public and written by an American who, driven by Americans' needs, took notice of the advantageous points of Japan's "social system" that the Americans were not aware of. It just happened that it was the time when the groundwork for Japan's high-speed economic growth was laid and when the bubble resulting from the strong yen emerged in Japanese society. This book was therefore convenient as Nihonjinron that explained the "anxiety" associated with the feeling of uplift connected to these changes. Namely, there appeared a fantasy suggesting that the great economic power, Japan, created by salarymen, may be "number one" in the world, along with the suggestion that with its twin deficit America is finished, and the book seems to have attempted to explain this neatly. When this situation reversed, giving rise in the 1990s to the idea that Japan is unable to become number one after all and to the realization that America is the sole superpower reigning over the world, the book *Japan as Number One* was dismissed as something that could no longer be taken seriously. Thus, deviating slightly from the author's intention, readers interpreted the book as discussing the fact of Japan's prosperity, and when the reality went against expectations, the book was abandoned.

However, the way Japan was then seen as a country with the potential to become number one is only one mode of describing reality, or a fantasy, and not a declaration of the reality itself. Yet, the reality is that a few of the aforementioned strengths of Japan pointed out by Vogel still remain alive and well.

As Vogel accurately predicted in "Can the Japanese Model Survive Success?", these strengths are under threat from such factors as other countries catching up with the leading-edge technologies, the increase of manpower costs, the aging society, the difficulties of corporate debt repayment, the downsizing of companies during recession thus affecting the weaker part of the workforce, and the decreasing efficiency of the government due to political instability.

Although some exaggerations can be found throughout Vogel's monograph, it is an enlightening book written by a scholar for ordinary readers. The reason why it was completely forgotten after being read so widely is not the contents of the book itself, but the fact that the Japanese –

who are prone to experiencing anxiety during both the rise and fall of Japan – wished to read something that would serve as an explanation. If anything, the book was originally addressed to the American public.

Vogel shed light on the salaryman as an aspect of postwar Japanese society. He describes the strength of the Japanese in one phrase, arguing that it is "the group-directed quest for knowledge" (Vogel 1979: 27). This is an extension of the "ingenuity" concept linked to "craftsmanship". The major theme of the Japanese documentary series *Project X* is the efforts and attentiveness of the unsung heroes. People depicted in *Japan as Number One* can be perceived as "the salarymen". As I have mentioned earlier, this category includes public officials, and is therefore not restricted to employees of a company but implies members of a group. In addition, this is not the salaryman as the descendant of the warriors of the Warring States period or the tumultuous final days of the Tokugawa shogunate, when the emphasis was on the "military" (*bu*) nature of the role, but of the warriors living in the peaceful feudal domains of the Edo period, who were focused on "literacy" (*bun*).

This salaryman is also a descendant of farmers living in a village (*mura*), which was the most standard unit of society when Japan was an agricultural civilization. However, their faithfulness to the group and nature as "group members", as highlighted by Vogel, suggest that rather than farmers who could secure their living in the village as long as they continued working, these salarymen resemble the warriors inhabiting the "military domain" (*han*) and ready to share the fate of the latter, which under the worst circumstances could mean complete destruction.

The abolishment of the military forces following the Second World War was a significant event. All the energy and talents of the human resources that had been absorbed by the army and naval forces were redirected towards companies and the bureaucratic system. Thus, a "corporate warrior" (*kigyō senshi*) – an expression used in Japan – refers to none other than the people who are engaged in warfare without the use of arms.

However, in the early stages of Japan's postwar rapid economic growth, corporate warriors who were fighting hard battles overseas were not seen as *samurai* in Europe and the USA. The *samurai* were essentially typified as armed warriors who valued rituals, and the post-defeat people who used the "absence of the army" as a public stance and were desperate to sell their products even at the expense of throwing away the rules of etiquette, were not viewed with respect, as reflected by the fact that Prime Minister Hayato Ikeda was called by French President Charles de Gaulle a "transistor salesman". We can thus understand that for Westerners, *samurai* was a stereotype first and foremost linked to "noble savages" with their "military" (*bu*) nature.

Nevertheless, the salaryman is the product of the model of being Japanese that was created by postwar Japan. He is the offspring of the "cultured" (*bun*) warrior of the Edo period, who disposed of his pre-war "military" aspect, replacing it with faithfulness towards the organization (*han*) and the "ingenuity" characteristic of craftsmen. These salarymen emerged as people who attained the postwar dreams of peace, equality, and prosperity.

"The False Realities of a Politicized Society": *The Dark Side of the Salaryman Model*

It is an established view that once Japan was at the peak of realizing of these dreams, downfall immediately followed. Karel van Wolferen's *Ningen wo Kōfuku ni shinai Nihon toiu Shisutemu* (English title on the cover: "The False Realities of a Politicized Society"; literally: "A System that Does Not Make Humans Happy"), which was published in 1994 following the collapse of the bubble economy, explains at great length the shortcomings of the salaryman model and Japan as the system it produced, as well as the negative impacts on the people within this system.

In this work, Van Wolferen makes a few exaggerations and gets a little carried away. For instance, he argues that the Japanese people possess an "innate" group mentality and keeps pressing this idea over and over throughout the book despite the fact that – as far as I know – there is no genetic theory to support such a claim and that he does not cite the source on which this allegation is based. Such claims are like idle suggestions that do not merit being called theory, such as saying that "all Indians are philosophers" or "all French are artistic". One may instead state that the Japanese learn group mentality "postnatally" through the Japanese culture and education, but while this is a plausible argument, there would not be much value in making this statement alone since it is too predictable. This would then be a completely worthless piece of Nihonjinron not worth the paper on which it is printed. The reason why I bring up Van Wolferen here is because his work forms a pair with *Japan as Number One*, as they describe the events on both sides of the peak – namely, before and after the bursting of the bubble – respectively.

Theoretical arguments also suggest that the advantages of salarymen, such as their willingness to work, enthusiasm for devising things, and faithfulness towards their organization, may all be accompanied by such weaknesses as poor values in regards to anything but work, unawareness of the effect that technology has on the whole structure, and sacrifices towards the organization. Yet, it would be wrong to assume that before the bubble economy they had only strengths, while after the bubble burst they exuded weaknesses. Both the strengths and weaknesses of salarymen coexist on the both sides of the peak, the bubble, as if two sides of the same coin. It is incredibly difficult to take only the positive outcomes and eliminate the risks. Freedom, equality, humanism, and tolerance – the values developed during the formation of the modern age – are all associated with such problems and dilemmas as overindulgence, egocentrism, anarchy, as well as fluctuation in norms of behavior depending on who is dealing with whom.

The purpose of calling a certain society "number one" or claiming that it has hurtful impacts on its people is not to make a logical argument, but to accentuate and highlight a certain aspect. In this case, if we speak in terms of Japan as a system or a human model, it is in order to highlight the existence of the "salaryman". Although it may seem that the two authors are arguing for two opposing positions, with a retrospective glance we can see that they are, in fact, collaborating with each other. They both attempt to identify why among many countries in the world it was Japan that succeeded in achieving striking economic growth after the Second World War and they chose the same phenomenon – namely, the social relationship between the individual and the group in Japan – to do so. Vogel, who wrote in 1979, prior to the bubble period, forecast the last leap of the Japanese economy as he focused on depicting the positive side of this relationship, while Van Wolferen, who indicated the problematic areas present in Japan from before the bubble, reasoned from the negative perspective. The Japanese people who read *Japan as Number One* – a book that was aimed at an American audience – did so in search for an explanation of the reasons behind Japan's success while those who turned to "The False Realities of a Politicized Society", known as a book meant for the Japanese readers, looked for the reason behind Japan's downfall. Such readings are the result of the anxiety of being Japanese in the contemporary world, the grounds for why Nihonjinron is read. While the two books assume opposing positions, they merely look at the same object from two different angles. The most useful way of interpreting these two pieces of literature is perhaps viewing them as two mirrors that have been set up to face each other so that one could see the front and back of the salaryman model of being Japanese.

CHAPTER 10

"A Human Being": The Form that Remains After Everything is Removed

Japanese Under the Name of "Human Beings"

Kaneto Shindō's *Hadaka no Shima* ("The Naked Island", 1960), a black-and-white film without any dialogue, depicts the life of a family of farmers inhabiting a small island in the Seto Inland Sea. It shows monotonous days of harsh labor, short-lived moments of rest, and tragedy striking the family. The final scenes, in which the characters resume their day-to-day activities, leave the audience deeply and quietly moved. At the end of the film, the words "yet, people continue to live" appear in large white letters across the screen as if seeking to arouse such emotion, and the image of these final words stayed in my memory for a long time. I later watched the film again on DVD to relive that memory, and while I found that the final caption was not included, the film still leaves just the same impression on the viewer. The introduction on the cover says: "This is a human drama about the real day-to-day lives of human beings". It seems that this film evokes the word "human being" (*ningen*) in the minds of its viewers.

This word, "human", is infused with the sense of a flesh-and-blood being that lives in a different dimension to that of words and concepts. It is for this reason that "The Naked Island" has no words or dialogue. We can also observe an emphasis on the existence of "naked" humans, whose way of life is rooted in something deeper than the long history and culture of the people described with the adjective "Japanese". In this sense, this film can be viewed as depicting not only "the Japanese", but also "humans" on a more universal basis. The film received a similar evaluation at the Moscow International Film Festival, where it won a grand prix.

However, I do not believe that this movie describes the universality of human existence. I believe that the view on humans it displays is highly "Japanese" and individualistic. What it conveys is that there is true importance in the feelings of delight, anger, sorrow, and pleasure that appear when one is leading a very hard life. However, it is also possible to suggest that as people express their feelings through the "culture" that has accumulated over the years (rather than expressing their "naked" feelings), only the emotions present at that level of culture are valuable to us. Both viewpoints are particular "ways of thinking" about humans. However, in Japan it is the former of the two – the way of thinking that places emphasis on "humans" – that appears in different everyday situations as a final solution, and is extremely powerful.

Contrast with the Jewish People

Isaiah Ben-Dasan argues in his book *Nihon-jin to yudaya-jin* ("The Japanese and the Jews", 1971) that the Japanese people hold a unique view on humans, as is also expressed in the connotations of the Japanese word *ningen* ("human beings").

"The Japanese and the Jews" initially attracted interest due to the secrecy surrounding its author. While it was published under the name of "Isaiah Ben-Dasan", who was said to be a Jewish author, no further details were provided about this mysterious new writer (Note 1). At the same time, the book also attracted great interest as it was unique, one might even say sensational, among the works dealing with the Japanese because it was a departure from the tradition of discussing Japan by means of comparison with the West or the neighboring Asian countries. It highlighted the uniqueness of the Japanese through comparison with the Jewish people and their way of life, a most unexpected comparison given how unfamiliar they were to the Japanese. The comparison of two strongly contrasting groups in this way was highly novel. In terms of its content, it did not bring up the customary topics of nature appreciation in the Japanese arts or the aesthetic categories of *iki*, *wabi*, and *sabi*, but focused instead on such phenomena as the Japanese perception of "safety" in daily life and on how it differs from that of the Jews, explaining and illustrating the behavior of the Japanese people in the everyday world.

The mysterious writer, who transpired to be Shichihei Yamamoto, the owner of publishing house Yamamoto Shoten, was seeking to provide a commentary on the Japanese view on humans, which he referred to as "Japan's religion", and a number of other aspects about Japan, through such concepts as "mood" (*kūki*) or "common sense" (*jōshiki*). Concepts such as "human being", "Japan's religion", "mood", "common sense" are all similar in that they are neutral in meaning, lack character, and are ubiquitous. They are therefore like "air" (primary meaning of the word *kūki)*, something which we are not conscious of despite breathing it on a daily basis. This conforms with the concept of "humans" in the context of "The Naked Island". That is, "human" is the form that one is endowed with from the start, the form that remains after all the gloss is washed off – the most natural, commonplace form.

A Human Being as the "Reason Beyond Reason" and the "Law Beyond Law"

Yamamoto states that this "human being" exists as the basis of all things, as the "reason beyond reason" and the "law beyond law".

For instance, after the war a law was introduced in Japan to crack down on the trading of food on the black market, but if one followed this law strictly, one could not have survived as a "human". As a result, the majority of people were breaking the law by obtaining food through illegal routes. At that time an incident occurred in which a judge who adhered to the law without exception died of famine. It would have been logical to say that the Japanese abiding by the law were doing the right thing, while all the other Japanese deserved to be called outlaws and criminals, but the "public sentiment" of those days did not perceive the matter this way. Rather, although people commiserated with the "followers of the law", the incident made everyone feel that "taking it that far was not 'human'".

If so, the solution may have been to abolish this law, but Yamamoto – writing under his pseudonym Ben-Dasan (and thereby avoiding giving the impression that a Japanese was "condemning" the Japanese) – states the following:

> If there are foreigners who would say that this law should have been abolished, it means that they possess absolutely no knowledge about Japan. That is, this law existed as an authoritative rule "within the framework that did not ignore one's human nature" and one was to be disciplined for breaking it (Ben-Dasan 1971(1970): 109).

In other words, even if a law is adopted by the Diet and its clauses state certain rules when interpreted rationally, the concepts of "Japan's religion" and "human being" are assumed to exist outside this logic, outside this law. Therefore if "inhuman" things contradicting these beliefs – such as becoming unable to survive or, in less extreme cases, becoming unable to live like a human – were to occur, everyone understands that the relevant law can be ignored. Yamamoto suggests that while black-market rice is a thing of the past, a present-day example would be tax, as if tax regulations were applied strictly, it would turn out that everyone is evading payment. It means that abiding by tax regulations too rigidly is against human nature.

This is indeed the case. Furthermore, this understanding is shared not only among taxpayers but also among those who collect taxes. When one inquires at the tax office about what can be included under "necessary expenditure", one is usually told that it will be fine as long as one sticks within the realms of common sense. This serves as an example of "common sense" being applied as the law beyond law. While this is only one case, such situations can be encountered very often in the course of daily life.

This concept in Japanese society of the "law beyond law" becomes clear when compared with the ideas held by Jewish people. This "common sense", this shared perception among the Japanese, does not, as it does for Jews, exist at the level of god, transcending human existence, let alone is it written into the law. In Japan, the highest value is placed not in god but in the people themselves, the "human beings". Therefore, no problem occurs if the "human beings" interpret and facilitate the use of the common sense that exists in the realm of humans.

This concept of "humans" itself is always perceived and reinterpreted at the concrete level of unadorned human flesh-and-blood, without the use of any abstract concepts to interpret it or abstract words to express it. For this reason, "humanness" and "common sense" differ from person to person and there is no wonder if the "air" of the situation that is supposed to be "read" is read differently depending on the individual. As a result of the ambiguity of the shared idea of "common sense", in daily situations we constantly test our mutual common sense and humanness by exchanging phrases like "That's common sense, isn't it!" or "This isn't what it means to be human!"

Yet, regardless of such ambiguity and friction, the Japanese society continues to function without falling apart and it is in fact often noted for its stability. To put it another way, the Japanese spend a lot of time adjusting mutual ideas in order to correctly understand the meaning of concepts such as "human beings", "common sense", and "air of the place", and therefore succeed in securing a significant degree of mutual understanding. This in its turn implies that if one is unable to achieve this shared understanding, they "cannot become Japanese". This should be the reason why Japanese employees are willing to stay (which does not always mean to work) at their workplaces longer than required. They spend considerable time building consensus on "common sense".

England and Japan: The Western and Eastern Champions of the Industrial Revolution

Another work of Nihonjinron, historian and anthropologist Alan Macfarlane's monograph *The Savage Wars of Peace: England, Japan and the Malthusian Trap* (1997; "England and Japan" in the Japanese edition, 2001) employs a comparative method similar to that adopted in "The Japanese and the Jews". However, while "The Japanese and the Jews" uses a distinctive contrast, Macfarlane's work focuses instead on the parallel commonalities. The book bases its discussions on the objective of exploring why only England and Japan were able to successfully achieve industrial civilization before any other country in Europe and Asia respectively.

However, in reality, prior to this individual problem of "England and Japan's Industrial Revolution", there existed another more complicated question linked to the history of men. This is the question that Malthus puts forward in his work "An Essay on the Principle of Population".

Until two thousand years ago the human race was at the stage of agricultural civilization. At that stage, even when mankind reached such heights as Roman civilization and Chinese civilization, food production could not catch up with the rapid population growth that resulted from prosperity, therefore the only means to limit overpopulation were the so-called three biggest traps of humankind: "war, famine, and plague". Civilization was therefore destined to repeatedly undergo the cycle of rising and then declining under the impact of one of these three traps. The most vexing question of modern history was then to understand why after the Industrial Revolution brought industrial civilization, we became able to escape this cycle by absorbing the excess population into cities and industries. In order to solve this, Macfarlane decided to examine the cases of England and Japan, nations that accomplished the Industrial Revolution in the West and the East respectively.

He consequently discovered a phenomenon that occurred in England and Japan, a phenomenon that was highly bizarre and even incomprehensible from the perspective of population theory. His analysis of materials on population levels in the past revealed that the mortality and birth rates were both at low, stable positions with the birth rate only slightly prevailing over the mortality rate, and this continued to be the case until the first half of the 18th century in England and until the second half of the same century in Japan. This shows that despite their prosperity these two societies did not experience overpopulation; instead, their populations increased at a low and steady pace. This was the first time in the history of mankind that something like this had occurred.

As I mentioned above, until then the population of every society, if left undisturbed, would continue to increase persistently as a result of the high birth rates, so the excess population would be rapidly reduced upon an encounter with the "three traps". Macfarlane speculates that in the case of Japan and England it became possible to abandon this kind of fluctuating graph and instead plot a graph in which the birth and mortality rates form two parallel lines, with the former just slightly above the latter, because they suppressed the "three enemies" and achieved stability through politics, economy, and ideas on livelihood. He then closely examines how Japan and England mitigated and suppressed war, famine, and disease. This is the highlight of the book, and gives it the excitement of reading a novel.

Having examined how Japan and England tackled the "three traps", Macfarlane asserts the following. If one assumes that a society possesses demographic stability as seen in these two countries and if the factors demanding larger population – such as, for instance, the expansion of foreign trade or new inventions, such as the steam engine –come into play, this society should be able to generate the necessary population by slightly increasing its birth rates. In the preceding history of mankind, when the population grew, it flowed into the cities thus aggravating their sanitary conditions and leading in turn to epidemics, or it created social instability, opening up the potential of war, which, once started, would result in the devastation of farmlands and famine. This vicious cycle was responsible for the reduction of the excess population. However, the societies and cultures of England and Japan had enough resilience and tolerability in place to combat overpopulation. England and Japan were granted with a few fortuities and their societies were thus able to move onto the stage of industrial civilization.

Macfarlane argues that the reason the Industrial Revolution happened in these two countries in the 18-19th centuries has to do with a chain of "intentions and coincidences". He suggests that Japan did not merely copy the way in which England experienced the Industrial Revolution after "inventing" the steam engine, one of the rings in this chain, by importing its technology. Macfarlane emphasizes that what is of true importance is not the trigger, but the fact that both England and Japan successfully created societies that were ready to respond to such changes well before the advent of the Industrial Revolution.

Macfarlane pinpoints the nature of England and Japan as "big" islands as the factor that made such success possible. Their position as islands allows them to avoid wars and plague to a rather high degree. Famine can then be prevented if the occurrence of war and plague is circumvented. After starting with the idea of England and Japan's distinctive qualities as "island countries", qualities that everyone can picture even just vaguely, Macfarlane thoroughly and tirelessly depicts both the commonalities and many differences between the two countries – such as, for instance, the scope of cattle breeding – that he has ascertained through a meticulous pursuit for materials to create this impressive work.

Not "Industrial" But "Industrious" Revolution

Akira Hayami, a scholar of historical demography, attributed Japan's success on that front to what he called "Industrious Revolution". This wordplay highlights the industriousness that was the key factor in Japan's process of establishing itself as a modern nation. In his tenacious portrayal of Japanese farmers transporting water to elevated farmland in "The Naked Island", Shindō Kaneto symbolically depicts the labor of the Japanese farmers and indeed of all the people of the Edo period. As I mentioned in Chapter 7 when discussing the "craftsmen", it is the ideology of diligence, of "busying oneself with work", that constitutes the "way of life" of the Japanese people, rather than poor labor conditions. This diligence is both the driving force and the outcome of Japan's stable birth and mortality rates described in Macfarlane's population theory.

Such daily life created in the Edo period is perhaps one of the best products of Japanese history. As one can see, Japan experienced no war then and managed for over two centuries to sustain a "peace" during which it did not suffer from big famines or epidemics, a contrast with many of the rest of the world's societies of the same period. As is clear from "The Naked Island",

at that time the Japanese society cultivated all arable land, consumed everything edible without making waste, transformed excretions into compost
and, largely relying on "women" for labor force and "care" (Note 2), presented
in itself a "sustainable, recycling-oriented society", achieved through untiring
hard work. I believe that the prototypes of various forms of "behavior characteristic to the Japanese" such as "ingenuity", *seken*, and "dependence" (*amae*)
that have been referred to in many works of Nihonjinron and continue to
exist until now were molded in the process of creating and sustaining such a
society.

First of all, in this society not only the economy but also human relations
were incorporated into a close-knit system. The transcendental aspects of
religion were weakened by the thoroughness of the systems that developed to
manage the people as a result of the prohibition of Christianity in feudal Japan,
which in turn led to the secularization of Buddhism – namely, ensuring that
emphasis was placed on the real world. This situation overlapped harmoni-
ously with the aspect of Shinto as a "natural religion" that does not have sacred
texts – although Shinto and Buddhism had already been mixed together in
a form of syncretism by then – and produced at the level of everyday life
what Shichihei Yamamoto calls "Japan's religion". The village organization
of the Edo period and the enhancement of the mutual surveillance system
paired with the sharing of collective responsibility in five-household groups
(*gonin gumi*) in towns and villages can be seen in the multiple practices and
rules present in the Japanese collectivity pointed out by Benedict, the vertical
structure with *ie* at center described by Nakane, and Abe's *seken*.

Macfarlane's *The Savage Wars of Peace* is thus an interesting book as
it adds historical grounds to the arguments brought forth in the works
of Nihonjinron that I have addressed in this book. For instance, let
us think of why Japanese society takes so long to solve the tasks it is
presented with and is unable to raise questions. In Japan a group strives
with extreme eagerness to eliminate even small differences (resistance),
rules out unsolvable problems by deeming them "inexistent", stubbornly suppresses people who cause problems, and does not consider the possibility that addressing such problems may actually take everything to a
new stage. These tendencies become comprehensible when seen as the
result of the historical experience of people who for over two hundred
years have intensively endeavored to avoid the risks that could destroy
the system that circulates both in terms of human relations and ecology,
and that have taken great pains to "sustain" this system.

From Marx to Malthus

By pursuing the discussions in "The Japanese and the Jews" under his Jewish pseudonym, Shichihei Yamamoto sought to distance himself from the left wing versus right wing structure that drove the pre-1970s "Japanese intellectuals" and the ideology and common sense that existed within it. In discussing Japan, he chose to compare it neither with the illuminating rationality of Western Europe nor Marxist ideology, but with Jewish thought, something of a completely different dimension. This helped him in his attempt to nullify the conventional wisdom of Japanese scholars and journalists.

Macfarlane's book is an academic work and its methodology is clear. It is positioned inside the trend led by a group of scholars from Cambridge University who created a new historical demography by taking over from Malthus's population principles from a critical viewpoint. Its approach of focusing on historical transition could be described as Darwinism, but the feature that distinguishes this work is the fact that it addresses not Marx but Malthus.

Here I would like to briefly refer to another book among the postwar works discussing Japan, *Bunmei no Seitaishi Kan* ("An Ecological View of History") by Tadao Umesao (1967). This book argues that Asia and Europe, placed on the opposite sides of the Eurasian continent, share a certain homology. In this sense it develops a theory that overlaps with Macfarlane's work.

It is possible to say that the work of Umesao, a descendant of the Kyoto School, links on from Shigetaka Shiga's *Nihon Fūkeiron* ("The Landscape of Japan") and Tetsurō Watsuji's *Fūdo* ("Climate"). It is also a hypothesis that perceives an ecological view of the "human society", different from the Marxist historical perspective.

It would perhaps be unfair labelling if we suggest that the three afore-mentioned works share criticism of Marxist historical theory as their common feature. Yet they do provide solutions to the problems of at-tempting to capture "Japan" from the Marxist perspective, which would mean taking the biased viewpoint on Asia of a philosopher who lived 150 years ago. Even if we do not think it strange to attempt to interpret the inescapable theme of individuality of Japan – the country that was the first to achieve modernization among the non-Western societies in the beginning of the modern age – by fitting it in to Marxism and other such theories of "modernization", it will inevitably result in there being something "left over". The works by Yamamoto and Macfarlane offer a solution to this by deliberating Japan's identity through comparison with other societies – from the perspective of the existential dimension of religious humans, and from the perspective of historical anthropology respectively – rather than historical theories of modernization.

Note 1: "The Japanese and the Jews" received the Ōya Sōichi Prize for Nonfiction the same year, and the fact that its mysterious author, Isaiah Ben-Dasan, was not present for the award ceremony made it even more popular. I was in Paris at that time and the Japanese students there were debating the possible identity of the author with great curiosity. However, like the Japanese depicted in Riichi Yokomitsu's *Ryoshū* ("Melancholy on a Journey"), we often engaged in discussions about Japan and I remember us, Japanese residing in a foreign land, reflecting upon the indifference that we had felt towards the "security" described in this book when we were at home in Japan.

Note 2: Macfarlane focuses particularly on the severity of the labor that the Japanese women engaged in. As I mentioned in Chapter 8, in the case of Japan this links to the fact that sexual activity between married couples decreases early on. This discovery by Macfarlane is due to his knowledge of and anthropological fieldwork on the Nepalese society whose people also live under harsh ecological conditions. Thus, while it is not openly stated, we can suggest that Macfarlane's work employs a comparative framework incorporating three societies, those of Japan, England, and Nepal, a framework that cultural anthropologist Junzō Kawada (2008) calls "triangular measurement".

PART 3

The Future of Nihonjinron

CHAPTER 11

The Role Nihonjinron Has Served Until Now

The Three Periods of Nihonjinron and its Respective Roles

Since Japan commenced its modernization efforts following the Meiji Restoration, there have been three distinctive periods during which Nihonjinron has been written: the period of elation following the First Sino-Japanese and the Russo-Japanese wars, the "gentle slope" of Shōwa, and the half a century of the lengthy postwar economic rehabilitation. I described the Nihonjinron of each respective period in Parts 1 and 2 of this book. Here I would like to compare each of the three periods and examine the "hypothesis" on Nihonjinron that I put forth in Chapter 1.

The hypothesis is as follows:

The nature of Nihonjinron lies in its attempt to explain who the Japanese are and thereby remove the anxiety associated with the identity of the modern Japanese. The existence of this anxiety stems from the fact that in modern times Japan occupied a peculiar historical position, namely, it was not a society that belonged to the Western history that produced "the modern age". Since Japan being an outsider in the so-called "Western" modern era is a historical given that cannot be changed retroactively, the anxiety arises again and again. When the "anxiety" rises, Nihonjinron is written, making interpretations in line with the features of that anxiety. However, as this anxiety over identity is ingrained and unsurpassable, a new form of "anxiety" always emerges and every time this happens a new work of Nihonjinron becomes a bestseller. Yet, by no means does this "anxiety" only increase in the event of crises involving "Japan"; it arises equally when the future of the country looks favorable, as its people do not feel certain about its success. Thus, the anxiety and the

Nihonjinron as a response to it appear both when the country's power strengthens and when it fades.

The First Period: Proactive and International

The first period, the elation following the First Sino-Japanese and the Russo-Japanese wars, is when the "anxiety" about what it is to be Japanese emerged for the first time. Until then, the national problem had been the anxiety that came from the fear of falling prey to the imperialist powers. During that time it had been self-evident that Japan did not belong to the Western civilization and while this fact in itself had presented a clear problem, there had been no anxiety of identity. Rather, it is when Japan in a sense "colonialized" Hokkaido and Okinawa, turned its sights to the Korean Peninsula, and developed the ability to take a high-handed attitude towards China that the problem of identifying what these resourceful Japanese people were became a concern.

Yukichi Fukuzawa's editorial *Datsuaron* ("Departure from Asia"), which was published in the *Jiji Shinpō* newspaper in 1885, is "antagonistic" in the sense that it states that Japan as a nation is seeking to stand up to Europe and the USA and the influence and control that they wield by attempting to establish its dominance in Asia and bring Joseon and China under its influence before they become civilized. While antagonistic towards the West, each of the four Nihonjinron works that were written around the time of the First Sino-Japanese War and Russo-Japanese War – Shigetaka Shiga's *Nihon Fūkeiron* ("The Landscape of Japan") (1894), Kanzō Uchimura's *Representative Men of Japan* (1894), Inazō Nitobe's *Bushido: The Soul of Japan* (1899), and Tenshin Okakura's *The Book of Tea* (1906) – emphasize Japan's resemblance and its affinity with Western society, asserting that while Japan is different in appearance it is the same in essence and possesses features that can be likened to those of the Western civilization. While separated from Yukichi Fukuzawa – who was born in 1835 – by only one generation, the four authors were able to identify themselves as belonging to the same current as the West.

As Japan's national power mounted, the authors each tried to relieve the anxiety associated with the grounds for that growing strength in their own independent way. They share their assertion that Japan has always possessed history and culture that is on a par with that of the West (as well as the rather questionable claim that Japan also enjoys equal geographic conditions). These four Nihonjinron works therefore differ from those written during the two subsequent periods in that they actively look outward.

Apart from "The Landscape of Japan", the other three were originally written in English and published for Western readers. They were then read by the Japanese audience whose members felt convinced that it was possible to assert themselves towards the West in the presented way. While appearing to target a domestic audience, Shiga's *kanbun* (Chinese prosaic style) manuscript was in fact the work of an elite who was well versed in foreign matters, a graduate of Sapporo Agricultural College, the most advanced institution of the times. In other words, he was giving the readers the seal of approval to compare Japan's landscape with that of foreign lands.

If these books, especially the three English-language works, are still read by the Japanese people, the reason for this lies with their reputation as works that were originally written in English for foreign audiences and were able to earn a certain degree of support and acclaim. In comparison with the Nihonjinron books written by the Japanese authors during the two later periods – with the exception of the works by Chie Nakane – these more than one-hundred-year-old monographs are for a fact still more widely known abroad as books introducing Japan. It is possible that in a sense these works provided Western readers with an appealing portrayal of Japan, which shaped Japan's overseas image, in turn laying the preparatory groundwork for the new readers to accept these books easily. Hence, the fact that these works are still read by foreigners and then soon after by Japanese means that the entrenched perception of Japan, or even the image of Japan compliant with the orientalist vision of foreigners, is still becoming ever more intense today.

Let us put that trend aside for the time being, and briefly return to the Nihonjinron works of the first period, the period following the First Sino-Japanese and the Russo-Japanese Wars. The four works written in this time helped to alleviate Japan's "anxiety of not being the West" while it was gradually acquiring confidence as one of the members of Western civilization. This is naturally not to suggest that they managed to eliminate the anxiety – they merely whited out its surface.

The Second Period: Defensive and Introverted

All four of the books that I introduced as Nihonjinron of the second period are based on the indisputable fact that Japan is a non-Western society, the issue that has continuously been present since the first period, and are thus the records of the struggles to ascertain the direction in which the ideals as a state and as an individual can be found. However, each of the authors combats the question from their own field. In contrast to the four writers of the first period who – possibly due to the fact that they were around the same age – seem to share a relationship akin to solidarity despite not being aware of each other's presence, the authors of the four books of the later period approach the issue completely independently, each tackling it from their own respective positions.

Shūzō Kuki's *'Iki' no Kōzō* ("The Structure of Iki") seeks to conceal its opposition to the West by focusing on *iki*, Japan's concept of internal, localized beauty. However, to achieve this it is necessary to make the book's content extremely direct and overly earnest. One should not lay one's opposition to the West bare in an attempt to throw off simplistic connections that suggest that Japan is in parallel with the West or shares common elements with it, and yet at the same time should not allow oneself to be seen as forcedly ignoring the West. After noting that one "should not be misled by the fact that we happen to discover *iki* in artistic forms of Western art" (Kuki 1930, translated by Nara, Hiroshi 2008: 58), Kuki carefully and defensively explains in great detail that *iki* is a phenomenon unique to Japan. This contrasts with how Nitobe, in his book *Bushido: The Soul of Japan*, draws comparisons between *bushidō* ("the way of the warrior") and the moral systems of knights in the Middle Ages, to present *bushidō* as a category of the "noble savages" that is easy for Westerners to accept. Perhaps this is why when one reads "The Structure of Iki", with its overly serious writing style and methods of analysis, one cannot help but wonder if it was written as a joke or a parody on the discourse on the Japanese culture.

Thus, Kuki sought to neutralize the hints of opposition to the West by applying the Western philosophical method, but ultimately produced a "Japanese-style" piece of literature addressed to the Japanese. Japan's future course was never mapped out by this book alone. Yet, the existence of this work serves as a foundation for defining "Japan". It caused a stir in response to the anxiety of being "Japanese" at the time, which had otherwise been kept pent up.

"The Structure of Iki" not only held such significance at the time of its publication, it also now serves as a "base ground" for writing about Japan solely due to its reputation as a monograph about Japan, despite the fact that it is not popularly read and the lack of recognition of the fact that it is a book describing the world of *geisha*.

In *Fūdo* ("Climate"), Tetsurō Watsuji carelessly expands the essentialist theory that as the Japanese people live in humid weather conditions that involve rainy seasons and typhoons, they have "intrinsic" sensitivity toward nature and have ultimately developed a submissive attitude and character that allows them to accept rather than struggle against it, above and beyond what their apparent intentions are. It is a defiant argument implying that rather than openly opposing the West, one should prioritize the Japanese circumstances since they are unique to Japan. The hopeful and yet resigned attitude towards Asia and particularly China is also inextricably linked with this assertion that the first problem to address is that of Japan and its place in modernity. Therefore while the argument begins with individual sentiments – the sense that the Japanese have no choice but to put up with what they have as they cannot swap the humid climate for the "pastures" of the West or make the West understand what it is like to live in such a climate – it links into questions of national attitude. There is a passage in Riichi Yokomitsu's *Ryoshū* ("Melancholy on a Journey") in which, following a lengthy description of the landscape of the pastoral Alps, the character Yashirō exclaims with a sigh: "When looking from here, Japan is really at the ends of the earth!" (Yokomitsu 1998(1937), Upper Volume: 166). This corresponds with the mindset encouraged by Watsuji's "Climate". Would it be an exaggeration to describe this mindset as one that accepts misfortune? It is not that "the Japanese" are the commonality of this "misfortune"; rather, the solidarity of "the Japanese" is born through the act of "acceptance" of the misfortune. This resembles the atmosphere in *Kindai no Chōkoku* ("Overcoming Modernity"), akin to a dark banquet where everyone is drinking silently, except just a few merry guests.

The reason why "Climate" is nonetheless still read by the Japanese is due to the clarity of its emphasis on intrinsic qualities and its composition that places Japan as part of the world, albeit feignedly. However, while this book seems universal in its description of the world, it is directed internally in terms of its content and assumed readers, as can clearly be seen in the fact that Japan appears at the very end of the book, like the "finish" square of a board game.

The anxiety that runs through "Melancholy on a Journey" had a devastating effect on both the novel and the argument that Yokomitsu wished to present in the book. The depiction of the ardent arguments pursued by the Japanese youths while they are in Europe – a situation which causes a particular increase in their anxiety of being Japanese – overwhelms the readers not only in terms of its content, but also through the compelling feeling that one has to engage in a similar debate. However, while this fictional discussion starts at the same time as the real occurrence of the February 26 coup d'état by Japanese army officers in 1936 and continues after the characters come back to Japan, it is outpaced by the actual situation and incidents of Japanese society. After the Pacific War began, Yokomitsu continued to portray the characters as sensing the impending war, however, it is unavoidable that the "hindsight" born following the onset of the war penetrates the novel's fictional world, which had already become the past. To address this, as a novelist Yokomitsu tries to ensure that the world and time of the novel remain fixed, however, if anything he lets in the hindsight as he stops himself from writing what cannot be known to the characters, rather than adding some afterthought and feigning ignorance about it. Moreover, this story's failure as fiction is possibly spelt by the tone of the last chapter, which Yokomitsu finished writing after the war, that unintentionally reveals a sense of mourning the characters and the fact that they may fall in the upcoming war. On the other hand, if Yokomitsu had restrained these emotions in the last chapter as well, this would have probably amounted to another kind of demise of this work as a novel, like a slow withering.

The two characters of the book, Yashirō and Kuji, use the words "no win" to express their inability to reach common ground in the discussion, but "Melancholy on a Journey" is a kind of a novel that was abandoned, having failed to accomplish reconciliation between its status as a Nihonjinron-novel and as a Nihonjinron-debate. Yet, through its depiction of the melancholy of journeying, sometimes even called the "poison of sorrow", the state of being that manifests itself in various ways, this novel has more than shown the breeding ground of Nihonjinron that emerges when the Japanese encounter foreign countries. I will write about one of its revelations, "studying abroad", later in this chapter.

The work that serves as an apogee of the defensive and internally-oriented Nihonjinron is *Kindai no Chōkoku* ("Overcoming Modernity"). The underlying tone of this piece is the anxiety surrounding the fact that Japan "was winning the war". Despite the fact that that war was against the West, only a very few people could say that the West was nothing to be afraid of, and the shared understanding among the participants was that their modernity was the one of the "West" and that unless they acknowledged it, it would be impossible to move forward or "overcome" it. It is a separate question whether they thought so intuitively or as a result of conclusions to logical investigations.

This work presents two distinct ideas in terms of how it attempts to alleviate the anxiety pertaining to the hypothesis on Nihonjinron. The first is the position like that of Fusao Hayashi, who suggests "acknowledging as felicitous and pure things" the "classics" brought up by Hideo Kobayashi and other participants as well as the newly developing aspects of Japan which he demonstrates through the education of "the young airmen". The other position insists that "a modern man can win over the modernity only by means of modernity" (Kawakami 1942, translated by Calichman, F. Richard 2008: 208). However, while the former view sounds like a discourse to be naturally uttered afresh in 1942, it is in fact a belated discussion. The latter view, due to its sensible nature, also carries nothing new, as when the historical given that Japan is an outsider in relation to the "Western" modernity is considered as a "problem", it is nothing but empty talk to suggest that modernity can only be surmounted by modernity. Moreover, Hideo Kobayashi's expression "to win over modernity" is interesting as it shows his ambiguous position, but this is perhaps due to Kobayashi's own separate issues.

The Third Period: Initially Reflective and Gradually Self-Affirming

A feature that can be consistently found in the Nihonjinron written during the long postwar period is a reflective tone related to the defeat in the "Greater East Asian War" (the Pacific War). This reflective mood questions why Japan ended up waging war and what should be done in order to avoid repeating it.

This sentiment is also predominant in *The Chrysanthemum and the Sword*, the first postwar piece of Nihonjinron. While it was not written by a Japanese, it was translated (in 1948) and read by the Japanese as a piece of literature that could be useful for such self-reflection. Although this can be seen as self-torture, reading such a book during those times and reflecting upon one's conduct must have felt all the more liberating. After "tormenting" themselves through reflection on past events, rather than feeling daunted, "the Japanese" were "then again" able to strive in the direction of recovery and live as part of the democratic Japan and the international society. It is not right to worry that it is a "self-tormenting" book and it is hard to imagine that the readers were "torturing" themselves. Rather, this work was widely read with the purpose of accomplishing recovery. The Japanese demanded some kind of explanation for the loss of direction that had arisen from the defeat in the war.

This "reflective" tone is equally present in the Nihonjinron that describes Japan in favorable times. *Kono Kuni no Katachi* ("The Form of this Nation"), *'Amae' no Kōzō* ("The Anatomy of Dependence"), and *Japan as Number One: Lessons for America* are works that give their readers the opportunity to perceive a positive Japan, regardless of the authors' intentions. However, each of these books adopt the approach of explaining the postwar reality by reflectively examining the defeat in the war and the pre-war system, posing questions such as what kind of a failure the defeat implied, what the problems of the pre-war emperor system were, and how the defeat was overcome. Of course, in such books as *Nihonjin to Yudayajin* ("The Japanese and the Jews"), *Ningen wo Kōfuku ni shinai Nihon toiu Shisutemu* ("The False Realities of a Politicized Society"), and *'Seken' to ha Nani ka?* ("What is 'Seken'?") that addressed Japan critically (negatively), the reflection upon the defeat in the war emerges as a starting point to contemplate the Japanese and the Japanese society. If we consider this in connection with my hypothesis on Nihonjinron, we see that the anxiety of identity of being a Japanese in the modern age took a discernible form as a result of the defeat in the war. If we think of this in terms of the story of "Japan", wouldn't it relate to Japan's actual failure, in which the concern that Japan was "playing with fire" turned out to be a superbly accurate perception? However, Japan's defeat can be attributed to various different factors: the country's pure military weakness, its inability to overcome the disadvantages of being a belated participant of the imperialist competition, or a series of diplomatic mistakes.

Yet, aside from such military, historical, and foreign policy perspectives, the narrative that has taken over at the level of Nihonjinron is that Japan lost the war simply because "the Japanese" were immature. This stance has made it easier for Nihonjinron to address the "anxiety of identity in the modern times". Namely, it means that the mainstream narratives that Japan is "behind in terms of modernization" or that it lacks "modernistic individuals" have become more convincing.

At any rate, these nearly seventy years have seen drastic vicissitudes for Japan. This period started immediately after the defeat with the resignation that Japan may not rise again, followed by gradually regained economic confidence and uncertainty about the unexpected prosperity that continued from the mid-1950s onwards, when the nation surmounted such hardships as the oil crisis. Although when Ezra Vogel's *Japan as Number One* first came out no one seriously thought of Japan as number one, ten years later people had started to imagine that it might actually be true. Then, immediately after the circumstances worsened, the collapse of the bubble economy and the defeat in the monetary war came along, leading to the present-day situation when one cannot help but wonder whether the lost ten years will continue forever. Thus, the ups and the downs plunge us into corresponding levels of anxiety, in line with the sentiment of the moment. It can be said that the postwar era has been characterized by the constant presence of anxiety. Nihonjinron works have repeatedly become bestsellers due to such societal transformations and Japan's changing position within international affairs.

However, the very fact that Nihonjinron works continued to be published serves as evidence that they did not fulfill their ultimate goal of relieving the anxiety of identity of being a Japanese. When one becomes conscious of the structure of this anxiety and feels how it functions as part of one's mentality, it is impossible to alleviate the anxiety unless the past history is blacked out, since it originates in the history. This is clearly demonstrated by the fact that the anxiety did not disappear despite Japan becoming – even if not the first – the second largest economy in the world or being admitted to the G7. Moreover, Japan's loneliness would not vanish, as even when Korea, China, and other Asian countries catch up with Japan, emerging as its non-Western allies in the modern age, Japan still tries to distinguish itself from such countries and achieve an upgraded status within the modernity.

Japan takes strong pride in its standing as the only country in Asia to be a member of the G7. Yet, this very status of belonging to the G7 makes Japan's identity unstable, compelling it to sway between Asia and the West, while China deliberately and cleverly stays away from this "Rich Club". An example that illustrates this situation at a glance is the lonely figure of the Japanese prime minister in the group photograph of the G7 leaders. The Japanese newspapers choose to print photos capturing such moments as the US president considerately initiating a conversation with Japan's leader, but in television and newspaper photos in the West the latter is seen left behind despite traveling as a member of the group. When considered from a distance, the Japanese Ministry of the Foreign Affairs' long-term attempt to secure a permanent seat on the United Nations Security Council seems like a belated struggle that reflects the anxiety of identity that has given rise to Nihonjinron since the Meiji period.

In order to discuss the Nihonjinron of the third period, we also need to consider the ongoing changes. The current discussion about Japan as a state is stimulated by reflection upon the genre of Nihonjinron, skepticism about the Japanese as a grouping, and the sentiment that discussion should be focused on multiple Japanese individuals, rather than the Japanese as a whole. It seems that the goals that the postwar Nihonjinron failed to achieve are now being discussed as the theory of the state (*kokkaron*). I will touch upon this in a separate section.

Nihonjinron as an Avocation

When we take an overview of the Nihonjinron of the past, a few features become visible. The first is that Nihonjinron works are rarely written as specialist pieces in a head-on, earnest manner.

Of the Nihonjinron works of the first period Okakura's *The Book of Tea* and Shiga's *Nihon Fūkeiron* ("The Landscape of Japan") are written within fields of specialization, but target a general audience. Uchimura and Nitobe are not specialists in the fields they address in *Representative Men of Japan* and *Bushido: The Soul of Japan* respectively. Of course, they both put their hearts and souls into these, writing their works for their own individual reasons. However, Nitobe, for example, specialized in agricultural economy and pursued a professional career in diplomacy, neither of which areas are related to the subject of *bushidō*. The authors of the Nihonjinron works of the second period were writing on topics related to their specialist fields but at the same time breaking away from their primary work areas. By creating these books the authors stepped outside their professional fields and attempted to make a broader investigation of Japan in general and the identity of being a Japanese that is existent as one's inner nature.

This became more apparent following the end of the war. When a series of books was labeled "Nihonjinron" and new ones started being published under the heading "Nihonjinron" it became natural to refer to them as a "mass consumption commodity", and thereby the tendency for Nihonjinron to be written as an "avocation", rather than specialized literature, increased.

Let us take another look at the postwar Nihonjinron that I introduced in this book. The postwar Nihonjinron that started with *The Chrysanthemum and the Sword* generated many works; yet there has not been much real development from there. As I already mentioned, it was read as a means of solving the "anxiety" that emerged from time to time, giving way to a circulation of a few keywords, and fading soon after. Yet, there were not many opportunities for these pieces of Nihonjinron to be examined, critiqued, and refined. Then, a few years later, a similar argument would be articulated using different expressions, leading to a publication of yet another book on Nihonjinron.

There is at least one reason why the Nihonjinron written to this day has been characterized as sporadic in nature and rarely accumulating or developing. It is due to the fact that many of its works were written as an avocation, and therefore the arguments they contained were not considered worthy subjects for discussion, criticism, or development. Being "an avocation" does not necessarily indicate that the level of the writing is low. What it means is that when its authors are scholars, Nihonjinron is written as a "by-product" of their research. Such authors strive to contribute to matters that appeal to everyone rather than focusing on their primary work, and are driven by personal interests and slightly distanced from their usual professional awareness. As in the case of the aforementioned Nihonjinron works of the Meiji period that simultaneously served as "introductions" to Japan for foreign readers, the authors of the postwar books of the same genre were more often than not professionals in different occupations and areas, and serving as diplomats or persons of letters. They would go abroad and be inspired to write about what the Japanese are on the basis of their own personal interests. As a result, the Nihonjinron they produced would be positioned outside their "primary" work. In reality, there is still no theory such as the "study of the Japanese" and there are no scholars specialized in Nihonjinron. It resembles the debates on the age-old controversy over the geographical location of the Yamatai kingdom (a state in the Yayoi period [c. 300–100 BCE]), an area in which no one is a specialist and anybody can freely join in like taking part in a game.

Furthermore, even if the author's intention were to write it as part of his primary occupation, it would not be perceived as such by the readers or commenters. To give an example, for Benedict, an anthropologist of the "culture and personality school", *The Chrysanthemum and the Sword* was her primary work, putting aside the fact that it was requested by the military. However, the Japanese people either fiercely disapproved of or supported her arguments, or dismissed them on the grounds that there were things she "could not understand" because she was a foreigner. This, along with Benedict's passing in 1948, has resulted in a simplistic assessment of whether the work hits the mark in terms of understanding Japan. The author's chosen anthropological methodology or her viewpoint as a whole received no attention, and all that came out of it was that a few mistakes were pointed out, a number of keywords ("shame culture") entered circulation, and several years later a handful of new books postulating similar arguments were published. Keiichi Sakuta, a sociologist, attempted to redefine the concept of "shame" from *The Chrysanthemum and the Sword* in his work entitled *Haji no Bunka Saikō* ("A Reconsideration of Shame Culture") (1964). Nonetheless, with the exception of this example, there has been no development on Benedict's impressive work to this day.

In the case of *The Chrysanthemum and the Sword*, the Japanese readers must have experienced a sense of resistance in regards to being critically examined by a "stranger", a foreigner at that. However, the refined works of Nihonjinron of the postwar period that I introduced in this book, with the exception of Tsuneichi Miyamoto's *Wasurerareta Nihonjin* ("The Forgotten Japanese") and Dower's *Embracing Defeat: Japan in the Wake of World War II*, also have features of "avocation", each of varying intensity. The other various works of Nihonjinron are more of an "avocation" and even lacking in skill.

But then, the reason why Tamotsu Aoki criticized in *'Nihon Bunkaron' no Hen'yō* ("Transformation of the Discourse on Japanese Culture") the very idea of writing Nihonjinron unless devoting oneself fully to the exploration of the "discourse on the Japanese culture" was not because he recognized its "avocational" nature. He was also taking precautions against it being used for a political debate, as under the political context writing and reading Nihonjinron could be interpreted as approving of or negating the contemporary social system. This sense of caution is possibly the reason why the authors adopt an "avocational" pose. On the one hand, the serious-minded Japanese have stopped getting involved in handling such a complex topic as Nihonjinron as a primary occupation, but on the other it has continued to be created as a response to demand from readers, in a manner below the level of an "avocation", even turning into a ridiculed genre. The outstanding examples of Nihonjinron that have emerged more recently – such as Dower's *Embracing Defeat* or the NHK documentary series *Project X* – were not initially created with the purpose of pursuing Nihonjinron.

Men Damaged by Studying Abroad and Women Who Do Not Write Nihonjinron

Yet, why do outstanding theoreticians step into the realm of Nihonjinron, be it as an avocation? This can be linked to the following part of the hypothesis on Nihonjinron.

> Since Japan being an outsider in the so-called "Western" modern era is a historical given that cannot be changed retroactively, the anxiety arises again and again. When the "anxiety" rises, Nihonjinron is written, making interpretations in line with the features of that anxiety.

In the extract above, "Japan" is the subject. However, we can replace "Japan" with "a single Japanese" and modify it as follows:

> "Oneself, a Japanese person" being an outsider in the so-called "Western" modern era is an "inborn" given that cannot be changed by going back to one's "upbringing", hence the anxiety arises again and again. When the "anxiety" about "oneself as a Japanese" rises, Nihonjinron that will provide interpretations in line with the features of that anxiety "becomes indispensable for oneself as well".

This kind of anxiety is not always present. As I explained in Part 1, one starts thinking about being Japanese when one becomes conscious of "foreign countries". For many writers this often happens when placed in the environment of "studying abroad", or during a relatively long stay abroad. In Yokomitsu's "Melancholy on a Journey" both the Japanese students and Japanese spending time abroad debate incessantly about Japan. These ideas are uttered and consumed then and there as the Nihonjinron that the participants need.

Most of the authors introduced in this book seem to have been motivated in some way to write Nihonjinron by their experiences of studying or staying abroad. For Nitobe, Uchimura, Sōseki, Kuki, and Watsuji, as well as Abe and Nakane, the point of departure was studying abroad, while for Yokomitsu it was staying in Europe and for Shiba and Yamamoto it was their experiences on the battlefield. This situation is likely to become clearer when compared to the authors of other works of Nihonjinron or the discourse on the Japanese society (*nihonshakairon*). To give some examples here off the top of my head, experiences of studying or spending time abroad clearly threw a shadow upon the works about Japan and the Japanese by Eiichirō Ishida (*Nihonbunkaron* ["Lectures on Japanese Culture"]), Shūichi Katō (*Nihon Bunka no Zasshusei* ["The Hybrid Nature of Japanese Culture"]), Masao Yamaguchi, Shunsuke Tsurumi, Masakazu Yamazaki, Jun Etō, Kanji Nishio, Yoshimi Ishikawa, and Norihiro Katō, to name the least.

I chose the word "shadow" for a reason. For an individual staying abroad, the relationship between oneself and the foreign society is built along two lines of communication: the words and the body. In order to be assured that one is accepted in the relevant society, it is essential that one is able to both communicate by means of words and to share a bodily relationship, namely, to partake in some sort of intimate relationship. The latter also includes sexual contact with the "local" people. For the Japanese, studying or staying abroad, experiences in which each respective environment is marked by each individual's personality – be they experiences studying abroad as a young or mature person or staying there for a short or a long time – have been a crucial "rite of passage" since the opening of the country, deeply affecting those who do go through it.

Even without invoking the case of Sōseki, who suffered from an emotional breakdown, we can say that anyone who studied or stayed in "the West" must have experienced a certain "gloominess" when going through various situations there. Namely, this gloominess could have been provoked by the anxiety that they endured when learning about the Western modernity in the course of their studies or time spent abroad, whether it was spent doing business with the West, building diplomatic ties, or sustaining relations. To repeat the adapted hypothesis above, one's status as "an outsider in the so-called 'Western' modern era is an 'inborn' given that cannot be changed by going back to one's 'upbringing'".

People do not usually talk about this gloominess, and they are even more likely to avoid speaking of it if it turned into a "trauma". In the preface to this book I wrote that Nihonjinron dealt with "the Japanese as a cultural being, and then proceeded to apply these theories to discuss the Japanese as a national being". In fact, this initially happens as an experience at the level of an individual. It means that among various "incidents" and "episodes" when studying or staying abroad one encounters situations when one has to strike back as if it was a personal matter at things that are deemed as characteristic to the Japanese on a cultural or national level. The reason why this is described in the generalized form of Nihonjinron is not in order to conceal that this problem is individual in nature, but because unless one's individual problem is explained by means of a compelling mechanism which generalizes it as an issue concerning "the Japanese", it cannot lead to a satisfying solution for a problem of an individual.

However, the structure of "orientalism", explained in Chapter 8, also reveals itself in this case. An inferiorly positioned Japan is expressed as a female and the bodily relations between the West and Japan are realized through a Western man and a Japanese woman (*geisha*), hence a Japanese man is not seen as a man in the face of the West. That being the case, a Japanese man is not recognized as a "man" in the situations of bodily communication with the West during his studies or prolonged stays abroad. This means that a Japanese man can "easily" get hurt as a "man" when studying or staying long-term overseas. Should one then develop a "trauma", this serves as a necessary momentum to write Nihonjinron.

If we look at this from a "female" perspective, we will see that when women study or spend long periods abroad, these experiences do not "traumatize" them for the same reasons that apply to the Japanese men. Of course one should exercise caution before stating this with certainty.

At the same time, the following supposition could be made in line with the flow of the discussion that I have developed so far. Japanese women, in comparison with Japanese men, are less likely to suffer from the "anxiety" that seeks an explanation in the form of Nihonjinron, an explanation in which an individual and the state (Japan) are superimposed. This may serve as an indication as to why so little Nihonjinron has been written by women. *The Chrysanthemum and the Sword* and *Tateshakai no Ningen Kankei* ("Human Relations in Vertical Society") are written by women, but they were created as scholarly works by the anthropologists Ruth Benedict and Chie Nakane and, although the works are read as Nihonjinron, the authors themselves did not set out with that intention. Moreover, neither of these two books was prompted by "anxiety".

In "Melancholy on a Journey" the discussion about Japan is carried out solely by men, and the two leading female characters either always keep distance from these debates or are portrayed as if distance can be maintained. This can perhaps be explained by the fact that women as individuals experience less anxiety of being Japanese in connection to the universality of "the Japanese".

The influence that these "studies abroad" and long-term sojourns overseas (known as *yōkō* or "traveling to the West") have wielded on the Japanese elites and intellectuals since Meiji, as well as the differences in the experiences of time spent in foreign countries depending on gender, constitute a deep trauma "inherent to the Japanese" that has rarely been discussed or debated.

CHAPTER 12

The Future Japanese and Nihonjinron

If Nihonjinron Becomes Unnecessary

At the end of the foreword to Part 2 I wrote: "When we are no longer able to discuss the newly written Nihonjinron together with the works on the subject created since the war, this will signal that Nihonjinron has begun to change intrinsically".

The "Nihonjinron today" is the discourse that I described in Chapter 1 through the "hypothesis on Nihonjinron". It did not merely have Japan and the Japanese as a subject of its discussion. A discourse that simply discusses a certain country and people belonging to its society can be found anywhere. Theories in historical science or social critique are precisely this, and it is common for them to take the form of a "discourse on the people of A (discourse on the Englishmen)", such as the biography of an important figure (like Churchill) of country A (England). At the risk of seeming repetitive, I would like to emphasize that the Nihonjinron I am addressing here is of a different nature; it is a mechanism to subdue and dispel the anxiety of identity regarding Japan's status as "an outsider in the so-called 'Western' modern era". It refers to discourse on the historical distinctiveness that Japan came to bear within modern civilization, discourse written and read by authors and readers who perceived Japan's distinctiveness as a significant problem, whether consciously or unconsciously.

There are people who liken the act of writing and reading Nihonjinron to narcissism, but I would not agree. I am not trying to suggest that it is not narcissistic because it is not always conceited and is even in some cases somewhat masochistic. The anxiety of identity of being Japanese that I refer to here decisively influences the value of "modernization" that oneself and the Japanese society have pursued until now and is therefore in demand of explanation. If modernization is not worth the efforts of oneself and the Japanese society, it will become a meaningless endeavor, and if its objectives do not suit the conditions inherent to Japan, it will lead to mistaken actions. It is therefore not a simplistic discourse engrossed in one's appearance.

The very problems that Nihonjinron deals with are not unique to Japan alone. While the way these problems manifest themselves is clearly particular of Japan, their essence is a universal matter lurking in modernization. When a non-Western society attempts modernization, the problems corresponding to such an anxiety always arise in their individual form for the people of this society. I think that for instance the "fundamentalist movements" of the modern Muslim societies share the same roots with the long-suffered problem of the anxiety of the "Japanese identity". That is, these are movements that aim to construct a new historical identity of Muslims in the process of modernization and that are marked by "anxiety". As Japan was for a long time the only society to achieve modernization outside the West, Nihonjinron addressed the problem of identity that emerged in the process of trying to accomplish modernization earlier than many other non-Western countries. Given this discourse's attempts to seek ways to determine what one's existence means, it has important implications for the societies that are undergoing similar historical experiences.

Let us consider the significance of the appearance of new Nihonjinron works in the future, which will in turn indicate fundamental changes in the approaches to Nihonjinron. The Nihonjinron of the future will not be aimed at dispelling the anxiety of identity of being Japanese. The Japanese will be freed from the anxiety regarding their existence inside the modernity. This means there will be a transformation in not only Nihonjinron itself, but also among the Japanese people who constitute the object of its discussion. I would like to conclude this book by providing an explanation of how such transformations will take place. To do this I will look back at how the Japanese have been portrayed in previous Nihonjinron works. I will also touch upon the extent to which the models of the Japanese that were proposed in the postwar Nihonjinron – such as the subjects (*shinmin*) and the craftsmen (*shokunin*) – are either still applicable or outdated. I will then discuss whether or not Japan is now seeing the appearance of "Japanese who do not need Nihonjinron".

Sōseki and the Japanese for Nihonjinron

One element of postwar Nihonjinron that I find quite strange is the popularity of Sōseki. Many people cite Sōseki. References to his works can be found in *'Amae' no Kōzō* ("The Anatomy of Dependence") by Takeo Doi, *Nihon-jin to yudaya-jin* ("The Japanese and the Jews") by

Isaiah Ben-Dasan, and, among the recent works, in *'Seken' to ha Nani ka* ("What is 'Seken?'"") by Kin'ya Abe. In fact, *The Chrysanthemum and the Sword* by Ruth Benedict, the first postwar Nihonjinron, cites a passage from Sōseki's *Botchan*. She recollects that Botchan worries about and tries to give back one and a half *sen* that he borrowed from his colleague Yama Arashi while not bothering about three yen from Kiyo, a maidservant who has taken care of him since he was little. This fits in perfectly with the feeling of "owing" (*on*) that we still possess a hundred years later. Having introduced this example, Benedict writes that "painful vulnerability" akin to that of Botchan's "occurs in American records of adolescent gangs and in case-histories of people suffering from nervous disorders" (Benedict 2006(1946): 108). She very shrewdly notes that in the case of the money received from Kiyo, since it is a situation involving a person who is clearly in a lower position as one's own servant and who "is fixed inside" the narrator's "hierarchal scheme" (Benedict 2006(1946): 109), the Japanese would pay no attention to this kind of indebtedness. A quarter of a century later, Doi drew upon the very same passage and made similar arguments, albeit in different words (Doi 2001a(1971): 124-127).

The fact that Sōseki is cited so frequently can perhaps be explained by the fact that his works are considered effective reference sources because they are so widely read. However, it is likely that an even greater reason is that the present-day life of the Japanese, even over one hundred years later, had or has not yet changed much from the descriptions found in Sōseki's novels.

Yet I am not fully convinced. While there are things that have not changed, aren't there things that have undergone transformations? Perhaps Nihonjinron is insensitive towards such things? It may sound strange to say it, but since Sōseki is cited that much, it is as if there is a game called "Nihonjinron" in which players are supplied with Sōseki's works as materials, and set the task of solving what it means to be Japanese using those materials. For instance, Sōseki's novels would not be of much help when contemplating women. The women he portrays are undeniably the women as seen by the men from the outside. To begin with, women have not been illustrated as leading characters in the Nihonjinron today, as if it was deemed sufficient to only theorize about men. Even in the *The Anatomy of Dependence*, while the "man" is described as being "spoiled", the "woman" who spoils him is left without attention. Doi's discussion about homosexuality also subconsciously refers only to relationships between two men and shows no interest towards lesbian relationships. This is possibly to do with the fact that there are not many women among the authors of Nihonjinron, as noted above.

What I would like to highlight here is not that everybody refers to Sōseki, or the same passage of the same novel at that. As I also utilized Sōseki's work in the discussion on the "people" (*kokumin*) in Chapter 5 to exemplify the uplift in the people's feelings toward the Russo-Japanese War, it is evident that Sōseki's portrayals of Japanese people give us certain hints. However, I would now like to focus not on the Japanese whom we can understand through Sōseki's novels, but on the fact that there must be Japanese in the modern-day Japan who we are no longer able to understand by applying Sōseki's works.

After all, when we attempt to capture "the Japanese" as a "whole", we naturally imagine a group of people, a community continuing along the axis of time. We look for the distinguishing features of the Japanese in the unchanged parts of the time flow of the modern age. As a result, we are left with the suspicion that rather than being limited to Sōseki, Nihonjinron is in fact creating something equivalent to "the Japanese for Nihonjinron".

For instance, the "limitations of the Japanese" has become a popular topic for dinner table debate since the collapse of the bubble economy. On such occasions there are people who highlight the fact that Westerners are a hunting people and the Japanese are an agricultural people, and insist that the latter have no aptitude for wars or aggressive competition in business. It is easy to dispute this by questioning up until what point the people of the West were hunters or remembering that until more recent history the Japanese were considered to be belligerent *samurais*. Nevertheless, this kind of rhetoric is still persistent. The discussion on the Japanese therefore slips into gossip about scandals in politics followed by breaches of the rules of logic where types of the Japanese people that correspond to the earlier arguments are brought in post factum. Of course the participants of the discussion remain unaware of this. Meanwhile, a few stereotypes of "the Japanese for Nihonjinron" take shape.

I wrote in the text of the *Human Lectures* television series for NHK in 2002 that I would like to turn Nihonjinron into a "public property". I expressed my wish for outstanding Nihonjinron theories to not be forgotten or labelled "outdated" but to be critically examined and carried on to form a common foundation for discussing the Japanese people. To distinguish this new branch of thought from Nihonjinron, I suggested calling it "Nihonjinron for the Japanese". It is likely that in transforming from a "mass consumption commodity" into a "public property", Nihonjinron will unavoidably become one of the political disputes. If this is the case, since there is no such specialization as Nihonjinron and since for everyone it is an avocation outside one's primary occupation, it becomes necessary to address it as "Nihonjinron for the Japanese" without shirking the political nature of it. This does not mean that it only concerns politics and there is no room for leisurely talk on *wabi*, *sabi*, and *iki*. For instance, even such a book as *Koji Junrei* ("Pilgrimages to the Ancient Temples in Nara") (1919) by Tetsurō Watsuji (the author of *Fūdo* ["Climate"]), which is seen as a discussion of the world of "beauty" (*bi*) detached from the political dimension, contemplates the future of Japan, a political issue crucial for everyone, by interpreting Japan's past and reconfirming its present.

Just as the image of the Japanese presented in Nihonjinron is frequently that of the Japanese from Sōseki's novels, perhaps we have emerged as the Japanese made up of the "unpleasant aspects" that we discover inside ourselves. Of course, it is impossible to properly theorize on the Japanese, as it would likewise be in the case that we had gathered together only very positive aspects. The form of the new "Nihonjinron for the Japanese" – in which the past Nihonjinron will be modified into public property – will depend on how "the Japanese" are perceived. We must start by stepping away from "the Japanese for Nihonjinron", and consider where we can find the Japanese that we can employ as a topic of discussion.

The Current State of the Postwar Model of Nihonjinron

Here I would like to think about how the models of being Japanese that were put forward in the postwar Nihonjinron – the "subjects", "people", "citizens", "craftsmen", "mothers", *geisha*, *samurai*, "salarymen", and "human beings" discussed in Part 2 of this book – are lived by the present day Japanese, and the transformations that they have undergone.

I wonder if it would be surprising if I said that the "subjects" (*shinmin*) still live among us. It must be admitted that the "subjects of the emperor" (*tennō no shinmin*) that I described in Chapter 4 have undergone tremendous changes. However, the model of "MacArthur's subjects" is still alive, overlapping with the tide of populism.

I believe that the emperor system of the modern age continued for one hundred and twenty years and ended with Hirohito's passing. Hirohito became an emperor under the Meiji Constitution, and had his status redefined by a new constitution after Japan's defeat in 1945, in his twentieth year as emperor. However, since the emperor's power as military commander-in-chief and other shortcomings present in the system of the constitutional monarchy of the Meiji Constitution were eliminated, the forty years following the end of the war were favorable times for Hirohito as a "monarch". For him, the forty years after the war were a culmination of the three eras – Meiji, Taishō, and Shōwa – a culmination that turned defeat all the more to the advantage of the imperial family and ensured it the possibility of maintaining a crucial position inside Japan's system.

The affiliation with the people created a new level of connection between the Emperor and his subjects, different from the relationship between the state and the people. It happened regardless of Japan's defeat in the Second World War. However, it is impossible to state with certainty that the current Emperor envisages an extension of the modern-age monarchy that emerged as a result of the three aforementioned eras. Much less, it is hard to imagine that the relationship between the emperor and his subjects that was in place until Hirohito's reign will continue without change under the present Crown Prince and his successors.

In this case the relationship between the emperor and his subjects alludes to a situation where the emperor is positioned at the top and the rest line up in one line as his "subjects". One should imagine the emperor making a balcony appearance and the people greeting him by waving the national flag and giving three cheers of *banzai*. In Chapter 4 I explained that it was actually after the enactment of the Shōwa Constitution that the relationship where one would voluntarily, rather than forcedly, wave the national flag and cheer *banzai* took complete shape "for the first time". It is conceivable that people like this will always exist. They are comparable, for instance, to British people who feel similar fondness towards the British royal family. However, the interest and devotion that these "emperor's subjects" – regardless of their numbers – have towards the emperor and his family is more in line with sentiment generated by mass-media and journalism than strong right-wing ideology. It is also a fact that apart from this consciousness as subjects, the emperor's "cultural" authority, which stretches beyond a thousand years and has this country's ancient literary and performing arts as the apogee of culture, continues to live within people's minds.

Yet, here we have to consider another kind of "subject", namely, "MacArthur's subjects". There is still a deeply-rooted mentality of devotion towards an absolute authority at times of change, which becomes a significant factor when revealing one's political standing in conjunction with the model of the people that is discussed below. In Chapter 5 I noted that after recession began to develop in Japan in the 1990s, there was little response to the Japanese leadership's attempts to address the crisis by drumming up a sense of awareness among the people of their responsibilities as the "people" (*kokumin*) of Japan, and instead people tended to see themselves as "subjects" (*shinmin*), as reflected in the popularity of former Prime Minister Koizumi and the great anticipation for him to take bold actions on their behalf. To briefly elaborate, this means that while discussion surrounding the theory of the state is flourishing and is gradually gaining more momentum, both from a conservative or a reformist perspective, discussion on the theory of "the people" is yet to get in swing.

If we look at these factors together, we can see that while the "theory of the state" that is related to a state that does something for its people is popular, and incorporates people's consciousness as subjects, it is not a discussion about state sovereignty, the question of entity in world politics, or about the people that move it forward. The interest is focused on the state as the "infrastructure of living environment" which includes national debt, pension, and roads. Of course, this kind of infrastructure is the state itself. Yet, there is no sincere interest about the characteristics of the people who set it in motion. This is a deep and substantial problem that requires a separate discussion, but I can say here with certainty that the ability to associate oneself with the model of the "people" is disappearing in a loophole that has repentance for the pre-Second World War "nationalism" on the one side, and the postwar "free" view of life in which one perceives oneself as an "individual character that is precious to oneself" on the other.

The model of the "citizens" addressed in the next section can be considered to have reached every part of the society and achieved its realization if it implies people engaged in "civic activities". Civic activities – from grass-roots political efforts to NPO activism – have swiftly become a familiar part of our lives; I have been involved in them myself. However, they differ from what being a citizen means in the sense of the Western model. While there are differences across countries, the "citizen" concept in Japan is not associated with the historical connotations seen in the West such as the facts that the status as "citizens" was gained in the struggle with the former ruling class of aristocracy or that being a "citizen" in a civic society is still regarded as a certain "privilege". A citizen in Japan is living not in the "society", but in the *seken* (one's social milieu). The term "citizen" in Japan is perceived and used as a synonym of "commoner". The inverted commas around "citizen" will not come off that easily.

However, when seeking ways to adjust the word "citizen" (*shimin*) to the Western model, we realize that the "citizen" model, while not without deviations, is becoming the model of being Japanese in the 21st century. This word is, "for the time being", used as the opposite of the "people" (*kokumin*), creating an ambiguity that is a truly Japanese postwar phenomenon. However, in the near future it will become necessary when debating revisions to the constitution or in other such cases to clarify whether or not a "citizen" appearing in the realm of civic activities in Japan simultaneously refers to any national. It will be interesting to see what kind of transformation *seken* will undergo at that time.

The way of life of craftsmen is still a valuable philosophy – or as one might even say, an ideal – for the Japanese society and the Japanese. In the times of economic malaise that Japan is currently experiencing, there is an ever growing appreciation of the traits of craftsmen, especially in relation to industrial manufacturing. As I explained in Chapter 10, the powerful effect of the craftsman model is strongly connected to the fact that the Japanese do not have an existential model of God or a religious outlook that determines values by means of words and governs people's lives. In the human society up to now, especially at the stage of agricultural civilization, both the worldly matters and those transcending it have been governed by religion. When this function performed by religion weakened in the Japanese society during the Edo period and when secularism became the foundation of life, beliefs associated with the existence of an afterlife receded, and people's immediate surroundings and tangible objects filled in the blanks they left. This also links to the concept of "human beings" addressed in Chapter 10, suggesting an outlook on life that one's surroundings and surrounding things are the bedrock of the human world that one cannot fall below, and that as long as this basis is solid, there is no risk of one's life or economy falling apart. Can this be called a belief functioning in place of religion? To compensate for the firm ground, there is also a ceiling, akin to a glass ceiling that stops words and concepts from soaring high in the sky.

Does the "craftsman" model also hold significance for the present younger generation? A "down-to-earth life" of craftsmanship seems to be far from the worldview of the current youth. Yet I do not believe it to be this way. There is a direct relationship between the tradition of craftsmanship and the attachment to tangible objects observed in Japanese consumer behavior today. Japan will continue to support the "craftsman" model that passes the love of objects and ingenuity to the next generation through the objects it crafts.

The models of a mother and *geisha*, or "women that provide care", seem to have remained unchanged, at least in the eyes of men. It even looks as if the demand for such care has increased. Does this not contradict with the establishment of feminism in society? This can be illustrated by borrowing the concept of "dependence" (*amae*) or referring to the strong relationship of interdependence between a mother and a child in modern Japan and the positioning of a child within a family expressed by the term "parasite single". However, here I would like to think about *geisha* and *samurai*. Namely, I would like to address how the Japanese are seen in the eyes of foreigners.

It is likely that nowadays Americans, Europeans, and other foreigners are unable to form an image of the Japanese. It seems that since Japan's defeat in the Second World War, the postwar Japanese have carried out various activities with their faces concealed. While the pre-war military Japan had a clear image, the postwar economic Japan does not have a visible face. Since postwar Japan has been avoiding various criticisms and offering up "things" (manufactured products) overseas rather than revealing "a human face", it has turned into a creature with a flat, featureless face. When living in the West one would be surprised how little information there is about Japan; yet, it is even more surprising that ordinary Western people do not have enough of an "image of Japan" to picture it concretely, having put the information about Japan together. While Japanese products are known, the Japanese people are not.

This therefore means that the images of *samurai* and *geisha* are still prevalent. However, this is the same as seeing Americans as cowboys. It is superficial and unrealistic. When identifying Americans as "cowboys" one is still able to have in mind a particular American as a concrete expression of this symbolism; yet it is likely that since the war there is little concrete information outside of Japan about real Japanese people that could be applied to such symbols as that of a *samurai*.

The model of a "human being" is a potent one. It was brought about and strengthened over the two hundred years of the Edo period. In all likelihood, this model has deeper roots that date back to an earlier period, but an important driving force in finalizing its establishment was the secularization of religion in the Edo period. It even has Western "humanism" flowing through it. Similar to the new Japanese religious doctrines that are created through a mixture of Buddhism, Shinto, and Christianity, this definition of "human beings" seems to be a pure concept related to the idea of naked existence, equipped with the basic conditions for surviving, while in fact it is a philosophical construct with strong defenses that owes its state as a sound, unbreakable "original image" to the synthesis of various "ideas" that entered the archipelago.

The model and concept of a "human being" still possess strong value nowadays. When one does not believe in the transcendental world, the only value is to continue living, and being a "human being" presently existing in this world becomes the foundation for various judgments. It functions as a line of defense drawn in advance that acts as point from which to recover when everything is lost. Together with the "subjects' democracy", this model played a major role in Japan's reconstruction following the Second World War, in which no matter the losses, people felt no hesitation or strong sense of deprivation in regards to restarting from this line at which being a "human being" is the foundation for judgments. The Japanese people, who were at the lowest points of their lives after the war, were fully determined to make that line their point of departure.

Shiba's Dilemma and the Japanese of the Future

In order to think about Nihonjinron for the Japanese of the future, I would like to once again discuss the problem repeatedly brought up by Ryōtarō Shiba, namely the question why the Japan that was in a sound condition until the Russo-Japanese War produced the forty terrible years that Shiba likened to a "monster", a period that ended with Japan's defeat in World War Two. In Chapter 5 I addressed this by focusing on the "dropouts" portrayed by Sōseki as well as the readers of his works. I also wrote that the people who assumed the burden of those terrible forty years faced the challenge of finding a new concept and direction for the further modernization of the inner aspects of Japanese society – a departure from the ideas of the previous forty years after the Meiji Restoration – but failed to accomplish this task, and it remains unsolved today. What is then the reason that, instead of being unable to solve this, they ended up turning the following forty years into something resembling a "monster"?

I understand it in the following way. Let us call Yukichi Fukuzawa and the founders of the Meiji government the first generation of Meiji. The second generation would then consist of the pure elites they educated, Nitobe and Uchimura, and the people described by Shiba in *Saka no ue no Kumo* ("Clouds above the Hill"). The first forty years of Meiji were created by these two generations. Their efforts and deeds need not many words. While whether the state was in a sound condition is a matter to be judged separately, what they did represents a success story, their efforts being rewarded. These two generations of Meiji adopted enlightenment as well as wealth and military strength as a national course, making the revision of the unequal treaties and recognition as an independent modern state their immediate goals. This was accomplished through the victories in the First Sino-Japanese War and the Russo-Japanese War and the signing of the Anglo-Japanese Alliance. The generation that came into the world created by such people in the Meiji period and was educated and entered society following the victory in the Russo-Japanese War, in other words, the generation of people like Sōseki's protagonist Sanshirō were the ones who shouldered those forty "monstrous" years.

The reason why these years turned into a "monstrous" period lies with the qualities of the people that were to carry its burden. It may be possible to determine their qualities by looking at by whom and how they were brought up.

The first and second generation that mentored them enlightened Japan and turned it into a country superior to the other countries of Asia. They raised Japan to the level of a strong global power ranking among the countries led by white people. They took pride in being different from China and Joseon and held a spirit of self-respect in believing that there was no need to be outdone by white people. This generation took solace in the fact that the subsequent generation would not have to start from the low position of having to fight the unequal treaties and was contented that they would be superior to Asia from the onset, without having to feel inferior towards the West. It was their dream to produce a generation that would not have to live under the unfavorable conditions that they themselves were burdened by, a generation that, as the people of a first-class global power, could live without experiencing a sense of inferiority towards anyone, and this dream did in fact become reality. They educated the third generation and the youth to follow by teaching them that it was acceptable to feel pride and self-respect and that the sufficient groundwork to achieve this had been prepared. As a result, the people who bore those forty "monstrous" years matured as a generation who received a green flag from their predecessors.

When one thinks that this generation was born during the sound forty years of Meiji and acted in accordance with the upbringing and teachings they received from the people who created those sound forty years, it does not seem strange that their pride transformed into a contempt towards Asia and they persisted in taking a strong attitude with no sign of weakness in diplomatic affairs and war against the West. It is perhaps possible to draw on evidence to theorize on the historical factors of Japan's pitiful defeat in 1945 or on the points in time and judgments that led to the irremediable mistakes. The answer I put forward to "Shiba's dilemma" is not a critical analysis of the decisions and actions of the people who shouldered the forty "monstrous" years. The leaders and many people who made such misjudgments were the people who had been destined to be born as "the Japanese" during the sound Meiji period.

Let me try to apply this vision to the present. During the forty years after the war, Japan's ideals were freedom, democracy, and peace. In terms of the country models introduced earlier, it sought to be "international Japan". To break the model down further, it means that people lead their lives freely and create lifestyles based on their individuality. Social class disparities are eliminated under democracy and social equality is achieved between men and women. Finally, the people devote themselves to peace and make it the ultimate value.

This was the aim of both the first generation that was active from before the war and bore its outcome, having deeply repented the pre-war times, and the second generation that became the vanguard of the postwar restoration and uplift. The Japanese people who would take responsibility for the upcoming decades were born during the forty postwar years, raised and taught in the spirit of their ideals. From my personal experience of over thirty years as an educator inside Japan, I see this post-bubble third generation that will shoulder the future of Japan for a few decades from now on as fulfilling the expectations of the postwar Japanese. They have been granted freedom by their parents and told to develop their individuality, becoming competent not only in their studies but also in "cultural" activities such as music and sports. They detest the idea of displaying superiority over others and are receptive towards the idea of equality among men and women. They believe in peace and that fighting and discord should be avoided by all means. The Japanese of the future are the embodiment of these ideas. The postwar dream is realized through them.

These young people refuse to understand that freedom exists within the limitations of certain conditions, believing that free expression of individuality means living as one likes. They use the ideals of equality to justify avoiding the responsibility of having to manage other people, and in order to materialize "peace" on an individual level, they minimize their relationships and discord with other people as much as possible, and in extreme cases withdraw themselves completely from society. Yet, none of these approaches seem strange when we consider that this generation is acting in accordance with how they were raised and what they were taught. I am not writing this pessimistically as a warning that another "forty monstrous years" are about to start. I am only saying that the generation raised in the forty years after the war is the embodiment of the postwar dream, entrusted with the mission of taking the lead in the new age, and by no means the entirely unwanted children of the "monster". This new generation is both a continuation of the previous one and at the same time completely severed from it.

From my perspective, it is likely that the Japan created by such a generation will gradually lose its features as Japan. The transformation of the sense of nationhood will take place whether it becomes a society made of a group of "individuals" whose only aspiration towards the state is to have infrastructure provided, or a society marked by an externally weakened sense of nationhood in terms of awareness and institutions beyond national borders. When thinking about this generation one can see that such questions as whether Nihonjinron will change and whether Nihonjinron for the Japanese will replace it are related to the hypothesis on Nihonjinron, the "anxiety of identity". It has to do with whether the future Japanese will experience the anxiety of being of alien descent inside the Western modernity. To give a familiar example, it links to whether one is traumatized by the difficulties associated with verbal and bodily communication when studying abroad. My observations have shown that these are becoming less of a problem. Should the future Nihonjinron address the current generation, it will be a discourse of a transformed nature. I already mentioned that the phenomena of *geisha* and *samurai* have reached their expiry dates. New stereotypical aspects of Japanese culture – such as *otaku* (nerds or geeks; people with obsessive interests, typically in anime, manga, and video games) – have developed to take their place. While terms such as *otaku* are ambiguous and encompass an excessively broad range of meanings, they are gradually gaining recognition in the world as the expressions produced by Japan's new generation and as the words describing its representatives. The difference between *otaku* and *samurai* and *geisha* is that *samurai* and *geisha* refer to the realities of Japan's pre-modern system and are images that were developed inside the orientalist gaze, while *otaku* was born in the modern age itself. *Otaku* is an expression of another modernity, different from that of the West, a "hybrid" that takes its roots in the modern times of both Japan and the West. Being a modern-era "hybrid" protects one from the anxiety of not being a descent of the Western modernity and simultaneously of stepping too far away from Japan and Asia. Identity is after all a result of interaction between the person and the society surrounding him or her. As a result of the *otaku* culture and the culture of clothing, food, and housing related to the physicality of the Japanese people gaining acceptance in the West, the gaze from outside has changed, further transforming the way the Japanese people, the recipients of this new gaze, look at themselves. The identity of the Japanese by *otaku* has firmly entered the age of transformation.

I feel it is difficult to proceed with the argument that the Japanese people, rather than Nihonjinron, will transform. When a certain individual lives as part of a society that is becoming increasingly pluralistic, their experiences are likely to become "multilayered". "Multilayered" refers to being a man or a woman of a certain religion, political conviction, and cultural affiliation, and living in a world of relationships created by family, friendships, workplace connections, and networks one is a part of voluntarily. Being a Japanese national, a Japanese person, constitutes one of the layers. If that is the case, it does not mean that when an individual speaks about oneself, they necessarily start by mentioning being Japanese, followed by other attributes. If I do not feel "fascination" with the narrative on Japan, my story will not involve saying "I, a Japanese". It is impossible to perceive such an individual in terms of the kind of Japanese person he represents, where being "a Japanese" comes as the very first characteristic. At this point it becomes clear that the necessity of Nihonjinron and the importance of Nihonjinron for the Japanese are waning. This is what I mean by suggesting that the argument about the Japanese is difficult.

Moreover, each of the layers is undergoing changes. Being a Japanese, a farmer, a Buddhist, serving an important role at Shinto festivities, being a husband and a father does not indicate that one is an "ordinary person" as depicted by Yanagita. The farming may be to deliver vegetables to an Italian restaurant, the religion may be a new Buddhist denomination, the work at festivities may have to do with promoting tourism, the wife may be a foreigner, and the children may all have left home. Then, having a foreign wife may be changing the person's characteristics as a Japanese and the Buddhist sect may be granting him with a network that transcends the area he lives in.

When a society is pluralistic and an individual's world is multilayered, it does not merely mean that the number of constituting elements increases. It means that the constituents of the society and the world one lives in intermingle in a complex way, giving way to changes. The increase of foreigners inside the Japanese society does not indicate that the black (the Japanese) and the white (foreigners) pieces run together but that the white constituents penetrate the black pieces and the black constituents penetrate the white ones, leading to chemical reactions that bring about changes. Both the identities of the Japanese and the foreigners transform simultaneously. The "I" and the "Japanese" of the "I am a Japanese" change, yielding the construction of a new meaning of what it is be "a Japanese".

While I am tempted to explain these phenomena using words such as "postmodern" and "globalization," I will refrain from doing so because the anxiety of identity that I explained with the hypothesis on Nihonjinron cannot be easily relieved with words alone. It is expected that "historical aftershocks" – that is, once again experiencing anxiety about one's positioning as Japanese inside the modern age – will occur repeatedly. Particularly when Japan takes a place between Asia and the West in the course of its relationships with Asian countries, it will no doubt experience an identity shift.

Nihonjinron is in its final moments. This is because the sixty postwar years gave rise to a generation that does not feel the anxiety that I illustrated in the hypothesis on Nihonjinron. Such a situation is being witnessed for the first time since the beginning of the Meiji period in the late nineteenth century. It suggests that both "the Japanese" and Nihonjinron have entered a stage of transformation that will stretch across a long period almost as long as the over a century since the Meiji period, a time when Nihonjinron was needed.

Chronological Table of Events Related to "Nihonjinron"

1853   Arrival to Japan of Commodore Matthew Perry.

1858   Treaty of Amity and Commerce Between the United States and the Empire of Japan.

1863   Chōshū clan shoots at the Western ships at Shimonoseki. Anglo-Satsuma War.

1867   Return of the power to the emperor. Order to restore the emperor to power.

1868   Boshin War (until 1869). Oath in Five Articles.

1871   Abolition of the *bakuhan* system. Adoption of the system of prefectures.

1873   Order of mandatory military conscription. Land Tax Reform.

1881   Meiji 14 political crisis.

1887   **Loti, Pierre, *Madame Chrysanthème*.** Translated into Japanese in 1915.

1888   **Miyake, Setsurei, Shiga, Shigetaka** and others publish a journal *Nihonjin* ("The Japanese"). The title changed to *Nihon oyobi Nihonjin* ("Japan and the Japanese") in 1907.

1889   Promulgation of the Constitution of the Empire of Japan (Meiji Constitution).

1890   First meeting of the Japanese parliament.

1894   First Sino-Japanese War (until 1895).
Uchimura, Kanzō, *Representative Men of Japan* (written in English).
Shiga, Shigetaka, *Nihon Fūkeiron* ("The Landscape of Japan").

1898   **Long, John Luther, *Madama Butterfly*.**

1899   **Nitobe, Inazō, *Bushido: The Soul of Japan*** (written in English).

1901   "Yawata Steel Works" begin operations.

1904   Russo-Japanese War (until 1905).
Okakura, Tenshin, *The Awakening of Japan* (written in English).

1905   Treaty of Portsmouth. Japan-Korea Protectorate Treaty.

1906	**Okakura, Tenshin,** *The Book of Tea* (written in English). **Natsume, Sōseki,** *Botchan* **("Botchan") and** *Kusamakura* **("Kusamakura")** are published in a journal.
1908	Serial publication of **Natsume, Sōseki,** *Sanshirō* **("Sanshiro").**
1909	Serial publication of **Natsume, Sōseki,** *Sorekara* **("And Then").**
1910	High Treason Incident. Annexation of Korea. Serial publication of **Natsume, Sōseki,** *Mon* **("The Gate").** **Yanagita, Kunio,** *Tōno Monogatari* **("The Legends of Tono").**
1914	First World War (until 1918). Serial publication of **Natsume, Sōseki,** *Kokoro* **("Kokoro").**
1918	Rice riots. Siberian Intervention.
1923	Great Kantō earthquake.
1925	Public Security Preservation Law. General Election Law.
1930	Lifting of the gold embargo. Shōwa Recession (until 1932). **Kuki, Shūzō,** *'Iki' no Kōzō* **("The Structure of Iki").**
1931	Manchurian Incident. Formation of the Tsuyoshi Inukai Cabinet.
1932	May 15 Incident.
1933	Japan withdraws from the League of Nations. Takigawa Incident.
1935	**Watsuji, Tetsurō,** *Fūdo* **("The Climate").** Serial publication of **Yoshikawa, Eiji,** *Miyamoto Musashi* (until 1939).
1936	February 26 Rebellion. **Taut, Bruno,** *Japanese Arts Seen with European Eyes.*
1937	Second Sino-Japanese War. National Spiritual Mobilization Movement starts. **Yokomitsu, Riichi,** *Ryoshū* **("Melancholy on a Journey").**
1938	First Konoe Statement against Chinese Government. Announcement of National Mobilization Law.
1939	Second World War starts.
1941	Pacific War (until 1945).
1942	**"Bungakukai"** holds the **"Overcoming Modernity"** discussion.
1945	Bombing of Tokyo. Battle of Okinawa.

Atomic bombings of Hiroshima and Nagasaki.
Acceptance of Potsdam Declaration.
1946 Humanity Declaration by the emperor. Promulgation of the
Constitution of Japan.
Benedict, Ruth, *The Chrysanthemum and the Sword*.
Translated into Japanese in 1948.
1951 Treaty of San Francisco. Signing of the Security Treaty
Between the United States and Japan.
1955 Establishment of the Social Party.
Conservation Fusion.
1956 Soviet-Japanese Joint Declaration. Japan joins the
United Nations.
1957 **Umesao, Tadao, *Bunmei no Seitai Shikan Josetsu*
("Civilization from the Perspective of
Ecological History").**
1960 Intensification of opposition to the Treaty of Mutual
Cooperation and Security between the United States and
Japan (from 1959 onwards). Formulation of Income
Doubling Plan. **Miyamoto, Tsuneichi, *Wasurerareta
Nihonjin* ("The Forgotten Japanese").**
**Shindō, Kaneto's movie *Hadaka no Shima* ("The
Naked Island").**
1964 Japan joins OECD. Tokyo Olympic Games.
1965 Treaty on Basic Relations between Japan and Korea.
**Odaka, Kunio, *Nihon no Keiei* ("The
Japanese Management").**
1967 **Nakane, Chie, *Tate Shakai no Ningen Kankei – Tan'itsu
Shakai no Riron* ("Human Relations in Vertical Society:
Theory of a Homogeneous Society").**
**Sakuta, Keiichi, *Haji no Bunka Saikō* ("A Reconsideration
of Shame Culture").**
1971 **Doi, Takeo, *'Amae' no Kōzō* ("The Anatomy
of Dependence").**
**Ben-Dasan, Isaiah, *Nihon-jin to Yudaya-jin* ("The Japanese
and the Jews").**
1972 Okinawa returned to Japan. Improvement of relations between
Japan and China. First oil shock.
1978 Treaty of Peace and Friendship between Japan and China.

	Said, Edward, *Orientalism*. Translated into Japanese in 1986.
1979	Second oil shock. **Vogel, Ezra,** ***Japan as Number One: Lessons for America***. Translated into Japanese the same year.
1986	Serial publication of **Shiba, Ryōtarō's,** ***Kono Kuni no Katachi* ("The Form of this Nation")** commences (until 1996).
1987	**Befu, Harumi,** *Ideorogī toshite no Nihonbunkaron* **("Discourse on the Japanese Culture as an Ideology").**
1989	Malta Summit (between US and USSR). End to the Cold War declared.
1990	East and West Germany reunite.
	Aoki, Tamotsu, *Nihon Bunkaron no Henyō – Sengo Nihon no Bunka to Aidentiti* **("Transformation of the Discourse on Japanese Culture: Postwar Japan's Culture and Identity").**
1991	Gulf War. Collapse of the bubble economy. Dissolution of the Soviet Union.
1992	United Nations Conference on Environment and Development (Earth Summit).
	Abe, Kinya, 1992, *Seiyō Chūsei no Ai to Jinkaku – 'Seken'-ron Josetsu* **("Love and Personality of the Western Middle Age: Introduction to the Theory of 'Seken'").**
1994	**Wolferen, Karel van, 1994,** *Ningen wo Kōfuku ni shinai Nihon toiu Shisutemu* **("The False Realities of a Politicized Society").**
1995	Great Hanshin and Awaji earthquake. Tokyo subway sarin attack.
	Abe, Kinya, 1995, *'Seken' to ha Nani ka* **("What is 'Seken'?").**
	Kishida, Shū, 1998(1995), *Hahaoya Gensō* **("Illusion of Motherhood").**
1996	**Ei, Rokusuke, 1996,** *Shokunin* **("The Craftsmen").**
1997	Governments of Japan and the United States agree on the new Japan-US Guidelines.
	Golden, Arthur, *Memoirs of a Geisha*. Translated into Japanese in 1999.
	Macfarlane, Alan, *The Savage Wars of Peace: England, Japan and the Malthusian Trap*. Translated into Japanese in 2001.

1999   **Dower, Edward,** *Embracing Defeat: Japan in the Wake of World War II*. Translated into Japanese in 2001.

2001   Formation of the Junichirō Koizumi Cabinet.
September 11 attacks in the United States. The United States starts bombing Afghanistan. Establishment of the Anti-Terrorism Special Measures Law.
Abe, Kinya, *Gakumon to 'Seken'* **("Learning and 'Seken'").**
Doi, Takeo, *Zoku 'Amae' no Kōzō* **("Sequel to the Anatomy of Dependence").**

2003   British and US troops invade Iraq. Iraq War.

2007   **Funabiki, Takeo,** *Migi deare Hidari deare Waga Sokoku Nihon* **("My Country Japan Right or Left").**

2009   **Uchida, Tatsuru,** *Nihon Henkyōron,* **("The Discourse on Japan as a Peripheral State").**

Afterword to the Japanese Academic Paperback Edition

After "Exploring the Anxiety of Being Japanese: A New Look at Nihonjinron"

This book is a paperback edition of the monograph published in 2003 by NHK Publishing under the same title. I have not changed the contents. At the end of the book, I noted the following two points.

1) When Japan takes a place between Asia and the West in the course of its relationships with Asian countries, it will no doubt experience an identity shift.

2) Nihonjinron is undergoing its final moments.

Around seven years have passed since that time, but I have not changed my mind. Rather, it seems that the accurateness of these two points is becoming increasingly clear as a result of the internal and external changes that have taken place during these years. In order to clarify this, I will start with a review of Japan from the mid-19ᵗʰ century onwards.

Starting from the times surrounding the Meiji Restoration, Japan set itself out as an "adherent" of the Western civilization, and secured victories in the First Sino-Japanese and the Russo-Japanese wars, becoming a fellow partner of the mighty Western nations. However, from the 1930s, misjudgments of the international situation by Japan's leaders turned it into an "orphan" of international politics, which lead it to a disastrous defeat in the Second World War. It then became America's "adopted child" and, having "appropriated the best" of democracy and capitalism, achieved its second round of success in modernization (westernization). However, amid the reorganization of international power relations and capitalism since around 1990s, the country's national policy and national identity have been unstably fluctuating "between Asia and the West".

It seems that the bewilderment resulting from being positioned in "between Asia and the West" has been deepening increasingly since the time this book was originally published. The mechanism responsible for this is as follows.

As the first to have achieved modernization as a non-Western society, Japan is now attempting to gain independence from it (precisely, from the US), but it has not been able to fully shape an individual image for Japan (or Asia) distinct from the Western modernization. To start with, Japan has not played a proactive role in leading Asian countries after the Second World War. Rather, its intellectuals have been experiencing a sense of affinity towards European culture in terms of polit-ico-philosophical principles while many people have become familiar with American entertainment and sports. However, it would only be a joke to suggest that Japan will actually assimilate with Europe or the USA in the sense of becoming America's fifty-first state or joining the EU. On the other hand, China's rapid rise in prominence, similarly fluc-tuating "between Asia and the West" and sharing the same location with Japan geopolitically, is progressing at a pace that transcends the imagina-tion. This is why Japan is unable to determine its position in Asia. If we attempt to depict the situation using the metaphor I employed earlier, we will have an orphan adopted as a child who, upon becoming inde-pendent from his foster parents (the US), returns home (East Asia) and briefly enjoys superiority and affluence as a top runner of modernization to only be pushed away by the son of the major household (China) who has regained his power, leaving the cousin (Japan) in a situation where his advantage as a returnee from the West is fading day by day.

To put it in concrete terms, Japan is positioned as a nation between the USA and China. While it is said that "better is a stranger that is near than a relative far off", this case is more complex, since after the Second World War Japan has been relying on a stranger that is far off (the USA) rather than a relative that is near (China).

As I have repeatedly emphasized, regardless of whether it has been succeeding or failing in modernization, Japan – as a society that does not belong to the regional history of the West that gave forth to "modernity" – has been doubting its own legitimacy and thus has until now been in need of Nihonjinron in order to explain the anxiety of identity. I think that currently, with its identity as an achiever of Western modernization established, Japan has developed a new form of uneasiness related to its attempts to assume an appropriate status in Asia.

If we adopt the Western modernity as a benchmark, this uneasiness is related to the fact that Japan's levels of achievement and sophistication slightly outrank those of the neighboring Asian countries. The country is in an ironic situation where it has realized that it has been "mod-ernized" to the degree of feeling discomfort when attempting to return from "the West" to "Asia". It occupies a place somewhat ahead of Asia in terms of "modernization", namely, democracy in political governance, individualism in the social system, and creativity in culture. In the genre of Nihonjinron the Japanese are always criticizing themselves by saying that in Japan democracy is not established in everyday society, an individual is not independent in the society, and that the culture is lacking originality, but if viewed by the Western standards or compared to the other Asian countries, Japan is in fact an advanced democratic state, governed by the rule of law, where individual values are recognized and original accomplishments are achieved in science and art.

When traveling around Asia, one can take in the material and physical affinity with Japan in terms of the outward resemblance to the Asians and Asian societies, similarity of clothes, food, and accommodation, and shared bodily sensations resulting from the shared climate. Not to mention that the "uneasiness" experienced in Asia thirty years ago is rapidly fading away in the face of the present-day Asia with its progressing modernization.

Yet, the mind thinks quite differently to the body. This difference can be likened to spending a few days together or having a long-term relationship. The comfortableness upon visiting a "relative" in a rural area does not last long. A long-term relationship with a "stranger" one shares the same views with can be maintained when a certain distance is kept. It depends on the level of cultural and social events and each individual Japanese person whether one would feel most comfortable with the relative that is near (China, Asia) or the stranger that is far off (the USA, the West). It is common to hear Japanese people say such things as "Since I am originally Asian, I am a representative of Asia", but the communality of being "Asian" is not clear from the outset. Amid the harsh political reality and economic competition, the extent to which "Asianness" can support the identity of the Japanese in Asia is disputable.

There are two more peculiar points that have to be taken heed of. Although I just wrote, "the communality of being "Asian" is not clear from the outset", the first point concerns the fact that in East Asia or, more broadly, in the region comprising China and the surrounding countries, the international order of the Imperial Chinese "tributary system" (*sakuhō taisei*) existed for nearly two thousand years until the 19th century. The rising China may recreate a system with China at the center as a 21st-century version of the power relations similar to that of the "tributary system". However – and this is where the second peculiar point comes into play – Japan kept distance from the tributary system at all times due to its nature as an island located somewhat remotely from the continent. This can be likened to how England has kept a certain distance from continental Europe. It is of great significance that during the Qing Dynasty India and Japan, among Asian countries, were not part of its tributary system. In 21st-century Asia, only Japan and India have the potential to conduct diplomatic relations distanced from China. In the course of this conduct, the discomfort towards Asia, in particular the combined feelings of closeness with and repulsion of China, is responsible for destabilizing Japan's identity as a "member of Asia". Looking back on the history, one will see that it is not that Japan has just been passively keeping its distance in terms of diplomacy from China in mainland Asia, but that it has actively created something that could be called an individual civilization at the frontier of Asia. This historical fact is another reason why Japan's position in regards to Asia is neither internal nor external.

I believe that similar to how the uncertainty towards "the West" brought forth Nihonjinron, this situation may trigger the appearance of Nihonjinron of another kind. Japan's success in achieving Western-type modernization as a society belonging to Asian regional history as well as its ability in the earlier times to avoid being subsumed into the Chinese tributary system and to create original culture and society have made it difficult for Japan to fit in Asia; the more the phrases like "as a member of Asia" or "East-Asia community" are exclaimed, the more likely it is that the Nihonjinron explaining the accompanying anxiety will be looming.

Since the publication of this book a few works have appeared in the Nihonjinron genre and I find *Nihon Henkyōron* ("The Discourse on Japan as a Peripheral State") by Tatsuru Uchida (Uchida 2009) particularly interesting. I will save a detailed discussion of it for another occasion, but as one can see from the book's title, its discourse that positions Japan on a periphery and starts its arguments from there is more focused on the "Asian" element in comparison with earlier Nihonjinron. While the following comparison may be uncalled for, it shares a similar standpoint with *Migi deare Hidari deare Waga Sokoku Nihon* ("My Country Japan Right or Left") (Funabiki 2007). More specifically, it concerns the awareness that Japan's geopolitical standing in Asia and the identity of the Japanese people overlap and constitute a problem amidst the transformation of Japan and the world around it, with three occurrences before and after 1990 – the end of the Cold War, the Gulf War, and the collapse of the bubble – as a starting point. On a general level, the contemporary fact that the "Japanese style" is enjoying a boom in popularity among the Japanese themselves is connected to them perceiving it as a means of securing individuality while remaining a member of Asia, as opposed to the initial concept of the "Japanese style" antagonistic to the West (as it is seen, for example, in *'Iki' no Kōzō* ["The Structure of Iki"]).

If Nihonjinron that explains anxiety towards not the West but Asia has emerged, is it wrong to claim that Nihonjinron is "undergoing its final moments"? That does not seem likely.

While a new Nihonjinron is being produced, there are many young Japanese who are not in need of Nihonjinron, as I mentioned in the concluding part of this book. There are also more grounds to address this kind of people and the society not as Nihonjinron but as "Nihonjinron for the Japanese". These grounds are "glocalization", rather than "globalization", where the local, provoked by and in response to the global motion, simultaneously exerts its individuality and becomes localized and established. There is an increasingly established way of thinking in which Japan is perceived as part of the world, neither as a peripheral state nor as occupying a central place, but as holding a "certain station" on the globe. Naturally, it will take time for the Japanese to free themselves from the way of thinking in which Japan is seen "in contrast" to some other location. It is because the way of doing things that was created in this way is filled with the advantages and virtues of modern Japan as it is. The advantages are the extension of the weaknesses. If the weaknesses are thrown away, the virtues too will vanish. As the wisdom of the society and culture cannot be "reshuffled" like playing cards, the transformation takes place slowly from the front, leaving a long-lasting tail behind.

The length of these traces will most likely exceed a few decades or one or two generations. This is due to the indispensable role of Nihonjinron as the stabilizer of the modernization of Japan. Whether it took the form of a cheerleading song or a requiem, in the end it has been sung in support of nationalism. Its ceasing to be recited is not only to do with how Japan will change, but also with the fact that modern "nationalism" itself as seen from the global perspective will start transforming. Further, in Japan's individual circumstances, the problem can be formulated as the Japanese liberating themselves from the view on Japan and the Nihonjinron constructed in "opposition to the West" or in the newly-emerging "opposition to Asia". If the period from Meiji and until the 1990s is the formative period of Japan's nationalism that deemed Nihonjinron necessary, I believe that approximately the same period of time, precisely until the end of the 21st century, may be needed for the transformation into a "Japan" free of Nihonjinron to take place.

Of course, it is not possible to calculate precisely how long will be needed. It might take much longer than that. This is rooted in the fact that for the country to become the "Japan that does not need Nihonjinron" means, from the current view, that Japan needs "to stop being Japan". Transformation of such magnitude is unlikely to lead to a tranquil state where the country would be "reborn as a better Japan". Nihonjinron will disappear when, as a result of endless debates suggesting that "there is no need to become such a 'Japan'" or "in such a case Japan would stop being Japan, so this is not something the Japanese have to think about", this land returns to being an archipelago in East Asia where the Japanese language is most likely used but that is no longer "Japan" and that is no longer populated only by "the Japanese". Until we reach that state, we will engage not merely in Nihonjinron but in discussions about Japan and discussions about the Japanese.

Takeo Funabiki
March 2010

Afterword to the English Edition

The utmost forms of pride and prejudice are born inside the current Nihonjinron – the discourse on the Japanese. Pride is expressed in the titles of books that glorify Japan (*Nihon Raisan*), and prejudice dominates the titles of books that promote sentiments that are anti-Korean (*Kenkan*) or anti-Chinese (*Kenchū*). In large bookstores these days, one finds displayed piles of books belonging to these two preposterous genres. Over the last ten years, not only books have been produced but also television programs and websites, all of which sing Japan's praises as an expression of pride. Meanwhile, special journal issues have appeared in which – as an expression of prejudice – Korea and China have been viewed with deep hostility. There have been cases of hate speech towards Koreans residing in Japan and towards Koreans and Chinese people in general. Although I have not authored any such books, I am embarrassed even to utter their titles. Yet I will mention a few here for the sake of example. Books such as *Why is Japan the Most Popular Country in the World?* and *My Experience of Living in Europe: Japan Wins 9 to 1* go out of their way to extol Japan. Books like *I am Glad I Was Not Born Korean* practically choke on their own hatred. Citing more titles would be unbearable to me.

The contents of such books cannot really be called fake. Rather, they merely repeat things that have often been narrated. Books that extol pride in Japan deal with topics such as the country's beauty, its artisanship, and the spiritual nature concealed within its material world. None of these topics is new. In 2017 a pamphlet was published by the Ministry of Economy, Trade and Industry called *Nippon that Astonishes the World*, providing a comprehensive collection of such works. Disputes were aired in the mass media about whether this collection should see the light of day, but the problem was not factual mistakes. The pamphlet presents a series of examples that evoke strong feelings of déjà vu and its shallowness makes one flinch. For readers familiar with Japanese history, this collection is reminiscent of the journal *NIPPON*, published in 1935 by the contemporary government as propaganda about Japan's imperial ambitions. Nearly 100 years have passed but the objects of praise remain intact. There is a reason for this.

Whether called *Nippon (*spelt in *katakana)* or *NIPPON* (spelt in alphabet), what is being praised is tradition that lies at the foundation of national identity. If tradition was "invented" at the Japanese archipelago, it is no wonder that the reinvented "tradition" would be the same. The available materials are limited to a few thousand years of history.

Prejudice is aimed at Korea and China. The content of this prejudice is again nothing new. Its main sentiment is that these two countries are essentially inferior to Japan. This is practically the same as the pre-war contempt that was expressed towards the Korean Peninsula and China. To thinly disguise this prejudice, the modern-day narratives promote the premise that pre-war Japan in fact helped to modernize the colonized Korea and occupied China. This is a common discourse among the world's former colonizing powers, built on the idea that colonization had its advantages.

Readers are surely familiar with these narratives pertaining to the discussion on modernization. The reason I allude to them here, in the context of Japan's present-day "pride and prejudice," is that such ideas are deeply connected with the subject of anxiety which I explored in this book. I argued that in the course of modernization following the Meiji Restoration, Japan's ability to become modernized was questioned. The anxiety of being Japanese surfaced regardless of the country's success or failure in pursuing modernity. To address these questions and anxieties, Nihonjinron has been written and widely read. In the book's final chapter, I showed how Japan's success in achieving western modernity destabilized its identity as an Asian country, leading to another type of anxiety. I expanded on this hypothesis in the book's "Afterword to the academic paperback edition". This forecast, if I may call it that, has been alarmingly accurate. Yet, I never thought that the public sentiments I described would give rise to the titles so reminiscent of the hyperbolized pride and prejudice of the country's pre-war militarism.

Perhaps I can say the following. Nihonjinron has a two-layered structure. The upper layer relates to the discourses on Japan's culture and society, while the lower layer deals with politics. Until now, what I have called "anxiety" is part of a political discourse that employs notions such as ethos and ideology, and is not devoid of an emotional component. At first glance, Nihonjinron looks fairly unthreatening as it focuses on culture and societal relations; nonetheless, its virtual purpose is political. The notion that Japan was in need of "political direction" in the relevant historical periods is always closely connected to political discourses. As such, Nihonjinron is not a mass consumption product that can vanish upon consumption. Unable to be consumed, it will result in unresolved problems until it is dismantled at some point in time.

I would like readers to pay attention to what is about to be mentioned. The significance of the discussion I have presented in this book has to do with the following argument. Today's accounts of praise or hatred were generated within the structure of anxiety that arose through post-Meiji modernization. Although its object has changed from the West to East Asia, the mechanisms underpinning this anxiety remain unchanged. Current catch-phrases such as "declining birth rates" and "rise of China" are in fact not new; they echo the themes of "backward agricultural society" and "threat from the great powers of the West" that occupied the minds of Japan's elites 150 years ago.

In reality the contents of these books of appraisal or animosity are not as extreme as their titles suggest. This trick is nothing but extravagant advertising, common among works that are made to appear sensational when in fact they lack any novelty. Perhaps, the inability to produce content that conveys sufficient self-conceit or satisfactory resentment is the result of a sort of self-discipline, developed as a by-product of never-ending cultural anxiety. Even if such books sell hundreds of thousands of copies, stereotyping and lack of substance in their contents soon leads to their being replaced by other similar works. But we should not forget that at its foundation, Nihonjinron contains a political statement. When and if a political incident involving some type of war suddenly happens against the backdrop of 21st century politics – particularly in the East-Asian geopolitical environment, Nihonjinron might just reach the level of utter self-conceit and hatred. This would result in actual harm being done to the country's political course through the ripening of radical trends.

Truth be told, we should be even more concerned about the possible emergence of a more sharp-witted Nihonjinron. The roundtable "Overcoming Modernity", discussed in Chapter 3 of my book, conveys a mood of skepticism and melancholy. The anxiety which Nihonjinron displays towards the West clearly functions as a limiting force that prevents the spontaneous ignition of total self-conceit. However, would anxiety towards Asia produce similar effects of self-restraint in relation to Nihonjinron? Possibly, Nihonjinron that determines the fate of the era will appear, having left behind today's disposable Nihonjinron – whose authors lack persuasive power. I have read countless books of

Nihonjinron and analyzed their respective historical contexts, and I have the feeling I could myself write this kind of "new Nihonjinron" – regardless of whether it turned out to be fake or parody-like.

Although the pamphlet *Nippon that Astonishes the World* by Japan's Ministry of Economy, Trade and Industry is nonsensical and literally makes me itch, looking at it I hear devils whispering in my ear! Perhaps it is my turn to finally produce some real discourse on the Japanese. However, what I see as my immediate obligation following the publication of the current book is to foresee the appearance of potent Nihonjinron, which might prompt Japan to chart the wrong course. My duty, therefore, is to start analyzing the historical circumstances surrounding its potential emergence. It seems that the time to tackle this task has arrived sooner than I had expected.

Takeo Funabiki
August 10, 2017

Acknowledgements

It is dazzling how a chain of kindness sometimes leads to unexpected things. This book's English translation has been precisely that. It all started when my former student and NHK TV producer, Marina Miyagawa, convinced me to appear for an hour each week in the television series *Human Lectures*, which would last three months. She suggested I choose Nihonjinron as a focal point, having graciously persuaded me that the ideas I originally contemplated for the series would be of limited interest to viewers. As an anthropologist, I was naturally not keen to engage in discussions about such a "mass consumption product". However, Marina Miyagawa showed me the deeper meanings concealed in the chosen topic, and helped me to renew my thinking in areas where I was aware of the topic's density but had been inclined to ignore it. Another student, Yumiko Tokita, made me aware that such discussions on Japan might interest people outside Japan too. She asked me why I had not written the book in English for a larger audience. In so doing, she pointed out that the essence of Nihonjinron has to do with the inherent indecisiveness of Japanese people like me. Nonetheless, despite my understanding the need for translation, it was too troublesome for me to convert into English – which is written horizontally – the vertically-written Japanese text.

This problem has now been overcome and resulted in the book's English edition. The English work is entirely due to the Japanese and English bilingualism and the enthusiasm and focus of one of my last students before I retired, Ksenia Golovina. If there are any problems in this book, they are solely due to the swirly writing style of the Japanese original. If the ideas put forward here touch the hearts of readers, this is fully thanks to Ksenia Golovina's skill.

Thank you also to James O'Sullivan and Jaimie Norman at Cam Rivers Publishing and my secretary, Kaori Oishi.

Finally, this book saw the light of day thanks to the encouragement and generosity of Professor Alan McFarlane. Our long-time friendship and discussions made me aware not only of many anthropologically valuable phenomena but also about matters pertaining to Japan. My work has been strongly influenced by Alan McFarlane's *The Savage Wars of Peace*, the translation of which into Japanese I supervised.

Takeo Funabiki
August 10, 2017

Translator's Note

In the course of translating Chapters 1, 2, and 9, I referred to the preliminary drafts prepared by Professor Jeremy Eades and kindly handed to me by Professor Takeo Funabiki. For the quotes from original Japanese sources, where not stated otherwise – and where not written in English or translated by the Japanese authors themselves – the translation into English is mine. As a general rule, I italicized Japanese terms. The Japanese names in the translation follow the name–surname order.

I thank my friend Helen Kenyon for kindly proofreading the English translation and for discussions we had on the connotations of both Japanese and English words, when I was trying to find the most suitable expressions for the relevant concepts.

Finally, I extend my endless gratitude to Professor Takeo Funabiki for entrusting me with the task of translating his book on Nihonjinron. The experience has been rewarding beyond measure – both translating the book, learning from it, and discussing it with Professor Takeo Funabiki in the course of preparation for publication. I remain humbled by all these events.

Ksenia Golovina

Bibliography

Abe, Kinya, 1992, *Seiyō Chūsei no Ai to Jinkaku 'Seken'-ron Josetsu* ("Love and Personality of the Western Middle Age: Introduction to the Theory of 'Seken'"), Asahi Shinbunsha.

Abe, Kinya, 1995, *'Seken' to ha Nani ka* ("What is 'Seken'?"), Kōdansha.

Abe, Kinya, 2001, *Gakumon to 'Seken'* ("Learning and 'Seken'"), Iwanami Shoten.

Abe, Kinya, 2002, *Sekengaku e no Shōtai* ("Invitation into the Theory of 'Seken'"), Seikyūsha.

Akutagawa, Ryūnosuke, 1989(1927), *Saihō no Hito* ("The Man of the West"), Akutagawa, Ryūnosuke zenshū 7, Chikuma Shobō.

Akutagawa, Ryūnosuke, 1989(1927), *Zoku Saihō no Hito* ("Sequel to the Man of the West"), Akutagawa, Ryūnosuke zenshū 7, Chikuma Shobō.

Aoki, Tamotsu, 1999(1990), *Nihon Bunkaron no Henyō – Sengo Nihon no Bunka to Aidentiti* ("Transformation of the Discourse on Japanese Culture: Postwar Japan's Culture and Identity"), Chūōkōron Shinsha.

Befu, Harumi, 1997(1987), *Ideorogī toshite no Nihonbunkaron* ("Discourse on the Japanese Culture as an Ideology"), Updated Edition, Shisō no Kagakusha.

Ben-Dasan, Isaiah, 1971(1970), *Nihon-jin to Yudaya-jin* ("The Japanese and the Jews"), Kadokawa Shoten.

Benedict, Ruth, 2006(1946), *The Chrysanthemum and the Sword: Patterns of Japanese Culture*, Houghton Mifflin Company.

Doi, Takeo, 2001a(1971), *'Amae' no Kōzō* ("The Anatomy of Dependence"), Kōbundō.

Doi, Takeo, 2001b, *Zoku 'Amae' no Kōzō* ("Sequel to the Anatomy of Dependence"), Kōbundō.

Dower, Edward, 2000(1999), *Embracing Defeat: Japan in the Wake of World War II*, W. W. Norton and Company.

Dower, Edward, 2001(1999), *Haiboku wo Dakishimete* ("Embracing Defeat: Japan in the Wake of World War II"), with a new foreword for Japanese readers, Iwanami Shoten.

Ei, Rokusuke, 1996, *Shokunin* ("The Craftsmen"), Iwanami Shoten

Fróis, Luís, 2000 (2nd part of the 16th century), *Furoisu Nihonshi* ("History of Japan", original in Portuguese: *Historia do Japōo* or *Historia de Japam*), Chūōkōron Shinsha.

Funabiki, Takeo, 2000, *Kaisoku Rīdingu Yanagida Kunio* ("Yanagida Kunio: Express Readings"), Chikuma Shobō.

Funabiki, Takeo, 2007, *Migi deare Hidari deare, Waga Sokoku Nihon* ("My Country Japan Right or Left"), PHP Kenkyūjo.

Golden, Arthur, 1997, *Memoirs of a Geisha*, Alfred A. Knopf.

Hara, Takeshi, 2000, *Taishō Tennō* ("Emperor Taishō"), Asahi Shinbunsha.

Iijima, Ai, 2000, *Puratonikku Sekkusu* ("Platonic Sex"), Shōgakkan.

Inoue, Takehiko, 1999-(1998-), *Bagabondo* ("Vagabond"), Kōdansha.

Ishida, Eiichirō, 1987, *Nihonbunkaron* ("Lectures on Japanese Culture"), Chikuma Shobo.

Katō, Shūichi, 1979(1955), *Nihon Bunka no Zasshusei* ("The Hybrid Nature of Japanese Culture"), Collected Edition, Vol. 7, Heibonsha.

Kawada, Junzō, 2008, *Bunka no Sankaku Sokuryō – Kawada Junzō Kōenshū* ("Triangular Measurement of Culture: Collection of Lectures by Junzō Kawada), Jinbun Shoin.

Kawakami, Tetsutarō, 1979(1942), *Kindai no Chōkoku* ("Overcoming Modernity"), Fuzanbō. **English translation quoted in this book from**: Calichman, Richard (translator and editor), 2008, *Overcoming Modernity: Cultural Identity in Wartime Japan*, Columbia University Press.

Kishida, Shū, 1998(1995), *Hahaoya Gensō* ("Illusion of Motherhood"), Shinshokan.

Kuki, Shūzō, 1979(1930), *'Iki' no Kōzō* ("The Structure of Iki"), Iwanami Shoten. **English translation quoted in this book from:** Kuki, Shczō, *'Iki' no kōzō/The Structure of 'iki'*, translated by Nara, Hiroshi, 2008, English-Japanese Bilingual Edition, Kodansha International.

Lee, Teng-hui, 2003, *'Bushido' Kaidai – Nōbulesu Oburiju to ha* ("Bushido", A Bibliographical Essay – The Meaning of Noblesse Oblige"), Shōgakkan.

Loti, Pierre, 1937(1887), *Madame Chrysanthème* ("O-kiku-san"), Iwanami Shoten.

Macfarlane, Alan, 2003(1997), *The Savage Wars of Peace: England, Japan and the Malthusian Trap*, Palgrave MacMillan.

Malthus, Thomas Robert, 2012(1798), *An Essay on the Principle of Population*, Courier Corporation.

Mishima, Yukio, 1983(1967), *Hagakure Nyūmon* ("An Introduction to Hagakure"), Shinchōsha.

Mishima, Yukio, 1983(1968), *Bunka Bōei Ron* ("Discussion on the

Defense of Culture"), Shinchōsha.

Miyamoto, Tsuneichi, 1995(1960), *Wasurerareta Nihonjin* ("The Forgotten Japanese"), Iwanami Shoten.

Nakane, Chie, 1967, *Tate Shakai no Ningen Kankei – Tan'itsu Shakai no Riron* ("Human Relations in Vertical Society: Theory of a Homogeneous Society"), Kōdansha.

Natsume, Sōseki, 2002(1906) *Botchan* ("Botchan"), Collected Edition, Vol. 2, Iwanami Shoten.

Natsume, Sōseki, 2002(1906) Kusamakura (*"Kusamakura"*), Collected Edition, Vol. 3 Iwanami Shoten. **English translation in this book quoted from**: Natsume, Sōseki, *Kusamakura*, translated with an introduction and notes by McKinney, Meredith, 2008, Penguin Classics.)

Natsume, Sōseki, 2002(1908) *Sanshirō* ("Sanshiro"), Collected Edition, Vol. 5, Iwanami Shoten.

Natsume, Sōseki, 2002(1909) *Sorekara* ("And Then"), Collected Edition, Vol. 6, Iwanami Shoten.

Natsume, Sōseki, 2002(1909) *Mon* ("The Gate"), Collected Edition, Vol. 6, Iwanami Shoten.

Natsume, Sōseki, 2002(1914) *Kokoro* ("Kokoro"), Collected Edition, Vol. 9, Iwanami Shoten. **English translation in this book quoted from**: Natsume, Sōseki, *Kokoro*, translated and with a foreword by McClellan, Edwin, 1968, Peter Owen.

Natsume, Sōseki, 2002(1915) *Michikusa* ("Grass on the Wayside"), Collected Edition, Vol. 10, Iwanami Shoten.

NHK Project X Production, 2000-2006 *Purojekuto X Chōsenshatachi* ("Project X: Challengers"), Nihonhōsō Shuppan Kyokai.

Nitobe, Inazō, 2002(1899), *Bushido: The Soul of Japan*, Kodansha International.

Odaka, Kunio, 1965, *Nihon no Keiei* ("The Japanese Management"), Chūō Kōronsha.

Okakura, Tenshin, 1994(1906), *Cha no Hon* ("The Book of Tea"), Bilingual edition, Kōdansha.

Ōmuro, Mikio, 2003, *Shiga Shigetaka Nihon Fūkeiron Seidoku* ("An Intensive Reading of Shiga Shigetaka's 'The Landscape of Japan'"), Iwanami Shoten.

Said, Edward, 1978, *Orientalism*, Pantheon Books.

Sakuta, Keiichi, 1967(1964), *Haji no Bunka Saikō* ("A Reconsideration of Shame Culture"), Chikuma Shobo.

Shiba, Ryōtarō, 1993-2000(1986-1996), *Kono Kuni no Katachi* ("The Form of this Nation"), Bungei Shunjū.

Shiga, Shigetaka, 1995(1894), *Nihon Fūkeiron* ("The Landscape of Japan"), Iwanami Shoten.

Taut, Bruno, 1992(1936), *Nihon bunka shikan* ("Japanese Arts Seen with European Eyes", originally in German: Japans Kunst mit europäischen Augen gesehen), Kōdansha.

Uchimura, Kanzō, 1908(1894), *Representative Men of Japan: Essays*, Keisheisha.

Uchimura, Kanzō, 1997(1894), *Daihyōtekina Nihonjin* ("Representative Men of Japan"), with a commentary by Suzuki, Norihisa, Iwanami Shoten.

Uchida, Tatsuru, 2009, *Nihon Henkyōron*, ("The Discourse on Japan as a Peripheral State"), Shinchōsha.

Umesao, Tadao, 1967(1957), *Bunmei no Seitai Shikan Josetsu* ("Civilization from the Perspective of Ecological History"), Chūō Kōronsha.

Van Wolferen, Karel, 1994, *Ningen wo Kōfuku ni shinai Nihon toiu Shisutemu* ("The False Realities of a Politicized Society"), Shinohara, Masaru **(transl.)**, Mainichi Shinbunsha.

Veblen, Thorstein, 1965(1899), *The Theory of the Leisure Class*, Transaction Publishers.

Vogel, Ezra, 1979, *Japan as Number One: Lessons for America*, Harvard University Press.

Watsuji, Tetsurō, 1979(1919) *Koji Junrei* ("Pilgrimages to the Ancient Temples"), Iwanami Shoten.

Watsuji, Tetsurō, 1979(1935) *Fūdo* ("Climate"), Iwanami Shoten.

Yanagita, Kunio, 1963(1910), *Tōno Monogatari* ("The Legends of Tono"), Collected Edition, Vol. 4, Chikuma Shoten.

Yokomitsu, Riichi, 1998(1937), *Ryoshū* ("Melancholy on a Journey"), Upper and Lower Volumes, Kōdansha.

Yoshikawa, Eiji, 1975(1935), *Miyamoto Musashi* ("Miyamoto Musashi"), Kōdansha.

Yoshikawa, Kōjirō, 1976(1972), Saitō Kanki ("Records of the West and the East"), Collected Edition, Vol. 24, Chikuma Shobō.

www.ingramcontent.com/pod-product-compliance
Lightning Source LLC
Chambersburg PA
CBHW070909270326
41927CB00011B/2496